God, Get Me Out Of This One…!

"An Addict's Prayer"

A True Story About Addiction and One Man's Journey Back From Hell

John A. Carter

To Jason;
Behold the turtle, who only makes progress when he sticks out his neck!
God Bless!
John A. Carter

Second Edition

INKWELL PRODUCTIONS.

Phoenix, Arizona

www.inkwellproductions.com

In this story I traveled a roller coaster of emotions through the life of an addictive personality. I found compelling insights and vital information that has helped me understand the power of addiction.

Judy McCoole, Portage, IN.

We all have life stories, but so few have had the courage to revisit them, much less share them with others. As someone who knew you as a child, I lived your pain chapter after chapter. God lifted you from the darkness and the pain so you could help others.

Joy Bronner

Having read this book, it has brought me back to the agony and the bizarre behaviors of life in addiction. Having been part of this book and being involved with the players on our road to recovery, I found this book to be a reality check of our past lives and a yardstick on how God has changed us.

Gary Stambaugh

I have been a Friend of John for about forty-two years. I read John's book and think it is great. John is a man with integrity. I know the book is true because I was there a lot of the time. I would like him to write another book, he left out some good stuff.

Marshall Keith (Tooter)

God, Get Me Out of This One…!

ISBN # 978-0-9814648-1-7
Library of Congress # 2009927920

Published by:
Inkwell Productions
10869 N. Scottsdale Road #103-128
Scottsdale, Arizona 85254-5280
Phone: (480) 315-3781
Email: info@inkwellproductions.com
Web: www.inkwellproductions.com

Illustration by Questin Lard

Printed in the United States of America

In Loving Memory

Richard Carter
My Lost Child Brother
May he find his way in heaven

1953-2005

Dedicated to

Frederick Hoil

A loving friend who has
since crossed over… he once told me,
"God has a few angels who need counseling."

1943-2001

Acknowledgements

I'd like to thank all those who have helped me with this project. I couldn't have done it without you. Cathy L. Kaiser, Laura Smith-Whaley, Glenn Kimball, Chase Kimball, Diana Wheelock, Laura George, Rachel Blanchard, Sean Carter, Steve Longhi, Erica Curtin, Jill Crook, Amy Crook, Roberto Sanchez-Garcia, Amy Aossey, Valerie Pyfrom, Jeff Bodner, Questin Lard, Tim Broderick, Penny DeBlois, Sheila Broderick, Ken Morgan, Jennifer McCoy, Patty and John Sloan, Larry Belliard, Joe Licci, Michael Bohley, Robin Green, and all others, of which there are too many to mention. I believe this book was God inspired, and you were all the angels He sent to help me make it possible.

Contents

Contents

Dead Reckoning

Have you ever danced in the arms of the Devil
For a momentary thrill,
Then foolishly thought you could just waltz away
Before he's had his fill?
Have you ever held in the palms of your hands
The lifetime of goals you'd set to meet
Then traded them all for your hungry desires
For the laughter of hell so sweet?
Well I've waltzed through the wastelands
Of my ripped apart dreams
That I carelessly traded away-
Then I tripped on the remaining threads
Of the seams and lay face down in my dismay.
There's nothing more trying than the horrors
That's faced in the dead reckoning of
All that you are lay to waste.---

Written by: Carol Robin Green

Prologue

Jimmy and I pulled out of the Show Low liquor store and into the full service gas station across the street to put our last $4.00 into Ed's 1953 red Ford pick-up truck. It was already dusk, and Jimmy knew that it got dark early here in the canyon. He expressed concern about the burned-out driver's side headlight. "It gets so dark here you can't see your hand in front of you, and the other headlight is as old as the truck, and I'm afraid it's not as bright as it used to be," he said with a worried look.

Jimmy knew we were taking a chance driving up here, but we had been drinking most of the day, and we were drunk. We ran out of alcohol around 3:00 p.m., and we weren't finished partying yet, so we exercised one of the only two options we thought we had: continue to swim in the Salt River with nothing to drink, or drive up highway 60 to Show Low and buy more. We chose option two.

Jimmy pulled up to the pump where the attendant was waiting. "$4.00 regular, please." Jimmy told him. As he pumped the gas, the other attendant washed the windshield.

"I noticed your driver's side headlight is out. We can replace it for another $5.00," the attendant told Jimmy when he finished washing the glass. A good deal no doubt, but we had no more money because we had spent it all at the liquor store.

"No thanks," Jimmy said as he started the truck. I sensed he was none too happy about driving down the mountain with only one headlight, but what else could we do?

We left town, heading back in the same direction we'd come. As we passed the Show Low city limits, I opened my first pint of wine. I put the bottle up to my lips and tilted my head back. I took in almost three quarters of the bottle before I needed a breath.

I'd had my first beer at ten o'clock that morning and had been drinking most of the day, so I had no business drinking this wine like I was drinking a soda on a hot day, but I didn't care. Two minutes later I killed the pint. I turned to Jimmy and said, "That's some good shit!." He just looked at me.

I dropped the empty bottle to the floor of the cab and opened another pint. I put it up to my mouth and took a long drink, and then I screwed the cap back on.

I could feel the wind blowing up against my arm as it hung out the passenger side window as we entered the canyon, starting our descent.

The next thing I remember, I was waking up. I felt like I was floating in mid-air, like the initial drop on a roller coaster.

I looked toward Jimmy, but he wasn't there. I instantly thought, "We must be going off the mountain! Jimmy must have jumped out before we became airborne!"

I was so drunk, I didn't even think about the possibility that I could be killed. It never even crossed my mind. My only thought was, "I better hang on to this bottle [Which I had hanging out of the window in my right hand.], because I'm going to need a drink when this ride is over."

Well, I did hang on, with every ounce of strength I could muster. Besides, I couldn't have pulled my arm in anyway, because it kept hitting the trees and bushes on the mountainside as I continued my solo descent downward. I couldn't see them in the darkness, but I could feel them just the same.

My only objective was to hang on to that bottle. I was determined to have that drink when that ride ended, and that was as complicated a thought as I could put together at the time.

I must have lost consciousness, because the next thing I knew, I wasn't flying anymore, and I couldn't see a thing. The darkness was so thick I felt smothered by it. The truck was on its right side, and my arm, still holding the bottle, was underneath the truck. We had hit with such force that only my nose hit the windshield and punched a hole clean through the glass with no other breaks or cracks. As I lay there on my side, my arm started to throb. Through my drunken haze I began to realize how serious my situation was.

I had just gone over the Salt River Canyon as we entered it from the Show Low side at its highest point. The locals referred to this gorge as the "Mini-Grand Canyon," and I knew deep down inside that I had come down a long way.

I wasn't sure how badly I was hurt, but I knew something serious was wrong. I didn't know what had happened to Jimmy. Hell, I didn't even know if anyone had seen me go over the side. I was in trouble, and I knew it.

Somewhere I had heard that when we are close to death our lives start to flash before us. However, it wasn't a flash of light that caught my attention at this instant in time, it was the abyss of complete darkness. It's weird how blindness in the dark triggers awareness in the mind. As the gears in my head began gathering a raging momentum from the lethargy of a drunken stupor, I found myself at war in my mind. Crisis has a way of sobering the thinking process. It was at this time that I went back and assessed the battlefield...

Chapter One

Tombstone, Arizona

"Are you ready to take the next thing to come along?"

The year was 1951, and Harry Truman was the President of the United States. The average yearly income was $3,515.00. You could buy a new car at the cost of $1,520.00 and you could buy a new four-bedroom house at around $9,000.00. Gas was 13 cents, bread 16 cents, milk 19 cents and gold $35.00 an ounce.

That year: Truman fired General Douglas McArthur in Korea, Winston Churchill was called on to form a new government, and a truce was reached in Korea.

By my birth, February 18, 1951, my parents, Wallace Leon Carter and Rachael Rose Broncato-Carter, would be married two years, and I would be the second of what would be six children in all.

My birth was a difficult one in those times—my mother was in labor with me for seventeen hours and she almost died. She once told me that after eight hours she was so weak she felt she couldn't go on. With hope in her heart she prayed… "God, please get me through this one…!" God must have heard her, because nine hours later I arrived. Her story must have been imprinted on my mind so clearly that I uttered this phrase instinctively many times over my lifetime, as if it were my own…a part of who I am.

I was eight pounds, four ounces and everyone was there. Everyone, that is, except my father. He was out celebrating my birth. The problem was, he had started celebrating nine months earlier, and he wasn't done yet.

I was born at St. Mary's hospital in Long Island, New York. I was three years old when we left New York for Arizona. I don't remember much about my life while living in New York. I only know what I've been told by my family.

I know I came from New York on a train and landed in the small town of Tombstone, Arizona. It was November 1954, and we would live there for the next year of my life.

I grew to love Tombstone because living there was an adventure. Being in a small town, my brothers and I were free to roam as we pleased. My older brother Steve, my younger brother Richard and I were about a year apart. We lived down the street from the O.K. Corral, where Wyatt Earp, his brothers, and Doc Holliday fought the Cowboys in one of the most infamous gunfights of all time, the gunfight at the O.K. Corral. I couldn't tell you how many times my brothers and I reenacted that gunfight, playing Wyatt Earp, Doc Holliday, or one of the Earp brothers.

I remember a small fire station behind the corral where we use to spend time with the head fireman, old Gus. He would often sit outside the station on a lawn chair when he wasn't polishing the fire truck or playing with his Dalmatian puppy.

I loved talking with him and spending as much time there as I could. His puppy loved me as much as he loved Gus. Old Gus was full of stories about the town, and I loved hearing them all.

For three days each year the town held a festival called Hell Dorado Days. People came from all over to celebrate. What a party that was. There were gunfights in the streets, reenactments of the gunfight at the O.K. Corral, and filming of movies. It was a rich ingredient in the recipe of my life; the stories and the people belonged to me because I lived there, too. I used to pretend the people of Tombstone were my family because I didn't feel that same connection with my own.

Looking back, I now know why. I grew up in what I know now was a dysfunctional family. My father was an alcoholic, and my mother was an unhappy, angry, co-dependent caretaker. We never used those terms back then; we didn't even know what co-dependency was. All I knew was that my family was different. As early as 1955, I remember feeling unique and separate. I was not like the other kids in town. In our family, my father was never home and my mother, God bless her soul, as hard as she would try, could never stop raging. She yelled at us constantly. My father worked in Bisbee, Arizona, in the copper mines. He was gone all through the week and when he came home, you would find him in the cowboy bars in town. If he spent any time at home, it would be with a beer in his hand. My older brother Steve must have known something was wrong because he always felt a need to take care of his brothers. This isn't normal behavior for an older brother unless he is forced to grow up early, because of crisis and to protect the people he loves.

I remember starting school in Tombstone. I was in a classroom with three grade levels. Sometimes being in school was so much better than the alternatives. My teacher, Miss Crawford, made class feel like home. She loved teaching and it showed. She didn't treat us like students, she treated us like family. One day Miss Crawford asked me if everything was all right at home. I was somewhat confused about the question; maybe it was because of the way my brother would watch over me, and maybe it was because she was so much like family too. Growing up in a dysfunctional family I grew a thick skin and a high tolerance for inappropriate behaviors such as anger, crisis, chaos, and arguments. When you need the feeling of family around, sometimes one reaches far and blood relations aren't as important as they are for others. I never learned what normal was. That would cost me dearly in the years to come. "Normal" has fences with green grass and safety. I guess I never figured out the magic of fences, or maybe I kept pushing back the boundaries hoping to find my green grass and safety. Innocence is a form of blindness that changes horror into something else, something we survive rather than understand. Survival itself is safety of sorts. At least the sensation of survival can be the pleasure for the innocents.

In my family "normal" was dad drunk and never home, and so dad was never the fence line we needed. Mom was always angry. When she became too frustrated, she would lash out and beat on us. My older brother was always there for us because that's what an older brother did under these circumstances, but somehow I knew he was looking for the fence, green grass and safety too. When there was a crisis, we'd all pull together and we'd get through it. The problem was, in our family, there was always a crisis. My mother would complain about my father's drinking, her family, and—paradoxically—how she missed them. She didn't know that she was teaching us about loving and hating the same people. She complained about how she hated Arizona, the heat, the bugs, and how she couldn't take it. With all her complaining my father would continue to drink. When he became drunk enough, Father knew he could get to my mother best by attacking her family and telling her that they were no good. Neither of them knew how confused they made us feel when it came to good guys and bad guys. How could Mother love her family so much when my father hated them with such vigor? When he attacked her family, they would argue into the early morning, and sometimes it would get physical. At first I would lie in bed scared, but it happened so often it became part of my survival. In the end, my father would pass out. My mother would go to bed angry and alone. The next day it would be as if nothing happened; all we had to do was get past the crisis of the night before, and we knew we would feel better tomorrow. My mother would kiss my father goodbye as he left to go back to the mines for the week. Steve, Richard and I would get the same lesson the following weekend as if we just didn't understand it the first time. Fence lines, green grass and safety were abandoned for the rhythm between crises… the eye of the storm.

Over those young years Steve became increasingly concerned. He often talked to my brother and me about running away, especially when my parents fought. However, he never followed through because there was always the survival to the next day, and after all, tomorrow was really only a day away. I see now that Steve felt responsible for us, but at the same time he must have felt helpless, because he was only a year older than me, and he couldn't have done much anyway. I now believe talking about it must have made him feel as though he was doing something, if only for a little while.

Steve (6 years of age) on the left and John (5 years of age) on the right.

Chapter Two

Tucson, Arizona

"Children should be seen, not heard!"
-- Mom Carter

One afternoon, I left school for home and when I arrived, my parents were loading up Roy's Chevy pick-up truck and our car with all of our belongings.

I was told we were moving to Tucson and that we would be moving immediately. My brothers and I had no warning. There were no goodbyes, just the knee-jolt command, "Get in the car, we're leaving!"

Our friends, Roy, and his wife, Grace, and their two daughters, Angela and Connie, had moved out from New York at about the same time that we had. They were the only connection my mother had with her homeland. Roy would help us move, but they would not be making the move with us. Roy and my father worked together in the mines and he was as much of an alcoholic as my father was.

I didn't want to move. I was terrified. I was leaving the town I loved and where the world made some sense. At least I knew where to hide. We all lived on the threshold of chaos and we were afraid of what unknown situation might tip the scales too far. We had learned to live with fear, but as a result we had become seasoned professionals with the effects of what fear can do. When I protested, my mother let me know I had no say in the matter. She told me, "Children should be seen, but not heard." That would be a line I would hear over and over again growing up. How many times can a child be told that their feelings don't matter before they begin to believe it too?

We moved to a predominately Hispanic neighborhood around 13th Street and Speedway. We lived in a five-room brick house on a quarter acre of land. To the right of us was a large Hispanic family and behind them an older couple. I can't remember most of their names, but what I do remember was that they were all proud and kind people.

Our neighbors accepted us without reservation. They could see that we were as poor as everyone else. Back then, people supported each other because there was a strong sense of community.

At that time my parents weren't fighting as much. The neighborhood seemed to rub off on them in some strange way. With the beginning of a little peace in our lives my father slowed down his drinking. He was only drinking at home and when he did it wasn't as much as before. This was also around the time my mother became pregnant with my little brother, Vance.

Chapter Three

My First Bank Robbery

If we had any money to buy groceries, it was limited.
There were times when
all we had to eat was a loaf
of bread that we would toast and butter.

We had been living in Tucson for about seven months when Joe, a friend of my father's, came from Ohio with his friend Jerry. They were invited to stay at our house. It was decided that Joe would stay with us for a while but Jerry would find his own place. Joe was about the same age and build as my father and if you didn't know any better, they could be mistaken for brothers. Jerry was different at 5'-6" and he outweighed my dad by twenty pounds.

Joe and Jerry seemed nice enough, and they were paying my parents good money to stay with us. They were also helping out with the groceries. They would often take my brothers and me along when they went shopping. I liked going with them, if for no other reason than they would buy enough food to feed a small army, including snacks and other luxuries my parents couldn't afford.

After three weeks Jerry moved into his own place, a small motel room across town. Jerry came over almost daily and would eat at least one meal with us. He and Joe spent a lot of time together and because they were gone so much, I assumed they were working. I never questioned it, I was just grateful they were so generous.

After Joe and Jerry moved from Ohio, I noticed that my father began working less and drinking more. That made my mother return to her complaining about her family and Arizona in general. As young as I was, I already suspected my father had a drinking problem, and somehow I had known that his slowing down would be short lived.

Jerry drove a dark green, two-door, 1953 Mercury. The car was two years old and still looked new. He was always washing it in our front yard. One Friday morning, Joe and Jerry were sitting outside on our front porch, and as they talked, Joe was taking notes. Steve, Richard and I were playing with Bobby and Alfonso from next door. Around 11:00, Joe asked my brothers and me if we wanted to take a ride with them. Jerry announced, "Could be an ice cream cone in it for you." They didn't have to ask me twice.

On our way to pick up the ice cream cones, Joe said, "Before we go get ice cream, we need to stop by the bank."

They pulled into the alley alongside the bank and Jerry told us they'd be right back. In less than two minutes they came running around the corner. When they reached the car, Joe told us to get on the floor in the backseat. Joe drove and Jerry navigated. It is amazing how children accept unusual circumstances. About a mile up the road we were told we could sit up. I was sitting between Steve and Richard and when I stood up and leaned over the front seat I saw a grocery bag full of money. I remember thinking, "They must have a lot of money," and that only raised my opinion of them. I didn't have a clue about what had just happened. All I could think about was that two-scoop ice cream cone I was getting on the way home. It wasn't until a few days later that my older brother told me that something about our venture to the bank for ice cream wasn't right. However, I was playing and I didn't want to hear it. Besides, if it were true I thought they would be arrested. I just couldn't allow myself to think that way about these nice men.

A month and a half later my little my brother Vance was born. My mother was in the hospital about a week, and when she got out she needed bed rest for a few more days, so my brothers and I helped as much as we could. She told me she was in labor with Vance like she was with me and it was very hard on her. Once again my mother let us know we had been the source of "labor" for her.

Vance cried a lot the first few months after he came home from the hospital. My mother went days with very little help from my father, because the tension poured him back into his bottle. With my father drinking more and my mother getting very little sleep, my parents really began to fight. There was always a point at which my mother couldn't take it any more and she would explode her frustrations onto anyone who might cross her path. No one was safe when it came to her wrath, not even our new brother. Sometimes she would shake him so violently I thought she would break his neck. I could live with anger, but violence brought on a new level of fear, one I didn't know I could survive.

One Saturday evening about a month after my mother came home from the hospital, we had just finished watching the Lone Ranger on TV, and Vance had been crying for about forty-five minutes, when all hell broke loose. Both the front and side kitchen doors flew open at the same time with such force they slammed against the walls. It scared me so badly I almost wet myself. Several men in black suits burst into the room with their guns drawn. They identified themselves as F.B.I. They handcuffed both my father and my mother and sat them down on the couch next to each other. My mother was pissed, and she had no trouble letting them know how she felt!

I noticed that my older brother Steve stood between Richard and me and the F.B.I. as if he was the first line of defense to protect us. To say the least, I was terrified and confused. What appeared to be the agent in charge held up some papers he had in his inside coat pocket and read them to my parents. He said they had warrants for Joseph and Jerry for a series of bank robberies from Ohio to Arizona. I noticed an agent had picked up the baby and carried him into the kitchen. He was trying to stop him from crying. He sat down with Vance at the kitchen table and held him close as he rocked him in his arms. Before long, Vance stopped his crying. I remember thinking he must be a father himself because he looked like he knew what he was doing.

My parents tried to explain that my father was not Joe, but the officers weren't buying any of it. It didn't help matters any when they found a large suitcase full of money in the back of a small closet in one of the bedrooms. Well, my father and Joe looked like brothers, so I could understand how they could mistake my father for him, no matter how much we all protested. They took my father out to one of the many cars parked in the yard. The agent in charge took the handcuffs off my mother and told her to be quiet and listen to what he was about to say. He then said, "If we hadn't heard your baby crying, we had full intentions of coming in shooting."

I could hear my father outside, still arguing, telling the police that he was not the one they were looking for. Just then Joe walked up and turned himself in. "I'm Joe and I think you're looking for me." he said. He pointed to my father and said, "Skip knew nothing about the robberies." Joe had his head down when he spoke. The police didn't listen; instead they handcuffed Joe and put him in the car next to my father.

My father was released the next day without so much as an apology. The family never talked about it again until many years later when I found a copy of the Tucson Daily Star in an old brown chest where my mother kept her important papers. In that paper was an article about the robberies and arrests by the F.B.I. It was an old pattern. When something terrible happened we just never talked about it again, as if it would magically go away.

After this incident my father drank even more intensely. Trouble always drove father into a bottle as if alcohol was a medicine for a new disease. Sometimes he would leave the house on a binge and be gone for days at a time. When he did come home, he was always drunk and that would enrage my mother, like lighting the fuse to dynamite. Alcohol may have caused dad to forget, but it caused mother to remember. There were days they fought all day long and the only reprieve we would get was when he'd either leave again or pass out.

During this time, there was rarely enough money for food. There were times that we had to depend on friends and neighbors and there were times we'd go to bed hungry. My mother's friend Vi was a waitress in a small diner downtown. Sometimes we would take a bus to her work and Vi would use her tip money to feed us at the counter. Her father was a retired barber and he'd cut our hair for free once a month. There were times when all we had to eat was a loaf of bread or a bowl of beans. I can still see in my mind my mother buying pinto beans in twenty pound sacks. Hunger would make me angry with my father because he seemed to have money to drink while we were starving. I would become even angrier as I'd watch my mother go hungry because there wasn't enough to go around.

One morning I woke up early. My father was home and his car was in the driveway. The front driver's side fender was damaged from a car accident my father had been in the night before. I found out later that it was a hit and run accident and my father was the one who ran. Of course, he had been drinking and had caused the accident. I was playing on the car. Father told me several times to stay off. He had a hangover and wasn't in a very good mood, but I wouldn't listen. When he went back inside, I'd jump back on and continue to play. I was on the trunk when I saw him coming. This time he looked really angry. I jumped off in an attempt to get away, and when I did, I passed by part of the crumpled fender that had several sharp edges. I cut my right forearm on part of the wrinkled metal that was sticking out. The cut was five or six inches long and it was deep. I was bleeding all over myself. My father was standing on the front porch with a belt in his hand when he grabbed me. He shouted, "That's what you get when you don't listen!" and then he beat my butt with his belt. "Now go to your room!" he screamed. He opened the door for me and shoved me into the house. I ran to my room, crying, and too scared to show him my injury. I was covered with blood as I lay there in bed with my left hand over my wound trying to stop the bleeding. The cut was too deep, and although the bleeding slowed, I couldn't make it stop.

I could hear my mother in the living room arguing with my father about all the blood on the floor and how badly I might be hurt. She thought I might need to go to the hospital. They argued for a good half hour before my mother came in and looked at my arm, as if the argument was more important than my being hurt. She wrapped a hand towel around my arm and took me to the emergency room. I was given a tetanus shot and ten stitches. When the doctor asked me what happened, my mother told him that I was playing on an old junk car that was parked in the back of our house. The doctor told me to stay off of it and I was discharged.

My father's binges were getting longer. One day, after being out for almost a week, my father walked through the kitchen door and he looked rough. We had just finished a bowl of beans and a slice of bread for lunch and I was getting ready to walk over to the little store on Speedway with my friends from next door. Bobby and Alfonso each had a dime, and I was that told if I'd walk over to the store with them, they would buy me some candy. I thought—now that my father was home—that I could get my own money. I asked him for a dime for candy.

"No, I don't have any money!" he angrily yelled at me. He was sick and I knew better, but having been raised in a dysfunctional family, I knew no boundaries, so I wasn't taking "no" for an answer. I thought that if I hounded him long enough, I would wear him down and he'd give me my dime.

Of course, I didn't take into consideration how sick he was. He had just come off of a weeklong binge. Worse yet, he was showing signs of alcohol withdrawal and probably couldn't deal with anything, let alone a nagging child. However, I was determined to complete my mission, come hell or high water, so I was not going to let up!

All of a sudden my father, in a rage, stood up and backhanded me across my left cheek. I was shocked and scared. I jumped up from the floor and ran out of the kitchen door holding my face and crying. Steve followed me out to see if I was all right. We were standing next to the chain-link fence that separated our house from the neighbor when all hell broke loose.

My mother and father were having a knock down, drag out fight. I thought my father was going to kill my mother. That was when Steve and I tried to run back in to help our mother, but our neighbors held us back. I could hear my mother yelling obscenities at my father, and what sounded like breaking glass and pots and pans hitting up against the walls. Fifteen minutes later, the screen door flew open and my mother walked out, brushing herself off with her right hand and holding an iron skillet in her left, and at the same time screaming, "I'll kill that son-of–a–bitch the next time!"

To tell you the truth, this was a sight to be seen. My mother only stood 4'-9" tall, a slightly overweight Italian woman from New York, and my father was a 6'-2" farmer from Delight, Arkansas. When we looked inside, we saw that my father was lying on the kitchen floor, semi-conscious, holding his head with both hands. He was out for the rest of the day.

John A. Carter

Chapter Four

Another Move

Living in a dysfunctional family,
our reality changes often.
It could change up to a hundred times a day.
It's like being a mouse in a maze.

The more my father drank, the more my parents fought. What had once been a weekly argument became a daily event. My father drank to escape, but in the process he enslaved himself even more completely with every drink he took. My mother fought to resist his behavior, but in that struggle, she became a part of the cause. Neither of them realized how they each fed the other's weakness. Neither of them knew that the real victims of their madness were innocent, impressionable and desperate. Somewhere in the cycle of abuse and anger we lost some sense of who we were as children and replaced it with an intense need to survive. We watched and learned from our parents. We loved them both but hated them at the same time. Our parents had lost their way in life, and as a result, never gave us a chance to find ours. All philosophy about happy families made little sense to children who didn't know if there would even be a tomorrow. As a result, we—as children—became pros at immediate escape and temporary solutions.

It was the beginning of the summer of 1957 when my Aunt Betty came to visit. She was living in Phoenix with Karl, her sixth or seventh husband (I never really knew), Karl's son, Lloyd, and Aunt Betty's daughter, Carolyn.

Lloyd had cerebral palsy, and he lived his life in a wheel chair. I had never experienced a severe handicap up close and personal. I didn't understand it and it scared me. The part that frightened me the most was that there was no end to his illness or escape from his problems. We knew what "escapes" were, well taught to us by our parents. However, there was a "finality" to his problem. Fear could not cure this one. Lloyd proved to be a very kind person. I soon learned that he was no one to fear. There was a sense of calm and peace in his life that didn't make sense. He wasn't running from anything and he didn't appear to be afraid of his situation.

On the second day of my aunt's visit, my parents told me that my brothers and I would be staying for a while with my aunt and uncle in Phoenix. My parents needed to work on their marriage. The only one who would remain with my folks would be my baby brother, Vance. I didn't want to go, but—as always—what I wanted did not matter. The next day my brothers and I were on our way to Phoenix. Once again, there had been a radical escape planned and executed based on something out of control.

My worst fears materialized when it was almost six months before I would see my parents and little brother again. That fear and pain evolved into anger as the explanations of the behavior of my parents fell apart one at a time. Anger was the last emotion standing when all of the rest of my feelings didn't make sense. Anger always makes sense of itself. It comes with its own set of reasons. I intrinsically sensed that I was a child and that children needed protection. However, there is a great difference between protection and abandonment. The only possible conclusion I could think of was that my parents just didn't love me any longer. Why else would they abandon me? From the minute I arrived at my aunt's house I would sit on her porch watching every car coming down the street, hoping it would be my parents coming to get us. My aunt and uncle were wonderful, but that isn't the same thing as parents. The minutes turned into hours, the hours into days, the days into weeks, and then months.

There were no calls or letters. The fear I felt came from the fact that there would be no solutions. There would be no more mornings when the arguments faded overnight. How many times can we feel rejected before we become numb to abandonment? This kind of numbness takes the sensitivity out of other emotions as well.

To make matters worse, it appeared that both of my brothers were adjusting to the move better than I was. It was as if it didn't matter to them whether our parents came back or not. They were having a wonderful time. As a matter of fact, I believe my older brother felt some relief. After all, he didn't have to be the parent in the home of my aunt and uncle. He could return to being a kid his own age. I wondered, "Why do I feel different?" I still didn't feel as if I belonged anywhere. I remember feeling like I was an alien from another planet. It wasn't long after that feeling came up that I stopped asking for my parents.

When school started in September, we registered at Garfield Elementary, which was at 14th Street and Roosevelt in Phoenix. It wasn't in the best neighborhood, but it was better than the ones I was used to. By this time, I thought I would never see my parents or little brother again. The numbness gave way to a sense of well being, like taking a pain pill. I just stopped thinking about them. I even pretended they were dead! {Dead was better than being abandoned and worthless. At least when I thought of them as dead I was still worth something.}

In December of 1957 my aunt told us that we were going to spend Christmas at our grandmother's house in Eloy, Arizona. My grandmother Carter was the elementary school nurse in Eloy and had been for the past five years or so. My grandfather had died before I was born. My grandmother was known in the town as Miss Carter, and she was well respected. I loved going over to Grandmother's house because she loved us so much! Besides, with her I belonged to someone. My aunt told us that our parents might be at Grandma's. When I heard that they might be there, I didn't want to go. I was angry and afraid.

Two days before Christmas I woke up with a bad toothache. By Christmas Eve morning, I was really in pain; I remember begging my aunt to get it pulled. I told her the only thing I wanted for Christmas was to be out of pain. I felt scared, hopeless and alone. My aunt became angry with me. She wanted me to wait until after the holidays to get my tooth pulled. They started to tease me. They told me I *was* being a baby and accused me of trying to ruin their Christmas. I was angry with them because I thought they were going to let me die! I was in so much pain and I cried so much, she finally found a dentist who would come in on a holiday. He was in Mesa, thirty miles from where we lived, and he was very expensive, but I just couldn't wait.

After having my tooth pulled, we drove straight to Eloy. I lay in the back of my aunt's station wagon, spitting blood into a coffee can. I had a high fever from the infection that had developed, and I was very sick. But the pain was gone and that was all I cared about.

An hour later we arrived at my grandmother's house. My parents were there. I was sick so I stayed in the car. I was also angry with my parents. My parents came out to the car and greeted me as if nothing had happened, like they were only gone for a day or two. I didn't want to see them. As I lay there in back of the car, different family members would come out to the car and call me names like "baby." They told me to "grow-up" and "get over it." They were relentless and would not let up. I could feel my anger turning into rage as each person came out and took their shot at me. One thing about anger, it has its own reasons that can't be explained. Anger is the only emotion that must be met on the streets at high noon and will not go away until the villain is slain. I began to feel guilty, but I pushed it aside. I let them all know how I felt and that this showdown would not be shamed into submission. But they weren't listening to me. After a while, waiting for them to cut it out or shoot, I decided to join the party. I was beginning to think maybe I was wrong, maybe I was being a baby. I just didn't know anymore, so I got out of the car and joined the rest of the family. I pretended for a while that everything was all right, as if six months of my life meant nothing. I think now that they won the showdown that afternoon and my feelings were again ignored. It was an old story.

My mother told us that afternoon that things were better between her and my father and that we could come home. After Christmas, my brothers and I moved back to Tucson with my parents.

At that time, my father was working as a television repairman for Flash TV. And then, when school was out for the year, we moved to Eloy and lived across the street from our grandmother's house for about three months. Then we moved back to Phoenix. Living close to my grandmother made a difference, but not the difference I needed.

Chapter Five

Phoenix, Arizona

He was really a good friend, and
I believed he really cared. But, in my family,
we didn't talk about what went on inside of it,
not even with our closest friends.

It was early in 1958 when we moved to Phoenix. We moved to a little five-room house on 21st Place and Roosevelt. My father looked for work for about a month, and then he landed a job as a janitor at the Salt River Project corporate offices on East Washington. He worked the graveyard shift, so he slept during the day. Because our house was so small we were constantly being told to play outside, so outside was where most of our time was spent.

That was when I met Tommy, who lived a block to the east. Tommy had three sisters, eighteen-year-old Amy, Janice was sixteen, and Jane was six years old.

Tommy introduced me to his two friends, David and Dale Stone, who were brothers. The Stone family lived on my street, about a block and a half away. Their father was a midget, nick-named "Stony," and their mother was an attractive woman who spoke with a southern drawl. They were a close family, and they had no trouble expressing their feelings to each other. I enjoyed being around them.

One day Tommy, David, Dale, my little brother, Richard, and I came up with an idea to build an underground clubhouse. It took us three days of digging. It was ten feet long by ten feet wide and seven feet deep. We built the roof out of old scrap lumber we found in the neighbor's garbage. We were very proud of what we accomplished!

Two days after we had finished it, the five of us were playing inside when Tommy's two older sisters came by. They asked if we wanted to play army with them. They immediately set the rules. Janice said, "Since there are five of you and only two of us, we get the clubhouse." Like men often do for women, we agreed.

It didn't take long after our "play war" began for me be taken prisoner. I was taken down into the clubhouse to be interrogated. Sixteen year old Janice held me while Amy performed oral sex on me. I fought them, but not for very long, because I soon discovered that what she was doing to me felt good! Then they helped me pull my pants up and they let me go. It was not long before I allowed myself to get caught again. This time I needed no help getting my pants off. Janice took hers off, too, while Amy took off her top. While Janice and I had sex, Amy rubbed up against my backside with her breasts. I was eight years old and I felt I had just died and gone to heaven. I had no idea how inappropriate this behavior was and that I was being molested. As we were getting dressed, Tommy's little sister yelled down for them to come home for dinner. They both kissed me, and then they left.

I never saw Tommy or his sisters again. And I have never spoken of this to anyone until now.

Having your first sexual experience at the age of eight is like building the roof on your house before digging the foundation. What made things even worse was that the rest of my life would be no different: first execute, then plan. I wonder to this day just how different my life might have been if I had been introduced to sex at the right time and place. I can only guess, without any other reference to compare, how my married life would have been different. Building the self-image of a child is a complex and wonderful process that can drastically be altered if something inappropriate is introduced into that process. Sex is a crucial part of one's self-image, and I can't help wondering how much of me was lost or destroyed by the predators in my life. I wonder now how many of my later problems came from a loss of self-identity as a child.

The next few months I spent more time with David than I did with Dale. Dale was more my little brother's age, so they spent time together. Because David and I spent so much time together, it didn't take long for him to see the dysfunction in my family. Sometimes he would ask me about it. He was a good friend and I believed he really cared, but in my family we didn't talk about what went on inside it, not even with our closest friends.

One Thursday morning, David and I were sitting in a lot that was half way between my house and his. We were sitting on a fallen tree, which had been blown down during a monsoon storm the year before. The two of us spent a lot of time on that stump, just hanging out. This particular morning, we were talking about how cool people looked when they smoked. We ended up talking ourselves into trying it. We both agreed to steal a carton of cigarettes from home and meet back there in an hour. His parents smoked Pall Malls non-filter cigarettes and mine smoked Viceroys.

We were both back before the hour was up, each of us with our carton of smokes. His parents weren't home and my father was asleep, so we both found it easy to get the cigarettes. Sitting on the tree, I handed him five packs of Viceroys and he handed me five packs of Pall Malls. Then we lit up. Neither of us inhaled. I didn't even know how! We smoked one right after another until both cartons were gone. We smoked all four hundred cigarettes in about an hour and a half. I don't think I've ever heard of anyone who accomplished that in an hour and a half.

Now, it was mid-August and it was a hot day—well over 100 degrees—and sitting on that log with no shade, smoking all those cigarettes like we did, it was no wonder I got sick. Oh, did I get sick! I told David I had to go and he looked like he needed to go, too. I just about crawled home, I was so sick. I made it to the front door, opened it, stepped inside and threw up all over the floor. And then I just lay there, I couldn't seem to move. Every time tried I to get up, I'd throw up again.

My parents never said a word to me as I lay there throwing up. They sat there on the couch watching me for almost an hour. When they thought I was through, my father walked over to me and pulled out a pack of cigarettes from his shirt pocket and offered me one. Just looking at it made me sick all over again. I yelled out, "No, thank you, I'll never smoke again!" My mother came over with a pail of soapy water and told me to clean up, so I did. I was told that David repeated the same act at his house, his parents reacting pretty much in the same way. I didn't smoke again for another five years. A month later the Stone family moved and I never saw David or Dale again.

When I started school that year, my mother had made arrangements to have me held back a year, and I repeated the second grade. M.T. Macken Elementary was on 22nd Street just south of Thomas Road. I was put into Miss Bailey's second grade class. Within a month it was obvious I couldn't keep up with her class either, so I was put into Miss Montgomery's class. Miss Montgomery's class was for the "special kids" who were having problems of all kinds, and for all sorts of different reasons. I thought maybe I was a dummy. How could I have known that the rest of the problems in my life were probably more at fault than my level of intelligence? The other kids referred us to as "the dummies class!" God, I hated that. I didn't feel dumb, but then again I wasn't sure. "They" said I was, so I figured I probably was, but mostly what I felt was "different."

What made matters worse was that we were poor and all my clothes were hand-me-downs, some too big for me and/or had patches. My shoes were too big for my feet and they had holes in the soles.

Worse yet, I still had my New York accent. I was constantly the object of taunting at school. I was so embarrassed that I tried to change the way I spoke. The way we speak is something that belongs to us on a very personal level. Again, I was abandoning who I was in an attempt to make myself more acceptable to others. I began to slow down and pronounced my words carefully, and my accent changed, but my life didn't.

I hated school! No matter how hard I tried, I couldn't stop the other kids from making fun of me. I tried on several occasions to tell my mother what was going on. I expressed how it made me feel when the other kids called me dummy and made fun of the way I looked and spoke. I even suggested to her that if I had new clothes, or even clothes that fit me better, it might keep the kids from teasing me.

The reality was that we were poor and we had no money to buy new clothes. There was nothing my mother could do and I knew that, but like most kids in dysfunctional families, I offered suggestions. I even suggested that if dad would slow down his drinking we'd have more.

Now that was probably true, but Mother slapped me and said that dad's drinking wasn't my business. She screamed at me that I was wrong for thinking this way, and that my father worked very hard to support our family. She told me that father was entitled to a little relief now and then. I learned this very thoroughly from her that day, and it took me a very long time to let go of that belief and allow myself to understand how unhealthy it actually was.

About a week later my father met Andy Nelson at the "Mecca," a bar around 7th street and Virginia. Andy and my father had a lot in common. They both were married and had children about the same ages. His children were also attending M.T. Macken Elementary. Dot, Andy's wife, and my mother also had a lot in common… drunk husbands.

Andy and Dot had four children. Drew was their only son. It didn't take long to figure out that their family was just as dysfunctional as mine. They lived only three blocks from our school and our families spent a lot of time together. Andy and his son were both outdoorsmen and enjoyed fishing and hunting. Soon after we met Andy he invited my father and us kids along on some of their trips. We spent most of the time on these trips alone as children while Andy and my father drank. I really enjoyed these trips. Drew seemed to know what he was doing and that helped me feel safe in the strange wilds of Mother Nature that were so foreign to me.

Living across the street from us were Arnie and Joy, and their two daughters, Suzie and Sherri. Arnie was a cross-country truck driver. He drove from coast to coast for Cudahay, a meat packing company based in Phoenix. Arnie had a drinking problem and was, to say the least, a scary drunk. Their family appeared to me to be every bit as dysfunctional as we were. There were times when Arnie drank that he would fight with his wife. When they fought it scared his daughters. I remember Susie and Sherri always talking about how relieved they felt when Arnie was on the road.

When Arnie fought with his wife, sometimes it got physical and my mother would often help clean her up. It wasn't called "Domestic Violence" back then. If police were called, they were far more interested in keeping the noise down than in the welfare of the combatants. Of course the police in those days didn't always come when husbands were beating up their wives. Police just didn't get involved with family fights back then. Why go through the hassle when the wife would drop the charges as soon as the husband sobered up?

It's clear to me now that sick or dysfunctional people attract each other. The old adage, "birds of a feather flock together" doesn't quite say it right. Perhaps when you are banished to a leper colony the only other people who will associate with you also have the same disease.

As young as I was, I felt my life was out of control. The more I tried to take control, the less control I appeared to have. The less control I had, the more frustrated I became. The more frustrated I became, the more I struck back in defiance. Each time someone shot me down it appeared to me more like war, and make no mistake, this was war! I was taking my frustration out on my family. I was fighting more with my brothers. I didn't care. After everything else disappears, "All's fair in love and war." I was miserable and by God I wanted company. I became the official gopher for my father and his friends when they drank in our yard. Each time I would get them a beer I began taking a drink or two before delivering it to them. On a good day, I could down two or three beers if I played my cards right.

At this time in my life I was experiencing tremendous pain in my feet and lower legs when I walked long distances, and boy did I do a lot of walking! When I told my mother about it she would tell me to stop complaining. Mother accused me of just trying to get attention. No matter how much I complained, she just wouldn't listen.

She would tell me, "You're not the only one in this family." But, the reality was that I hurt, and the pain was getting worse. I complained daily. I just couldn't help it.

My Aunt Mary was a lab technician at the Crippled Children's Hospital on 18th Street and Roosevelt, less than six blocks from our house. She told my mother about the services they offered and she suggested that it might be a good idea to take me to see a doctor.

The following day my aunt brought over an application for my mother to fill out. It didn't take long to get approved and I got an appointment. I was assigned to Dr. Allen, an orthopedic specialist. After a month of x-rays and examinations, mother was told that I had an abnormal birth defect. I was born with brittle cartilage in between the bones in my feet and ankles. He explained to her that it would continue to get worse and the pain would persist if I didn't have corrective surgery. He said they would work on one foot and ankle at a time and that he would schedule the first surgery within the next month.

I had spent six months trying to convince my parents that there was something wrong and they had refused to listen. I was relieved when the doctor told my mother what was happening, but at the same time I felt hurt that they hadn't believed me the first time.

I was nine years old when I entered the Crippled Children's Hospital for the first time. The day of my surgery, when I awoke, my mother was by my bedside. She had brought me some comic books. I thought I must have had a bad reaction to the ether because I was sick; I threw up for two days. It reminded me of when David Stone and I smoked all those cigarettes on that hot August day.

After two days, I was put in a large dorm, which had ten beds, all of which were occupied. My aunt would come and see me on her breaks. My parents, on the other hand, didn't come by to see me much at all. Mother brought me comic books a couple of times during my two-month stay, but that was it. And my father never came to see me at all. I would ask my aunt, "When are my parents coming?"

"Soon," she would always tell me.

I wondered how long it would take my parents to notice if I fell off the back of the truck or if I didn't come home for a few weeks. I wondered if they would come to my funeral if I died. Then I wondered, after they missed my funeral, if they would even remember that I was ever their son. Gradually, self-pity turned to anger, and after a while I began to wonder if the only thing my father would ever miss would be a can of beer. Somewhere in my head, in my struggle to be important, beer rose with my self-image, too. "If I were a beer, dad would visit me." All hail the mighty beer! Beer was the home I never had, or perhaps beer was the home I never was.

I felt like I had when we were forced to live with Aunt Betty when I was six. Again I was sitting on the porch waiting for my parents to come. Minutes turned into hours, hours to days and days to weeks. After a few weeks I stopped thinking about them. I wondered if they stopped thinking about me too. I think my Aunt Mary gave up on them as well, because she made it a point to spend more time with me. What I didn't know was that my father's drinking was getting bad again and that things were crazy.

The day I was discharged from the hospital, my mother was there to pick me up. She acted as if it was no big deal. When I said something about it, she told me I was being a baby. She'd had to endure so much rejection in her own life that my feelings of rejection must have seemed trivial to her. I was different and really didn't belong to them anymore. The more I was separated from my feelings, the more my feelings died inside me. At the time I was unable to see that my mother was just as sick as my father. Like I said before, anger is the last emotion standing, and in the case of my mother, she was losing control as she lost everything else in her life. My brothers and I represented what she had lost, and she lashed out more fervently against us as the rage took control of her.

It was June of 1959 when my mother became pregnant with my sister Lynn. Three months into her pregnancy, my father was fighting with my mother out in the front yard when my mother tripped over my brother's bike. In the fall, she broke both wrists. My father picked her up and drove her to Doctors Hospital on 20th Street and Thomas. She was in casts the rest of her pregnancy. She made do with the help of her good friends, Joy and Dot.

Chapter Six

Ol' One Eye

"I believe that in a dysfunctional family, we learn to look at inappropriate behaviors as normal. Then we move as quickly as we can into acceptance, because if we don't, we get stuck in the injustice and it causes more pain."
-- *John Carter*

Because of the way I was treated, it wasn't uncommon for me to avoid school whenever I could. This day was no different. I spent forty-five minutes with the covers over my head, in ninety-five degree weather, trying to create the mood of illness. I kept telling myself over and over again that I was sick. I psyched myself into believing I had a fever and I played the role to convince my mother. That day, as it had so many times before, it worked like a charm. She felt my forehead with the back of her hand and said it felt warm. She told me to stay in bed. Just before eight o'clock mother walked across the street and Joy let her use the phone to call the school. At eight forty-five Dot came over for coffee with my mother. During their visit, Vance and I slipped out the back door to play.

I found an old frog gig in the irrigation ditch that ran along the back fence. A frog gig resembles a small three-pronged pitchfork with barbs on the end of each prong so that when a frog is speared the barbs kept them from sliding off. The two prongs on the outside were bent slightly and it had been outside for so long that there was rust where the red paint used to be. I asked Vance if he wanted to play chicken. I said, "I'll throw it up in the air as high as I can and see how close it comes to you. If you move out of the way, you're a chicken." He agreed, but with some reluctance.

About ten minutes into the game, Vance took his turn. He took the frog gig in his left hand to steady it, and with his right hand pushed it up as hard as he could. It reminded me of a missile being launched straight up into the air. It went so high I was mesmerized; I couldn't take my eyes off of it! I watched it go up about eighteen feet or so, turn around in the air and come back down. Vance yelled, "Get out of the way!"

But it was already too late. When I looked up again, the frog gig hit me in the face. It felt like my face exploded. The middle prong hit me right between the eyes and stuck into my nose. One prong stuck part way into my left eye and the other, slightly bent, laid against my right eye. I felt my face go numb. I must have lost consciousness. When I awoke I was on the ground. I could see out of the corner of my right eye. The handle stuck out so far that it weighed my face down. I could hardly lift my head. I grabbed hold of the handle and tried to pull it out of my face, but the barbs were so embedded that the handle came off in my hands. I was scared and confused; I just knew I was going die. I had to fight to stay conscious.

I stood up to get my bearings and found the south sidewall of my house. I tried walking along it in an attempt to get help. As I was feeling my way along the wall like a blind man, my mother, Dot and my little brother Vance came running around the corner of the house. My mother, seeing the frog gig still in my face, started screaming, "Why are you trying to kill me you son-of-a-bitch!"

Dot grabbed me and told my mother to get in the car. Joy, from across the street, had heard all the commotion and come running. When she saw what had happened, she grabbed Vance and told my mother and Dot to just go!

All the way to Doctors Hospital, my mother continued to yell and scream at me. "I can't take this! Between you and your father, I don't know who's going to kill me first! Why are you trying to kill me?" I tried to reason with her, but she wouldn't listen. All I could think about was how I made my mother feel and that I was sorry. I really had to fight blacking out and feared that if I did, I would die. I didn't mind being sick and missing school, but I most certainly didn't want to die for real. It was important for me to convince my mother I wasn't trying to hurt her and that it was an accident. I didn't want her to feel responsible. She wasn't to blame for the problems I was feeling deep inside.

It didn't take long to get to the hospital. Dot pulled up to the emergency room door, jumped out and ran inside for help. Out of the corner of my eye, I saw a nurse running toward the car with a wheelchair. I was half out of the car when I turned around to face her. She looked startled. She told me to sit in the chair; and then she adjusted my feet and hurried toward the emergency room doors as fast as I've seen anyone move, while Dot helped my mother out of the car.

As we entered the emergency room, I noticed that it became deathly quiet. Everyone stared as the nurse wheeled me by. Even those who worked there stopped what they were doing. Some ran over to offer assistance. My heart was racing and I felt light headed. I was terrified!

I was transferred from the wheelchair to a gurney and wheeled into a private room. As I lay there, still thinking about my mother's reaction, a doctor came in and introduced himself. "Hi," he said, "I'm Doctor Aiello, and I'm here to help you. I'm not going to tell you it's not serious, because it is." I was glad he was talking to me, because if left up to my mother, I knew instinctively that she wouldn't have told me the straight truth.

Doctor Aiello was an eye surgeon from New York who had been getting ready to catch a plane to go home. It was lucky for me that he happened to see me as he was exiting the building through the emergency room to a waiting cab.

He now examined me and said, "I think I can help." He was frank with me, which I appreciated. "I can save your life, but I'm not sure I can save your eyesight."

I was scared of being blind and I told him so. The doctor assured me that he would do everything he could but that he was making no promises. Some hope was better than none, right? I had felt that ray of hope many times in my life, and would again. It's like getting a second wind in a race. I prayed, "God, please don't let me go blind. I don't want to live blind." To my right, I could see my father walking up. He took one look at me and fainted. Now that didn't give me any confidence at all!

They wheeled me into a much larger room, where they cleaned me up and gave me several shots in preparation for surgery. Within five minutes I was out cold.

When I awoke the next day, I was in my own room across from the nurse's station. My left eye and nose were bandaged, but I could see out of my right eye. Being able to see was all I cared about. My prayers had been answered!

I had turned on the TV, and was gratefully watching it, when my doctor walked in and asked me how I was feeling. I thanked him profusely for saving my eyesight. He told me that I was very lucky the prongs on the gig had been bent, or I would have lost both eyes. I shuddered when I thought about it.

When my mother came to visit, I asked her when I could go home. She told me that when she was talking to the doctor earlier, he had mentioned that I could go home as early as the following day, if I didn't have a fever. Mother looked tired. She told me the police had questioned Vance about what happened. He was terrified by what happened and thought the police were going to take him to jail. That made me angry. I felt sorry for him. I knew he didn't mean it. Hell, if the truth were known, it was probably my fault. He was really happy to see me when I came home from the hospital.

I wore a black patch over my left eye for about three months. At first I thought it was cool, but that was short lived. It was my thought that maybe things would be different when I went back to school, now that I had been injured and lost my eye. Yeah, right. They made fun of me even more they had before. Cynically, I had to ask myself what had ever possessed me to think the kids at school would show me any compassion. They started calling me "Ol' one eye."

This was the point in my life in which I really stopped caring. I hated school, I hated my family, and most of all, I hated myself! I continued to distance myself by misbehaving. This only caused my alienation to get worse. One thing about isolating yourself from everyone is that you're left with the only person you can count on: yourself. These partial rescues from crisis had set a pattern in my life. Each time there was a crisis, there were consequences. But each time I escaped, even partially, nothing was really ever resolved. Things only got worse.

My father's drinking continued to escalate. He spent more time sitting out in the front yard with his drinking buddies. {At least they accepted him when he couldn't drink around mother without her approval.}

Drunks drink to get approval to begin with. Alcohol depresses the senses of guilt and shame for a while, especially if one is drinking with those who are looking for the same effect. When that one drinks around someone who instantly disapproves, the whole effect is lost.

The wives would cook or sit outside and gossip while the kids played, and I continued to be gopher for my father and his friends. Hell, I even had my own church key. I loved my job as gopher. On a good night, I could get a pretty good "buzz" going. Loneliness is a dish that is always served cold. Alcohol warmed that feeling.

My sister Lynn Ann was born on March 16, 1960. She was the first girl in our family, and I wondered if things would change now that we had a sister.

W. L. (Skip) Carter

Chapter Seven

THE BOXER

"...I equated waiting for my parents to show up
with watching a pot of water, waiting for it to boil;
it always took forever for either of these things to happen,
if it ever even did happen...I was preparing myself for
the day when I would be completely without
the support of my family."
-- John Carter

My brothers and I fought constantly. My parents were always breaking us up. One day my father brought home two pair of boxing gloves. He told my brothers and me, "I'm tired of all the fighting, so next time you get into it, you boys can take it outside and beat the hell out of each other." I started most of the fights to begin with, I thought, so why not take it to another level? I didn't care beyond what was safe inside of me! I had developed quite an attitude by this time in my life. The only feeling left standing inside me was anger.

One Saturday evening, with a yard full of people, I'd been drinking more than usual, and I had a good buzz going. I started giving Steve a hard time. He told me to back off several times, and of course I wouldn't, so it was on! The next thing I knew, we were in the middle of the yard, boxing. Steve wouldn't hit me back, so I won. Everyone congratulated me. Arnie from across the street called me "slugger," and others called me "champ." I was the center of attention. I loved it, and all I had to do was start it! My father and his friends enjoyed it so much that it became a weekly event. We became the entertainment.

I have always suspected, even then, that I didn't win because I was the better fighter. I won, I think, because my older brother didn't want to hurt me. I remember times when he would beg me to stop. Instead, though, the more he begged, the more brutal I became. I could even see the frustration on his face. I didn't care, because I was the man of the hour. I felt like I mattered and I didn't want to give that up. The look on his face still haunts me today as I look back on it. He must have hated having to perform for our father and his friends.

As for me, though, for the first time in my life, I felt like I was somebody. Whenever there was a gathering in our yard, I would start an argument, the boxing gloves would come out, and once again – victory! I was the champ! It worked out well for me, even at the cost of my older brother's dignity. I am sorry for that, but in a dysfunctional family someone had to be on the bottom, and for once it wasn't me. Of course, my reign as champ didn't last long. Within a few months it got old, the boxing gloves were retired, and all went back the way it had been before.

It was the summer of 1960 when my parents were able to put together enough money for a down payment on a new house in Tempe, Arizona. It was a large block home with four bedrooms, two bathrooms, a living room, a family room and a kitchen. It was perfect for a family our size. My mother had just had her fifth child, so we were going to need more room. It would be great not having to sleep three in a full-sized bed. I hated my nights in the middle, as I'm sure my brothers did as well.

Arnie and Joy bought a house on the opposite side of the street three houses to the east of us, and the Brook family, who lived next door to us on 21st Place, bought a home behind us on the next block. It was as if the whole neighborhood were moving to Tempe with us. Our house was used as the model for the other houses under construction and when the other houses were built, we would move in. The neighborhood was completed in late 1962. My parents were very excited, and they checked often on the progress of construction.

One day I was home by myself, the rest of the family having gone to Tempe to check on our new home. My brother's friend Stephen knocked on our door. I opened it and told him no one was home except me. He asked me if he could come in and wait for Steve.

At first, I was hesitant. I thought Stephen was strange; he had always reminded me of "Lumpy" on the "Leave it to Beaver" show. Once inside, he became sexually aggressive. Stephen molested me, and he told me that if I told anyone he would come back and kill me. Then he threw a dollar on the bed and left. I was scared, and then angry, and then just confused. Confusion turned quickly into shame, so I didn't tell anyone until many years later. Nothing causes isolation and feelings of loneliness like having your body personally violated. Whatever trust I had previously had left for the world had turned around one hundred eighty degrees into defensiveness.

I misbehaved constantly around people as a defense mechanism. My self-esteem, if I had ever had any at all, was now gone. I didn't like myself, and nobody else liked me, either. I was feeling less and less a part of this world, and I began to wonder what it would be like to die. Would it hurt? Was there really a heaven or a hell? I had heard somewhere that if you killed yourself you would go to hell. I wondered, if you were already dead, would it hurt to burn? I thought about it a lot. I was only nine years old and I felt I had been living forever. I know now I really didn't want to die, I just wanted to be out of this emotional hell I was in.

My father's drinking seemed to stabilize again. This time he wouldn't drink on days he worked, but on days he didn't, he would drink until he passed out. I was also drinking more now. When my father or his friends asked for a beer, I would drink almost a fourth of the can before I gave it to them. When I would drink too much and my mother noticed, she got angry and said something to my father; then my father would get his own beer the rest of the evening. When I drank too much and my father would notice, he would tell me to slow down. I'd tell him I would, but never did. I was drinking three to four times a week. I stole beer a time or two out of the fridge, but my father noticed, so I stopped.

In 1962, just before we moved to Tempe, I went back into the Crippled Children's Hospital. My stay there this time was for six weeks. I had the same surgery on the other ankle and foot. I received one or two visits from my mother…no big deal. After all, they were moving, and my mother had my little sister to take care of. This time I knew what to expect from my family. I knew they would leave me abandoned.

In a dysfunctional family one learns to look at inappropriate behaviors as normal, because if we don't change our perceptions, we get stuck in the injustice and it causes more pain. Besides, I equated waiting for my parents to show up with watching a pot of water, waiting for it to boil; it always took forever for either of these things to happen, if it ever even did happen. I was not going to go there this time. I was preparing myself for the day when I would be completely without the support of my family.

Chapter Eight

MOVING ON UP TO THE EAST SIDE

"It has always seemed ironic to me how
friendships created out of conflict
endure so well through the years."
-- *Paul R.*

The day I was released from the hospital, I was taken to our new home in Tempe. Steve had his own room, Richard and I shared a room. Vance and Lynn shared the other room. My brothers and I shared the bathroom in the hallway and my parents and little sister shared the bathroom off their bedroom. The house was huge—it was bigger than any place I'd ever lived before, and I loved the new feeling of freedom.

The following Monday, I started my new school. It was on 68th Street and Continental Drive. The school was called Supi Elementary and I was entering the fourth grade. My teacher was Mr. Castillo. I started a month late because I was in the hospital and I had some catching up to do. I began the year under pressure. I had a cast on my right foot and ankle up to my knee and walked on crutches.

I always hated the first day at school. In the past, it had always proven to be disastrous. During lunch, I was standing in line talking with my new friend, Carl, who sat next to me in class. He was telling me about the bully who terrorized the school. The bully was in the fourth grade, but even kids in the eighth grade were afraid of him. Carl then leaned over and whispered in my ear, "I heard somewhere, he even killed a kid from another school."

I remember thinking, "I hope I don't run in to this guy." I didn't need any trouble in this new school.

As Carl was talking, some kid no bigger than me walked up and said, "You're in my way, move it."

He didn't look very tough so I said, "Go fuck yourself!" I thought there was more than enough room to get around me.

I don't think he liked the response I gave him, because he started poking me in the chest with his right index finger as he glared into my eyes, trying to intimidate me. He then said, "Be on the upper playground after school. You're dead!"

"What an asshole," I thought. He could see I was wearing a cast up to my knee and that I was on crutches. I looked back into his eyes and said, "Yeah right," and then I turned away as if to say, "Get away from me. I'm busy." I then turned back to Carl and said, loud enough for the chest-poker to hear me, "I think he's just trying to impress his friends."

This kid then looked back at me and mouthed, "Be there." He pointed again to the upper playground. He then walked to the front of the lunch line and took cuts in front of everyone.

I couldn't believe this guy. I went back to my conversation with Carl and said, "Tell me more about this bully I need to avoid."

"His name is Danny." Carl's eyes got real big "And, too late. You just met him." Carl was now shaking his head from side to side.

I freaked! I thought about leaving school and not coming back. All of my emotions left me at once. With the exception, of course, of anger—anger that I had found another problem. It was as if I was wearing a sign that read, "Loser." I couldn't even eat lunch. All I could think about was having to fight this guy.

In class, as I sat there preoccupied with what was to come when the bell rang, I started to get angry. I thought, "Screw him, I'm tired of running." I decided to take a stand.

When the bell rang, I swung myself outside. I was met there by a group of kids, and standing in the middle was Danny, pointing to the playground.

With a shit eating grin on his face, Danny asked me, "Ready to get your butt beat?"

I didn't say anything. I refused to show fear. I was afraid that would add to his pleasure. I could tell he was enjoying the moment. He walked in front of me, and as I followed, I was taunted by his friends.

"Ready to get your ass kicked?" I heard one ask.

Another said, "You're a dead man!"

I was angry, and I was getting even angrier as I hobbled to my death. There I was, on crutches, with a cast up to my knee, and the school bully was about to kick my butt.

What was wrong with this picture? I couldn't turn my mind off. I was so angry, I was seeing red. By the time we reached the upper playground and he started to turn around, I was holding my crutch like a baseball bat! I was ready for him; I swung it and hit him in the back of his head as hard as I could. Danny went face first into the ground. I then started beating him with my crutch. Danny's two friends grabbed me, so he could get up.

I thought, "This is it." I closed my eyes, stopped fighting, and waited with anticipation for the beating to commence.

After what seemed like a long time, I opened my eyes and saw Danny stagger as he stood up. He reached back to rub his head where I had hit him with my crutch and discovered he was bleeding. He looked at the blood on his hand and smiled. He then told his friends to let me go. I knew I was dead. I just stood there. I had made up my mind that I would use any means I could not to get hurt too badly, but Danny didn't move. He just stood there with this half-assed grin on his face. He looked down at the blood on his hand, and then back at me. He did this four or five times.

No one said a word, and no one made a move. I had clearly made my stand, and as far as I was concerned, I wasn't backing down at any price. I think Danny saw that, and I also believe he gained a new respect for me that day, because Danny's next move was as much of a shock to me as it was to the forty or so kids who were watching. Danny wiped the blood from his right hand, onto the front of his shirt. He then extended it out to shake my hand, offering it in friendship. Next, he turned to the other kids, including his two friends, and said, "This guy has more balls than anyone here." He then told me I was his new best friend and that he would see me tomorrow. He turned to his friends and told them to get lost, and then Danny left by himself.

I am not sure how this experience contributed to my addictive behavior except to say that I used this memory many times when I sought acceptance from others or when I was in real trouble. It was like a secret medicine to heal my wounds inside.

Danny was true to his word; he and I spent a lot of time together over the next year and a half, and I was as respected as he was in school. I was known as the only living person who ever stood up to the school bully, although I do have to say that as I came to know him, I don't believe he was a bully at all. I learned to know him as a very kind person, who—quite paradoxically—really cared about people. It has always seemed ironic to me how friendships created out of conflict can endure so well through the years.

Being Danny's friend turned out to be some of the best times of my life. His family made me feel welcome in their home. Danny had a younger sister, Debbie. She was beautiful and I had a major crush on her, but I didn't feel like I was in her league, so I never told her how I felt.

I had other friends that I spent time with when Danny wasn't around. A couple of them were Randy and Steve. The three of us were in Mr. Castillo's class together.

Randy loved joking with people, but sometimes he took it too far. For instance, I remember one time he put a thumbtack in another teacher's chair. She turned out to be a diabetic and it almost killed her. He was expelled from school for a week, and his parents were extremely angry with him. Randy came from a good family. His father worked at the Auto Safety House on 44th Street and Washington in Phoenix. I remember that they built school busses and I thought that was cool. His mother was a house wife. When I was at their house, I pretty much had a standing invite to eat with them. They never asked if I wanted to stay, they just set a plate for me at the table. Lunch, dinner, it didn't matter. They always made me feel welcome. Randy had a younger brother, Steven. Steven was a good kid, who didn't talk much and stayed mostly to himself.

Steve, on the other hand, came from a dysfunctional family like I did. I didn't know his family like I knew Randy's, but I could see things weren't right. Steve's father was an angry man. If the truth were known, he was probably an alcoholic. His mother was a very docile woman who waited on her husband hand and foot. Steve had three brothers and a younger sister. The times I was there, the whole family walked on eggshells around their father, and if things didn't go his way, he would become violent and would beat them. From what I could see, Steve could never please his father.

One Saturday morning I went over to his house to see if he could hang out. "I have some work to do in the back yard and then I can go," he told me.

"I'll help," I said.

In the back yard, I trimmed and he mowed. We were almost finished when his father came out the back door with a beer in his hand. There was no telling how much he'd already had to drink, but he was slurring his words. He pointed out a spot that Steve had already mowed and said, "You missed a spot."

When Steve came back with a smart answer, his father went off! He turned to Steve and hit him on the side of his head with his fist. Steve went down. When he stood up, his father gave him a beating like he would give another man.

I felt embarrassed for Steve and angry because his father wouldn't stop. His father then turned to me and screamed, "Get the hell out of my yard!" I left without a word because I thought he would take it out on Steve if I didn't.

I saw Steve two days later at school. I told him I was worried about him. He said, "I'm used to it, I'm fine," as if it were an everyday occurrence. I truly understand this today. You see, Steve thought his father's behaviors were normal. It was on that day that I realized I was not alone. There were other families out there just as dysfunctional as mine.

On October 15, 1963, my mother gave birth to my baby sister Penny Ann. She was the last of six children, and that would complete our family.

Chapter Nine

The Fall of A Kennedy

"The only time
I felt any emotion was
when I didn't get my way.
Life was all about me!"

It was the morning of November 22, 1963. The clock over the chalkboard at the front of the classroom read 9:30. My friend Steve was being funny and making me laugh. Our teacher, Mr. Castillo, was telling us to pull it together when an announcement came over the P.A. system. It was the office telling all teachers in all grades to turn on their TV's. I was in the fifth grade now and Mr. Castillo had moved up a grade level so he remained my teacher.

Our class watched in horror, as people were milling around the streets of Dallas, TX. Walter Cronkite was announcing that "John F. Kennedy, the President of the United States, had just been shot and is being rushed to Parkland Hospital."

Some of my classmates were crying, most sat there in disbelief. I didn't know how to act. By this time, I was so out of touch with my feelings that I couldn't feel anything, so I told myself, "When in Rome, do as the Romans do." We watched for maybe ten minutes when another announcement squawked over the P.A. and told us that all schools were being let out and we were to go straight home. I thought, "Only in America!"

When I walked through the front door, my mother was sitting in the recliner watching the TV and crying. They were announcing that John F. Kennedy had died and that Vice-President Lyndon Baines Johnson was being sworn in as our new President. Over the next week or so, the world mourned. All I could think about was that it was on every channel and that it was interfering with my shows. The only time I felt any emotion outside of my own existence was when I didn't get my way. Life was all about me!

It wasn't long after John Kennedy was shot that we moved again. We rented out our home because of financial problems my parents were having. The plan was to move back when things improved.

The Salt River Project owned several homes that employees could rent if they were available. The rent was $11.00 a month. My father had put in his request six months earlier, and one came available around the end of May 1964. The house was located at 43rd Avenue and Peoria and at the time it was surrounded by farmland.

My father once told me that the bar and store in the neighborhood was a co-op owned by the farmers. The laborers could drink and buy food for their families on an account and it would be deducted from their wages.

With the money my parents were saving on the rent, it enabled them to work on their finances. Of course, my mother hated the move. She started to complain again, like she had when we lived in Tombstone. She hated the bugs and the heat. She didn't like all the animals that were starting to accumulate on our four acres of land. She was miserable and she went out of her way to let everyone know it. We had chickens, ducks, geese, rabbits, guinea pigs, a jackass, a pig and a black German Shepherd named "Sam."

My mother hated the pig most of all because my father, when he was drunk, named the pig after her. He named her "Rosie," and this made our lives a living hell for about two weeks. Mother never let things go, and I believe she took that resentment to her grave.

My parents fought over every little thing, but mostly finances because of my father's drinking. I often wondered why anyone would put up with the things my father put my mother and our family through. The only conclusion I could come up with, at this young age, was that my mother was just as sick as he was, if not sicker.

I personally liked living there; we had a room off of the barn that my parents let me live in for a short period of time. One rainy monsoon evening around seven thirty, all hell broke loose. My roof leaked so badly it was as if someone had put a water hose on my roof and turned it on full blast. Ten minutes later, everything I owned, including myself, was drenched. I moved back into the house that night.

It was great living out of the city. I loved the quiet, the animals, and all the things there were to do that I'd be in trouble for if I still lived in Tempe, like shooting my BB gun. Let's face it, I enjoyed not being around people. I thought that if there was no one around maybe my parents would get along better as the time went on. That was my thinking. But, as usual, I was wrong. After living there a few months it became obvious that wasn't going to happen. I tried so hard to understand them better so I could fix them. What was I thinking, anyway?!

Chapter Ten

The Hispanic Elvis

I have always admired Jesse and his determination to succeed. That time with him was more of an education on life than I could have ever realized at the time. He was only fourteen years old, and he was my hero. I still benefit from my encounter with him.

It was the end of summer and time to go back to school. Richard and I would attend Cholla Elementary, and my older brother Steve went to Cortez High. Our bus stops were on 43rd Avenue, across the street from each other. Our bus stop included all the kids from the farm labor camp, across the street from my house.

Going to a new school was again hard for me. Having to start over with new friends and teachers was like starting at ground zero when I already felt like I was there to begin with.

When my brother and I got off the bus, I noticed several kids gathered around what looked like six tetherball poles. I had seen a few poles at other schools that I had attended, but I had never paid attention to how the game was played. I watched for a while, and then asked Richard if he would hold my books so I could try it. He told me he would, so I got in line. I asked the kid in front of me how it was played. It didn't look difficult. It looked like a twelve-foot pole connected at the top with a chain and a rope with a soccer sized ball on the end.

The kid next to me said the objective was to hit the ball hard enough to wrap the rope and chain around the pole until the ball touched the pole. Your adversary stands facing you from the other side and tries to wrap the ball around the pole in the other direction. Sounded simple enough, I thought, so I waited in line. The same person continued winning in the line I was standing in and it didn't take long. One, maybe two minutes and he was inviting the next person in line to join him. He was good, there was no doubt about that. But, that didn't scare me. I knew, even without trying, that I could do it.

The kid standing next to me told me the winner's name was Jesse. I thought Jesse looked like a Hispanic Elvis, the way he combed his hair and wore his clothes. He said, "Jesse has been playing tetherball for about two years, and he's known around school as "Champion of the Poles." I've never met anyone who could beat him, but they all try." As we talked, the kid in front of us was walking away in defeat. Jesse told my new friend to wait a minute and that he needed to catch his breath. While Jesse rested, my friend continued to tell me about him. "Jesse has a reputation and is well respected. He doesn't go around bullying other kids, but if there's a challenge, he always ends up on top."

"He sounds like a good guy," I said.

Jesse waved him in. He was out in less than a minute.

It was my turn and, only knowing the mechanics but never having played the game before, I thought I did very well. As a matter of fact, I did so well that I was accused of lying about never having played the game before. He was good, but so was I. As we went back and forth we both came close several times, but neither one of us could pull off a win. We continued playing until the second bell, maybe fifteen minutes or so. We had drawn a large crowd, and they cheered when we stopped the game. Jesse walked over to me and put his arm around my neck as if we were old pals, and then he walked me to class.

Jesse and I developed a bond that day and we stayed friends until I moved a year or so later. When we weren't in class, we were out at the poles. One day on our bus ride home, I asked him if he could come over and hang out.

Jesse lived with his family in the camp across the street from our house. He turned to me and politely said, "I'd love to come over, but I can't." I didn't understand. I thought we were friends. Then Jesse explained, and what he told me made me feel proud to be his friend. He said, "Living in a Farm Labor Camp I have responsibilities. When we are hired, the whole family works. My day starts at 4:00 in the morning. At 7:00 I get ready for school. When I get home from school, I eat, do my homework and then I go back to work in the fields until dark. On weekends I work twelve hour days."

I just listened while he talked. He continued, "I am grateful to my family that I can go to school. I have two older brothers who never went, but my family knows that I want to be a doctor or a lawyer. I'd like to be able to take care of my family someday. That's my dream." When Jesse finished, I sat there thinking how fortunate I was. I've never been expected to take on that kind of responsibility and wasn't sure I could. Here he was, only fourteen years old, but he appeared much older. I knew then that, as determined as he was to succeed, and with his willingness to work toward his goals, someday Jesse would realize his dreams.

I always admired Jesse's determination. The time I spent with him at Cholla was more of an education on life than I could have ever realized at the time. For only being fourteen years old he was wise beyond his years. He was my hero, and I still benefit from my encounter with him.

As the year unfolded, I developed a closer relationship with Jesse than I'd ever had with anyone in my own family, and when we were at school we were always together. That year I was treated with high regard. Even though Jesse remained "Champion of the Poles," I was known throughout the school as someone equally as good as the Champ, himself. Somehow I always felt that we both were winners because of Jesse's character and presence.

Chapter Eleven

The New Gang

"The company you keep will
determine the trouble you meet!"
Author Unknown

I feel as if I'm repeating myself, but I have to say it—during this year my father's problem became worse. And the more he drank, the more I drank. Mother's anger became worse as a result. Mother finally talked Dad into moving again. Somehow, she must have thought that changing locations might make things better. I learned about the Nomads in school that year. They were a tribe of people in the Middle East who roamed the desert, never settling down because they had no country. I started calling my family Nomads after that.

It was August of 1965 when we moved to another cheap house owned by the Salt River Project. Starting a new school was becoming old hat. This was my seventh school, and I was entering the seventh grade. My teacher was Mr. Gannon. This would be his last year to teach, because the following year he became Principal.

My first day of class I met Ted. He was considered to be cool. Ted liked me and it wasn't long before I was hanging out with him. Ted was a good looking guy. He reminded me of a young Dean Martin. He was very popular with the girls, mostly the older ones. He and his older sister lived with their mother.

I thought his mother was a strange woman. She had a rule that nobody was allowed in her house alone with Ted without supervision. I could understand needing supervision in the streets, but I didn't understand why we would need it in his house. Ted could do no wrong in his mother's eyes. Whenever there was trouble and he was involved, his mother would blame those around him.

Now, Ted had two associates, Linda and Mary. Linda was a tall, slender girl with blonde hair that hung down to the middle of her back, and Mary had beautiful red shoulder-length hair. Mary was a little heavier than Linda, but she was every bit as pretty. The three of them had this business, which Ted's mother did not know about, in the garage in the back of their house. Ted had set up a bed in the garage that the girls used whenever they had a customer. They would do their business and split the money with Ted. I guess you could say that Ted was their pimp. He made bank with this "business"—he always had a pocket full of money.

Another friend, also named Mary, lived across the alley from Ted. She was very outgoing and fun to be with. Ted told me that she was a year older than he was and that she had stopped going to school half way through the eighth grade. Her father was never home; he drove truck for a well-known moving company and was gone for weeks at a time. Her mother was a waitress in downtown Phoenix. She worked six, and sometimes seven, days a week. So Mary spent a lot of time at home with very little supervision. I believe today that both her parents were alcoholic, and they spent a lot of time in the bars downtown when they weren't working.

Katie, Mary's mother, would close down the bars, and she wouldn't come home until two a.m. almost every night. When Bobby, Mary's father, was in town, he and Katie would stay out and close the bars together.

As I got to know Mary, we spent a lot of time together at her house. Only a select few were ever invited. Her house became a haven for those of us who really didn't want to go to school. At first, I would ditch school once or twice a month, but as I continued to get away with it, it wasn't long before I was ditching school one or two times a week. At Mary's house, we pretty much had free rein to do whatever we wanted—just as long as we had her house clean before her mother came home. What freedom! It was great. Mary was so popular. She knew everyone, and everyone loved her. It was Mary who introduced me to the neighborhood.

I met Mac and Marge, who owned the Log Cabin Bar, "Mac and Marge's." It was a beer-only bar and if you were caught drinking anything other than beer, they would confiscate your bottle and ask you to leave. Of course, if you were a regular, they were more apt to turn their head. Getting to know Mac and Marge was great. They never knew how old I was. They never asked, so I started drinking in their bar at seventeen years old.

Mary also introduced me to Milt and Lucy; Milt owned "Milt's Liquor Store." And then there was George, who owned the Pool Hall, which was located between Milt's Liquor Store and Mac and Marge's. The pool hall was a popular hangout for most of the people that would play a significant role in my life for the next eight years.

It was toward the end of the seventh grade when I started smoking again. I thought there was nothing as cool as a Marlboro cigarette hanging out the side of my mouth as I walked down Van Buren Street. I really thought I was tough!

This was also about the time that my father changed jobs at the Salt River Project. His new title was Zanhara. He was provided with a Salt River Project truck, and his responsibility was to open and close the gates to let water into the neighborhoods for irrigating. He worked twelve eight-hour shifts, with four days off in between. He had rotating shifts—twelve days on the day shift, twelve on swing, and then twelve on the graveyard shift. He hated the graveyard shift the most, because it interfered with his drinking.

At this time, my mother was working swing shift as an aide at the Arizona State Hospital.

My parents' schedules left my supervision up to me. I was fourteen years old, smoking, drinking and ditching school. (I thought I was old enough to take care of myself.) At night, I would sneak out my bedroom window, and sometimes I'd stay out until one or two o'clock in the morning. And then I'd be too tired to get up for school. When I did attend school, I did so poorly that I almost flunked the seventh grade. Because I did so badly in the seventh grade, I would end up in Miss Crabtree's eighth grade class the following year. That class was for kids who couldn't quite make the grade, but who hadn't quit school. But we'll talk more about that later.

For now, back to the seventh grade. I met Tommy shortly after school started that year. He sat behind me in class. I had seen him around school, but did not actually meet him until we sat by each other in the seventh grade.

One day during recess, I was sitting on the bleachers when Tommy came over and sat by me and started telling me about his uncle David. His uncle had a reputation for being a gangster and involved with the Mexican Mafia. Tommy asked me if I'd like to try something very cool. "Sure," I said. Being as cool as I thought I was, I was willing to try just about anything to maintain my image.

After school, we left to go over to Tommy's house. His Uncle David met us there, and Tommy introduced us. As I got to know David better, I learned more about his fighting and criminal activities. I was sure glad he liked me, because he was one of those people you didn't want as an enemy. This particular day, though, Tommy and David introduced me to glue in Tommy's back yard. That day I became a "Glue Sniffer," which was my very first addiction. Don't get me wrong, I liked beer, but I truly loved glue!

I watched as Tommy reached behind a pile of bicycle parts alongside his back fence and pulled out a red and white tube of model airplane glue. The tube read, "Testors model glue." He then went into his house and came out with a white hand towel. He ripped it in half, and handed one of the halves to me. "Watch," he said. He poured a generous amount of glue on one end of his rag, and then he rolled it up, starting at the end with the glue. He poured the remaining glue onto my rag and instructed me to do the same. Next, he put the glue rag over his nose and mouth and took in four or five deep breaths.

I followed his lead, and I felt the effects immediately. It felt like my brain was going in four different directions at the same time. There was mass confusion at first, and then light-headedness followed by a floating sensation. I took a few more breaths and I could feel it down in the pit of my stomach. I loved the way it made me feel! I couldn't remember ever feeling so good before, and I wanted more.

When I came to my senses, it was dark, and I saw that I was lying next to Tommy in his backyard. As high as I was, I had lost all track of time. It was late and I knew I was in trouble. I ran all the way home.

On my way home, I was thinking of what to say. When I walked in the back door, expecting to be yelled at, I saw my father passed out in his armchair in the corner where he always sat and drank his beer and tomato juice and watched TV. I looked at the clock in the kitchen. My mother was still working. I thought, "Maybe I'm okay. We'll see in the morning." I went to bed, but stayed awake for a long time, thinking about the high I had experienced. I couldn't wait to do it again! I couldn't get it out of my mind. I knew right then that I was going to have a very intimate relationship with glue.

I half expected to be yelled at the following morning, but nothing was said, so I knew I had gotten away with it.

That day Tommy was not in school. I stuck around for about an hour, and then I went over to Mary's. I told her about the glue the night before. She was upset with me and let me know it. "You've got to be crazy trying that stuff. I heard it can give you brain damage!" She was livid!

It was hard for me to conceive that anything that could make a person feel so good could possibly hurt them, and I told her so. She shrugged her shoulders and walked into the kitchen.

I didn't do it again until the following Saturday. That day I saw Tommy at the Park and Swap flea market at the Greyhound Dog track on Washington Street. He was with Janice, a girl from school. "Did you get in trouble the other night?" he asked.

I told him what had happened, and he said he could relate. He said it sounded like his family. We laughed, and then he leaned into me and said, almost whispering, "Are you ready to do it again?" He didn't have to ask me twice!

We walked Janice home and he kissed her goodbye.

From her house, we walked to a little gas station on Washington Street. "Two tubes of Testors," Tommy told the clerk.

"Twenty cents plus tax," the clerk said to Tommy as he turned around to reach for the glue on the shelf just above his head. He put the tubes in a small paper sack and set it on the counter. Tommy handed him twenty-one cents and picked up the bag.

We left the store and headed in the direction of school. On the way, he was explaining "the art of clothes line shopping," as he called it. "When shopping for a glue rag, one must know what to look for. Not just any material will work. It has to be cotton!" He smiled. I thought that was funny.

We stopped at a backyard about a block from the school. Tommy walked up to the clothesline and grabbed a pair of cotton socks. As we trotted the rest of the way to the school, he handed me one of the socks. We climbed a six-foot fence and walked over to the swings behind the Phoenix Drive-in. I looked at my watch; it was 1:00 in the afternoon.

Tommy handed me a tube of glue and I opened it. I squeezed a portion of it into the sock, rolled it three, maybe four times, then put it over my nose and mouth. I took several deep breaths and again the effects were immediate, a repeat of my first experience, but even more intense. It was such a great feeling I couldn't begin to describe it. I just didn't want to stop.

It wasn't long before the glue dried and I opened the sock to put more into it. Tommy stopped me. He showed me how to get more "high" out of the existing glue without wasting any. He taught me how to break up the glue when it started drying on the rag. He took the rag and popped it as if it were a shoeshine rag being popped by the old black man shining shoes in the lobby of the Caravan Inn on Van Buren Street. He told me it would make the glue last longer on the rag. Tommy was truly a master in the art of glue sniffing.

I loved this new high. I was hallucinating, and I kept going in and out of blackouts. I lost all track of all time. When I finally came to my senses, I looked at my watch. It was midnight. I didn't care. I knew I was in trouble, but as far as I was concerned, it was worth it. I ran home and when I got there, my father was passed out in the corner. Good sign I thought. My mother walked into the back door five minutes after me. I acted as if I had been there all night. She wouldn't have suspected anyway. Again, I had gotten away with it and nobody was the wiser.

Now I knew the "where" and the "how" of sniffing glue, and I was developing the art. I wasn't getting high all the time, but I did it two or three times a week and in between I was drinking with Mary and the gang. Sometimes when I got high, situations would develop around me without my having any clue of how they developed. And sometimes they were not very good situations to be in, but my attitude about that was, "Oh well, shit happens!"

I am not really sure how some of the people I hung around with ever entered my life. It appeared I just woke up one day and they were already there. There was Marshall (we called him "Tooter"), Randy his older brother, Dennis or "Denny" and his brothers, David, Richard and Roger. There was Leonard, and Tommy, who was Leonard's little brother. There was Joe, a very good friend who played a role in my recovery several years later, and the Kraft family—Marty, Sam, George, Ida and Terrie. The Kraft's lived in a trailer park across the street from me.

All of these people played a major role in my life and we were all very much a part of our neighborhood. We never judged each other, and I always felt safe in my neighborhood, day or night.

I remember walking home one time, by myself, at about two o'clock in the morning. All of a sudden a car full of Mexicans pulled up as I was crossing 40th Street to enter my driveway. I heard one of them yell, "We're going to kick your white ass!" My driveway was about an eighth of a mile long with a canal on one side and a six-foot fence on the other. I had nowhere to run. I was really scared as I watched them make a U-turn and stop in front of me. They climbed out of their car with baseball bats and tire irons and I thought I was dead. As far as I could see, there was nobody around to help me.

The next thing I knew, a black '57 Chevy pulled up behind them, with several men inside dressed in cowboy attire. When they climbed out, I recognized the Kraft brothers, Sam and George, Randy (Tooter's brother), and three guys that worked at Martin's Gas Station; Roy, Bobbie and Willie, and they all looked like they were ready to do battle. I knew that Roy always carried a gun with him. Willie had a tire iron and Bobby, the jack. "Are you all right?" Sam asked me.

I was sure glad to see them! "It's really up to them," I said as I pointed at the five Mexicans who were now just standing there contemplating, not sure what to do next. Then, without a word, they turned around and jumped back into their car. As they drove off, they yelled out something in Spanish that none of us could understand.

I thanked my new friends for being there.

"Any time," George said. They jumped back into their car, and then they were gone as quickly as they had appeared.

That was actually how I met Sam, George and some of the other guys.

The first day of eighth grade wasn't bad. We were the challenged population, so there really wasn't that much expected of us other than to show up and stay out of trouble. I was convinced I could do it. How hard could it be? There were kids in my class that couldn't even read. At least I could do that! Maybe not very well, but I could get by. My teacher, Miss Crabtree, was great. She never got angry or even appeared frustrated. She would approach each kid in her class on his or her own level. If you didn't want to learn, she would respect that and leave you alone. Then she would check on you throughout the school year and if you changed your mind, she'd be there to help. Because she was such a good teacher, you couldn't help learning something in her class by just being there.

Even though I missed a lot of school, I worked hard to get through the eighth grade, and I almost made it the whole year without an incident. Three weeks before school ended, I was in class when the bell rang for our last fifteen-minute recess of the day. As I walked up to the upper playground to sit on the bleachers, some kid ran into Mr. Carol, almost knocking him down.

Mr. Carol, who was acting playground monitor at the time, turned around and saw me walking by and assumed I was the one who ran into him. He grabbed me and told me to watch where I was going. I reacted by grabbing him back and as I tripped him on to the ground, I raised my left hand to hit him.

Mr. Gannon, the Principal and Mr. Vic, the shop teacher, tackled me. I tried to explain what happened in the scuffle, but the appearance of raising my fist to a teacher was all it took to get me in trouble. My reaction became the issue. I was marched, under guard, to the office. In Mr. Gannon's office, he told me I would receive three swats for threatening a teacher. Well, I felt it wasn't fair, and told him so. He chuckled. I got mad and told him, "No, I won't take any swats." I told him that I wanted to call my mother. I was angry too! My mother would tell him I was right. I didn't feel I had it coming and that was that!

He was angry, but he let me call her. I used the phone on his desk. When I called and told her what happened, she said, "Tell Mr. Gannon I'll be right there and not to do anything until I know more." Without saying goodbye, she hung up. I knew she'd be in my corner. After all, there's nothing worse to deal with than a co-dependent mother protecting her child. Does the term "junkyard dog" mean anything to you? Mr. Gannon didn't stand a chance and I knew it.

My mother was there in less than ten minutes with both of my sisters. Penny was perched on her lift hip, while Lynn followed close behind. She looked hot, tired, and—most important of all—angry! She held the door for Lynn, and then she blew past the office help as they tried to ask her what she needed. She opened the door to Mr. Gannon's office, again holding the door for my little sister to clear the doorway.

Now, I love my mother, but she could be scary at times. She clearly had a psychotic side and you could see it in her eyes when she became angry. She would be looking in your direction, which gave you the impression she was looking at you. In reality, she was looking through you with these piercing, slanted eyes.

"Get him, mom," I thought.

He was in trouble now. Mr. Gannon started telling her what happened, and what he planned to do about it. He told her my choices were limited and what they were. "Either take the swats offered or be suspended." Then he looked at me and said, "If you choose to be suspended, you will not be graduating with the rest of your classmates."

My mother then asked Mr. Gannon if she could speak with me alone. He excused himself and stepped out of his office, leaving us alone to talk. I told her in great detail what had happened. She believed me. I stuck my head out and called him back in.

When he sat back down, my mother went off. She had a fire in her eyes and a fight in her heart. She explained to him—in no uncertain terms—that the list of choices was incomplete and that a third option would be added. "You will not be giving him swats or suspending him, is that understood?"

Mr. Gannon looked scared. He thought for a moment and then he backed down. He looked down at the papers on his desk and nervously moved them around. He then looked up at my mother and said, "Let's just call it a day, go home, and come back tomorrow." My mother agreed. I was grinning from ear to ear. I had won!

My victory was short-lived, however. When she got me home, she called me into the kitchen. She yelled at me as she smacked me across the face. "You have no right to disrespect any elder for any reason whatsoever, and if I hear of you doing it again, I will beat you within a half inch of your life. Do-you-understand-me-mister?" What could I say? She was pissed, and she had knocked the smile right off of my face, but it was worth it.

And three weeks later, I graduated with my class.

Chapter Twelve

My 8th Grade Graduation… I Think!

What I didn't know was that my negative behaviors were now controlling me as I crossed over that invisible line they call addiction. When this line is crossed, there is no turning back. The more I would fight for control of my life, the less control I seemed to have. I did not understand this paradox until years later.

I felt a strange sense of pride the day of my graduation. I had completed something for the first time in my life. And what's more, I think my mother was proud of me too. This was one occasion she attended with pride. In the past, mother would only attend Parent-Teacher conferences or a few other occasions necessary to get me out of the trouble I managed to get myself into. Now, for the first time in as long as I could remember, my mother was proud of me. This was a new relation between my mother and me. What could possibly go wrong?

At the school, I was so nervous that I decided to go outside and smoke a cigarette. I walked out back and stood next to the swings with Tommy and our friend, Ted.

Ted had been drinking, and he smelled like it, and Tommy was high on glue. Tommy held out the rag that he had just filled with glue and offered it to Ted. "No thanks," he said, "I'll stick with my beer." Tommy then offered it to me.

I thought it might take the edge off of how I was feeling, so I covered my nose and mouth and took three or four deep breaths. WOW! I could feel the rush. I handed it back to him; he took a few breaths and handed it back to me. In no time at all I was feeling it. I was angry with myself. I hadn't intended to get so high. I tried to pull it together, but I was having a difficult time. I told myself to get back in there and get dressed in my cap and gown. Don't blow it now! I walked inside and staggered over to my mother; she handed me my cap and gown and I put them on over my street clothes. I sat down directly in front of her in the second row as they were lowering the lights to get started.

I was trying to focus and I thought I was doing a good job. The problem was that as I was sitting there waiting for them to call me up, I started feeling more and more loaded. When Mr. Gannon finally called my name, I was too busy thinking about how messed up I was and I didn't hear him, so I didn't respond until my mother slapped me from behind to get my attention. She said, with a look of disgust and in a loud whisper, "Get up there!"

I stood up and staggered over to the red velvet rope. When I passed the third pole, I bumped into it and it fell over. It was like dominoes, they continued to fall clear up to the stage entrance. I just stood there in disbelief. I realized, as I watched the last pole fall, that the whole place was completely silent. I looked back at my mother, only to see a look of complete shock on her face.

When I walked out on stage I was so angry and embarrassed that I walked up to Mr. Gannon, grabbed my diploma without shaking his hand and hurried off the stage. When I looked for my mother, she was nowhere to be found. I walked back outside to where my friends were and continued to get really wasted. I finally went home at about 2:00 the following morning. My mother and I never once discussed what happened that night, not even on her deathbed.

During the summer months, I decided that I needed to get all the partying out of my system because it was time for me to pull my head out of my butt and put my life in order before I entered high school. Besides, I was going to show everyone that I could do it, that I wasn't a screw-up. All I needed was some willpower. What I didn't know was that my addiction was now controlling me.

Through the next few months, my addiction advanced. I kept justifying it to myself by thinking that I would stop when school began.

This was about the time that my brother, Steve, was getting ready to enter the priesthood. This was a life-long dream that my mother had for him, although I've often wondered if he was pushed in the direction of the clergy because of the dysfunction in our family. In any event, a year later Steve was in the Seminary, in his first year of study.

Meanwhile, I was coming home at three or four o'clock in the morning, if I came home at all. There were times I came in and it was obvious I was high and/or had been drinking. At those times I could see the hurt in my mother's eyes and I hated it. I never wanted to hurt her. I would get mad at myself and tell myself to cool it and I would mean it, but a day or two later I would do it again. When it got bad, Mother would ask Steve to talk with me. I would listen to him and tell him I'd work on it, but then I'd keep right on using.

I really believed that they loved me and meant well, but what they didn't understand was that I didn't love myself. (They loved their son, but they didn't understand that there was someone else inside me at the same time). Addiction often causes a separation between the good and the bad deep inside. The worse the addiction, the more separate the personalities. I'm sure that if you had known me at the time, you would have thought that I only cared about myself. But that was far from the truth. I hated myself because of the things that I did. I was filled with shame and guilt. And the more painful it became, the more I drank and used drugs in order not to feel at all.

It felt like I was riding a bicycle with no chain; I worked really hard, but I never got anywhere. The spiral downward has no bottom. Being high most of the time, I would wake up in the early afternoon, start sniffing glue and stay high until early evening. I used drinking to take the edge off and mellow me out. I'd come home around two or three in the morning and the next day I'd start all over again. It was a corkscrew downward into a darkness that had no thought of tomorrow.

It wasn't long before I started losing all concept of time. I kept telling myself, "Pull it together John," but that side of me wasn't listening, even to myself. I felt that I was still in control, but nothing could have been farther from the truth.

One afternoon, I was sitting at the kitchen table eating an egg sandwich, feeling bad about how my life was going and trying to think of a way out of the madness when my mother walked in from her bedroom. She said hello and then she asked me what my plans were. "I have no plans, I thought I might go over to Mary's and just hang out."

Then my mother said something that really hurt. I almost cried, but I didn't! She asked me, "Why can't you be more like your little brother, Richard?"

"Why aren't I more like my little brother?" I repeated in disbelief. I would rather she kicked me in the groin. I was so hurt and angry I just walked away. I couldn't believe she had said it and what's more, I didn't even care why. I now had even more reason to "Chase the Dragon," so that's what I went and did.

It may have appeared to my family that I was out of touch with my feelings, but that wasn't at all true. I felt every horror and anger known to man. I had a rage inside of me that was a monster out of control. It scared me and the only way I could harness it was to feed the dragon and stay high.

I didn't go home for the next three days. The only reason I did go home then was because I woke up there. I often found myself on one of the couches we had in our living room, like the monster had taken my unconscious body and placed it there sometime in the night. I still had the same clothes on from days ago and I was ripe. The dragon didn't seem to care if I had taken a bath.

My father went to work and mother left for her shift at the hospital without saying a word other than to remind me that there were leftovers from last night's dinner in the fridge. Both of them left as if nothing had happened. I resented this pattern, even though I recognized it as the way they treated each other when they, themselves, were having this kind of trouble. They had taught me well that ignoring the immediate problem was simpler than to confront it and let Pandora out of its box.

I became hostile toward my family and more loyal to my friends. They became the family I had never known. Somewhere inside I blamed my family for what was happening to me. If only they had cared as much as my friends, the addiction would never have happened. But the addiction wasn't the problem in my head. The only thing that mattered was to be accepted somewhere. I was spending a lot more time over at Mary's house with people like Denny, Tooter and Leonard.

Denny, Tooter and I would sniff glue while Leonard drank and Mary watched us get wasted. Leonard was a melancholy drunk and he was always putting his arm around my neck and telling me how much he loved me. He would express his concern for me about sniffing glue. He would often tell me he was afraid that it would mess up my mind or worse yet, kill me. I was sniffing three to four tubes a day, but if anyone asked, I'd tell them maybe two. Addicts are always liars. I would tell Leonard I was okay and then he would look at me, with his head cocked to the right, his eyes half closed and his eyebrows raised, as if to say, "Yeah right," and then he'd go back to drinking his beer. Leonard was my friend and I believed he really cared. But the real truth was, by this time in my life I was using against my will and I didn't know how to stop.

Chapter Thirteen

Superman

I have learned that sometimes, especially when we have no defense, it is better not to say anything at all. This was one of those times.

It was mid-afternoon when I left my house on my way to Mary's. I could feel the humidity in the air. It was still the monsoon season, but it hadn't rained in almost a week. So, after my bath, by the time I was dressed, I felt like I needed another one. I hated days like this. It was two weeks before high school was to start and I was thinking, as I walked out my back door, that maybe I should slow down so I didn't have to stop all at once. Maybe I'll only drink today and not use anything else.

As I was walking out of the house, I noticed that my father, who had been passed out in his chair in the living room fifteen minutes before, was now opening the door to the station wagon. I remember thinking, "How can he drive in that condition?" As I walked toward the gate I noticed that my father had left it opened part way. I walked out and when I turned around to close it, I saw movement from the corner of my eye. It was my baby sister Penny crawling under the back wheel of the station wagon. At first, I was stunned and couldn't believe what I was seeing.

I screamed at my father, who had already started the car. He had the windows up and was hard of hearing anyway, so he didn't hear my scream. All he had to do was put it into reverse and he would run over her. Without thinking, I stepped behind the station wagon and as he put it in reverse, I grabbed the bumper and picked the back of the car up until the back tires were a couple of inches off the ground. He accelerated, the back tires spun, but nothing happened. He kept accelerating.

My mother, who was on the other side of the house hanging up clothes, heard the commotion. She came running, and when she saw what was happening, she pulled my sister out from underneath the car. When my sister was safe, I dropped the car and jumped out of the way. Father had revved the motor so high that when the back tires hit the ground they grabbed, and the car almost went into the canal behind him. (Had he not slammed on his brakes, it would have). He was so drunk that he wasn't even aware of what had just happened. Father put the car in first gear and headed out of the driveway without noticing a thing. My mother, still holding my sister in her arms, watched me drop the car and jump out of the way. She shook her head, put my sister down and walked back to the clothesline. I left, and by the time I walked into Mary's house, it was all but forgotten. I didn't really tell anybody because I didn't feel they would believe me; after all, I wasn't Superman.

Mary was sweeping the carpet in the living room when I arrived. She told me to turn on the TV while she finished. She handed me a beer and I watched a re-run of *Dark Shadows* while she swept around me. When she finished she jumped into the shower. She was dressed and ready to go by the time the credits rolled across the TV.

We walked over to the pool hall. Greg was working, and I asked him for a dollar's worth of nickels. We went over to the pinball machines along the north wall. I put the front legs of one of them on the tips of my shoes, carefully bending my toes in, so the machine was only resting on the tips of my shoes, thus changing the pitch of the machine. This prevented the balls from going past the flippers and down the chute. This enabled me to rack up points and win free games. I'd play for hours on a nickel…cheap entertainment. Of course, I didn't want George or Greg, his son, to catch me. George used to say, "Five balls is all you get. Anything more is cheating and I hate cheaters!" If we were caught, they would kick us out for the day. Mary's job was to be the lookout.

We went back to Mary's house around 6:30. We watched TV and drank beer until around 8:30. We were alone and we both had a good buzz going. We started to play around and it became serious. It wasn't long before we ended up in her parent's bed together. As we continued our little frolic in the bedroom, I heard some noise in the living room. I stopped what I was doing and sat up on the bed. The next thing I saw was her father standing in the doorway. We were both naked. I tried to cover myself with a pillow. He looked perplexed as he walked through the door carrying an overnight bag, and he was drunker than a skunk.

In a very calm voice he asked, "What are you doing to my daughter?"

I didn't know what to say, so I just jumped out of bed and put on my pants. My heart was pounding so hard it took my breath away. I was scared and embarrassed. When I looked at Mary, she didn't appear to be a bit concerned. She was lying on her left side, making no attempt to cover her body, with her head resting on her left hand.

She asked him, "What does it look like we're doing, playing checkers?"

He said, "Oh," and then he staggered out of the room and into Mary's room and passed out.

She told me not to worry about it and that he probably wouldn't remember it tomorrow anyway. She must have been right, because he never mentioned it again. The rest of the evening we just hung out. I went home around 11:00. That was early for me, because by this time my parents had given up trying to tell me what time I needed to be home. As a matter of fact, they both agreed that as long as I was able to get up in time for school the following day, it was up to me what time I went to bed.

When my parents were both working, they didn't see much of each other throughout the week. This kept their fighting to a minimum.

The first day of East High School I remember telling myself with every step I took, "This is it John, no more bullshit!" I reminded myself of the promise I had made to myself about pulling it together. School was more difficult than I thought it would be, but I worked real hard to follow through with my promise. I did really well the first few months. I studied hard and stayed away from the people who could get me into trouble. I began feeling a new sense of pride, and I think my mother was starting to notice. There was a time or two that she even said something to that effect.

In October of 1966, my father was confronted at work about his drinking. His boss, along with a co-worker, Kenny, performed what has become known as an "intervention." During this intervention Father was told, "Get help for your drinking problem or find a new job."

Kenny was a member of a 12-Step program and he suggested that my father start going to meetings with him. Well, that made him mad, but when your job is on the line, your choices are limited. So, he went with Kenny to some meetings. He attended two a week at first. He hated them. He used to say, "Too much God talk." He didn't believe in God. It didn't take long before he was going to one meeting a week and then none at all—all the time telling himself and others that he wasn't drinking and that he didn't need them.

The problem was that he was miserable. He had stopped drinking, yes, but he became an asshole in the process. Every little thing made him angry. My mother used to tell us he would get through it, but it only seemed to get worse. For the most part I stayed out of his way, because I had a way of making things worse just with my presence. When I did come home, it seemed he would go out of his way to engage me. No matter what I did, it was wrong.

After two months of this, I just couldn't take it anymore. We were arguing out in the front yard over me not taking out the garbage. He told me to get my lazy ass out of the way and that he would do it himself. Well that was it! I had taken all that I was going to and said, "Fuck you, old man!" I was still arguing with him when I started to cross the street by the trailer sales. I was about ten feet from the crosswalk when a police cruiser turned into my path. I was in the middle of 40th street, screaming back at my father again to go fuck himself, when the officer told me to get out of the road. I was very angry at my father and I guess I directed some of my anger back at the officer, because when he asked me to get out of the road, I said, "Can't you see I'm busy, you fucking moron?"

He looked pissed. He drove past me, made a U-turn, and then drove back. He honked his horn to get my attention and waved me over to his car. I walked up to his window and proceeded to tell him I didn't appreciate his interference. At first, he said nothing; he just glared at me, looking up and down my body for what seemed like forever. I was starting to become anxious. He then reached for the door handle. "Oh shit," I thought as I stood there in complete shock. I watched as one of the biggest men I had ever seen leapt out of his police car like an angry animal. "How does he fit in that car?" I wondered. He was huge! I backed up. He came angrily toward me, still not saying a word. I was petrified. I didn't even come up to his mid-stomach.

He backed me up against the hood of his car. "Ah, shit," I whispered under my breath.

He laid me back across the hood as he leaned over me, with his face about six inches from mine. He said, "I usually take punks like you to jail." He was poking me in the chest with his right index finger, "But I think I'll just kick your ass instead!"

I thought, "What the hell do I do now? This guy is a giant." I felt absolutely helpless. I just gave it up. I tried to tell him how sorry I was and that I was angry at my father and that I took it out on him and that I didn't mean to and that I wouldn't do it again and that…! I just kept talking; I didn't care, I just didn't want this big goofy bastard to hit me. OK, so I sold out. I guess he saw that because he backed off. He told me that I should treat my father with a little more respect. I told him that he was absolutely right and that, again, I was sorry. He told me I could go. I thanked him and left.

I headed in the direction of Mary's house. By the time I crossed Van Buren I had played it out in my head a couple of dozen times. I turned my rage on my father. I was thinking, "Why try anyway, he only sees the bad." Then my thoughts went back to the Officer, when had he said, "I think I'll kick your ass instead!" Hell, I hadn't even gotten his name. "What a butthead. The son of a bitch was as big as a Georgia pine tree. Who wouldn't have backed down? Even a moron knows when he's in a no-win situation." The bottom line was that I felt angry for not holding my ground.

I saw Denny coming out of the pool hall when I crossed Van Buren. I told him what had just happened. He said, "Gee, that's too bad," and then he said, "You know what we should do?" He was looking at me and smiling.

"What should we do?" I asked.

"Let's get high," he blurted out.

I thought about it for about a second, and then I reached into my pocket to see if I still had that five dollar bill my mother had given me before my father and I got into it. I said, "Lets get wasted!" I showed him the five dollar bill. He pulled out three more dollars. We had more than enough to get some glue and a few white cotton face towels. Somewhere in our minds, we thought we deserved to get wasted. We felt we were justified. This is one of the biggest lies an addict will tell himself.

We walked over to the little store next to the laundry mat. Behind the counter was the owner, who was a bald, heavyset man who was always chewing on his mustache. "Can I help you?" he asked. He already knew what I wanted.

"Give me a box of Tester's Glue."

He looked sideways at me. "A box? You know that's twelve tubes?"

"I build a lot of models." I told him defensively.

He said, "I know, you've told me." He knew I was lying, but I didn't care. He shrugged his shoulders, turned and reached for a box on the shelf behind the counter. He set it down in front of me and said, "$1.20 plus 6 cents for the government." I handed him the five and he gave me back my change. After he put the box in a paper bag and handed it to me, I turned and walked out. I went over to the laundry mat where Denny was waiting and showed him the bag. He was going to buy the face towels next, but he didn't have to. He had stolen two of them out of the dryers.

It was 6:30, and it was starting to get dark, so we headed for the school. At the school, we sat on the swings that faced the screen at the Phoenix Drive-in. The only thing that separated the drive-in from our school was a six-foot chain link fence that someone had cut a hole in as a neighborhood entrance for those who dared to use it. There were two sections of chairs underneath the movie screen for those who didn't want to sit in their cars to watch the movie, and of course, for those who entered through the back entrance! There were many attempts made through the years to repair that hole in the fence, but it never lasted more than a day or two. After several attempts they finally gave up trying.

As Denny and I sat on the swings facing the movie screen, we each had a towel and a tube of glue. I set the box between us. I poured some glue into my towel, folded it, put it over my nose and mouth and started to breathe in.

I noticed the movie was in black and white. I thought that was a bit odd, because most movies by then were in color. The movie was called, "Your Cheatin' Heart," with George Hamilton. It was about the life and death of Hank Williams, Sr. Why I remembered that I couldn't tell you, other than I liked Hank's music.

I remember waking up several times in different parts of the movie. The last time I went out, I could feel someone shaking me as I was coming out of it. When I opened my eyes there were two Phoenix police officers standing over me. One of them asked me if I was all right, while the other stood behind him.

At first, I lay there confused. I couldn't remember where I was, but then it came to me. I noticed the movie was over and there were no cars in the drive-in. I wondered what time it was. "Are you all right?" the officer asked me again as he shined his flashlight into my eyes. I could clearly see his look of disgust when he saw the glue on my face. His partner picked up my glue rag with his index finger and thumb and held it out to show him. He shook his head as he held it out. I remember feeling embarrassed as I lay there. I tried to stand up and fell back. One of the officers reached out his hand to pull me up.

"Where do you live?" one of them asked as I tried to force myself to come out of my fog.

"The white house that sits back from the road on 40th Street," I managed to get out. I still felt really high.

They each grabbed an arm and walked me out of the gate to their police car. One opened the door and they put me in the back. "They must have a key," I thought as one closed and locked the gate to the school, while the other started the car. I was really unsure at first if I was going to jail, but the car turned left on Van Buren Street heading in the direction of my house.

I found out later that when my mother left for work that day, my father used our argument earlier as an excuse to drink again and by the time we got there, he was drunk and passed out in his chair.

The police car turned into my driveway and parked behind the station wagon. The officer helped me to the back door where one of them knocked, but there was no answer. He knocked again and then turned to his partner and said, "I can hear a television on." He tried the door and it opened. He looked in. After assessing the situation, he opened the door wide enough to help me get through the door. When they brought me in, I couldn't help but notice my father passed out in his chair, with the TV blaring "The Star Spangled Banner" as a flag waved across the screen. There were beer cans on the floor that had fallen from the brown Safeway bag he had next to his chair. There was an open beer on the table next to him. They tried to wake him but he was out. They both looked at him, then at me. They looked at each other, then walked me over to one of the couches and laid me down. They were both shaking their heads from side to side as they walked out. I felt ashamed. I can't tell you why, I just did. I have never forgotten it. I can still see in my mind, when I think of it, the disgust on their faces as they both walked out of my house. I heard them drive out of our driveway and they were gone.

My father didn't drink again for a few months. He told my mother that he was sorry and would not do it again. He still didn't return to his 12-Step program, and he was still miserable. Nothing changed between him and me. All I had to be was in his presence and I would make him angry.

I woke up at about 2:00 the next afternoon. There was a note on the door of the refrigerator that read, "Johnny, tried to wake you for school, but you wouldn't wake up. You need to do better. I called you in sick. There's food in the fridge. - Mom."

"The hell with school," I thought. I was still angry at my old man.

I was hungry, so I ate two bowls of left over spaghetti. I took a bath and got ready to go out. My father would be home at four and I didn't want to be home when he got there. I didn't need any more crap right now, so I needed to be gone. It was 3:10 when I looked at the clock in the kitchen as I was getting ready to head over to Mary's house. Tooter, Denny and Leonard were there. I asked Denny what happened to him last night.

He said, "I went around the building to go to the bathroom and on my way back I saw you with two cops. I went back the other way, jumped the fence and went home. Hell, I thought you were going to jail." They wanted to know what happened to me when I got home, so I told them. I also shared how it made me feel. Leonard said he understood the feelings. I knew he probably did.

We sat around Mary's house until dark, and then we walked over to the Phoenix Drive-in. We entered via our private entrance in the back and headed for the seats in the front and sat down. On Friday and Saturday nights, the drive-in was a popular hangout for those in the neighborhood. It looked like a scene from the movie "The Outsiders," a movie from the early eighties about two rival gangs who meet in a drive-in movie to discuss an upcoming fight in a nearby park and to set down the rules. The setting was a small town in Oklahoma in the mid-fifties. They each were a good group of kids with a very strong set of values, but they were different, so they couldn't get along. This scene has always reminded me of how it was on a weekend night at the Phoenix Drive-in, and this Friday night was no different.

A lot of the guys were there with their girlfriends. There would always be drinking and a fight or two between those who dared to enter the neighborhood uninvited. It had always been that way, and it continued to be that way until it showed its last picture in the mid-eighties. There was George with his girlfriend Wanda, Sam with Carrie, and Randy had some girl with him I didn't know. Roy was there with Bobby. So were Willie and Andy, Roy's nephew. Ted was there with Ida, just to name a few. It looked like everybody who was somebody was there, and they were all drinking and raising hell.

Tooter, Denny, Leonard and I went out on a campaign to see how many beers we could bum off of them, while Mary stayed with our seats. We asked everyone we knew. We would collect as many as we could and then meet back at our seats to split them up.

We were younger than most of them, so when I asked for beer it would always come with a lecture on how to be a responsible drinker. I would very politely thank them, tell them I was grateful for their concern and go on to someone else. We met back at the seats thirty minutes later. When we pooled all of them together, we had more than a case. Mary only drank one, maybe two, and we drank the rest. I drank about seven beers in the two hours that the movie played. I was feeling like I had a good buzz going, along with everyone else.

We then realized that we were hungry, so we walked over to the Ramada Inn Coffee Shop, where Marie, a single mother of two who was maybe thirty-two years old, was our waitress. She had worked the graveyard shift for the past two years or so, and she always took care of us when we had no money. She would tell the cook who was working to burn a couple of steaks and make us a double order of French Fries. In return, if she ever had a problem with someone who'd had too much to drink or just happened to give her a hard time, we would help in any way we could. I always thought Marie was a very attractive woman. The problem was, I was fourteen years old with no hope of ever having a chance with her, but I always protected her as if she was my woman. That night she told the cook to burn us three steaks between the five of us.

I left the Ramada Inn around 4:00 a.m. and headed for home. The following afternoon I woke up at about 3:00. It was Saturday, so my parents let me sleep in. My father was at work and my mother was in the kitchen cooking. She asked me how I was doing. She hadn't had the chance to talk with me since that Thursday when my father and I got into it over the garbage. I told her how I felt. She told me to try and be more understanding and that he was doing better.

That's mom. For some reason she always felt a need to step in between my father and I when we were going at it. It was cool that she was there, and maybe it kept us from getting physical, but with her always in the middle we could never find resolve, so it continued to get worse.

"I love you mom," I told her. She meant well. I cleaned up and left before my father came home. As I crossed 40th Street, heading toward the pool hall, I saw the white SRP truck turn into our driveway.

Before I had left the house, my mother had given me five dollars in change. You see my mother had two rules or beliefs that she always pushed on us. One was, you never leave the house without any money in your pocket because you never knew if there was going to be trouble and you might need to call for help, or if you're hungry and needed food, or for whatever reason. Secondly, you never leave the house without clean underwear, because you never know if you might get into an accident. I always wanted to tell her that if I ever got into an accident and I was hurt really bad or even killed, I'd probably mess my underwear anyway.

When I arrived at the pool hall, Randy and Greg were playing a game of straight pool. It was really something to watch. They would run the table two, sometimes three times before one would miss a shot. They were good! I was sitting in one of the tall-backed chairs that were lined up against the east wall, watching them play, when Tooter and Denny walked in and Tooter asked me what I was doing.

"No plans, why?" I asked.

"Have any money?" He was fishing.

"A few dollars," I said. I was holding out because I wanted to keep enough money to buy something to eat later.

Tooter bummed a dollar from his brother and Denny was broke as always. "Lets get some glue and get high," Tooter said as he held up his dollar.

Randy came up from behind and cuffed him in the back of the head. He said, "I don't want you doing that stuff, and if I catch you, I'll kick your butt." He then turned to face Denny and me. "That goes for you guys too." He pointed at me.

Well, I've seen Randy fight, and he was as good at fighting as he was at pool and I wanted no part of that, so I said "No problem!"

He then gave Tooter another dollar and said, "If you're going to get high on something, buy some beer!" Tooter took it and we headed out the door. In the parking lot, Tooter put his two dollars with mine and we headed for the little store next to the laundry mat. Tooter and I went next door to the laundry mat while Denny went into the store. I walked over to a dryer, opened it and pulled out three white hand towels, hoping that the two women sitting in the back talking wouldn't say anything. Neither of them seemed to even notice we were there. Denny walked by the window with a brown paper bag. That was our cue, so we stepped out and headed for the school.

I hopped the fence first. I'd done it so often I was getting good at it. Denny handed me the bag over the fence and then climbed over himself. Tooter followed. We sat in our usual spot on the swings behind the drive-in. It didn't take long before I was off and running. I went in and out of consciousness and each time I did, things around me were different. It was like watching the movie "The Time Machine," where Rod Taylor turned on the machine and as he went back through the years, things would change around him.

We were sitting on the swings while it was still daylight, then it was dusk, I couldn't find Tooter, but Denny was passed out to the left of me on the ground. Then the movie was playing and Tooter was lying next to Denny and I was on the grass sitting Indian style. When I woke up again, Tooter and Denny were both gone and the movie was ending. The next thing I remember was waking up in my own bed without any clue of how I got there. I do know that it was the next day and it was in the afternoon. "That was intense!" I thought, thinking back, trying to put some order to the previous night.

I don't know about anyone else, but I always had an uneasy feeling in my gut, along with mass confusion, when I woke up from a blackout. This was always followed by the fear of not knowing what I might have said or done that could come back to bite me in the butt later. However, I was a survivor. I always landed back on my feet and what's more, I was becoming a master at it.

Boy, it didn't take me long to fall back into my old self, missing school and running amuck during the day. Addicts get to a point at which they just don't care about anything. In January, I stopped going to school altogether. I got up, pretending to go to school every morning, and then I would go over to Mary's house and sleep on her couch, or sometimes I'd hang out at the pool hall. It didn't matter; I always found something to do or someone to be with, and you could bet I was drinking and/or using, depending on who I was with. I would come home and everyone in my family thought I had been at school. No one was the wiser. I was back to my old self and I liked it.

The problem was that you could only get away with ditching school for so long, and then someone started putting two and two together and you got busted. It was great for a while but it didn't last.

A week before my birthday, when I arrived home one Friday afternoon, I walked through the back door and sitting on the couch opposite the door, drinking a beer, was my father. I didn't know what to say. He was glaring at me. He pointed at me with his right index finger, the rest of his hand wrapped around his beer and yelled, "This is your fault, you little bastard! That's right—it's your fault!" He continued drinking his beer. He then threw his empty can at me. He said, "Your school called me at work today and told me you haven't been in school in over a month and that they were dropping you."

I didn't know what to say so I just kept quiet. I have learned through the years that sometimes when you have no defense, it is better not to say anything at all. This was one of those times. I stood there as he continued.

"Now you need to explain to your mother why you got me drunk!" I couldn't believe what he was saying. I was numb at first. I was also sorry I made him drunk. I knew my mother would be disappointed in him for drinking and angry with me for pushing him into it, so I left.

I dropped my books onto the couch closest to the door and ran out, trying to hide my tears. It didn't take me long to turn my hurt into anger. I ran up the driveway screaming, "Fuck him! Fuck him!" I hated him for blaming me, but at the same time, I felt responsible. I had made my father drink and I was sorry. I didn't know where I was going. I walked down the canal bank and found myself in a clump of trees. I sat under one of them and cried. Before long, I was sobbing uncontrollably for what seemed like forever. The harder I tried to stop crying, the harder it was to control. I was truly sorry! I never wanted to hurt my father, I just didn't know how to love him, and I was pretty sure he didn't know how to love me. I wished I had the courage to kill myself but I didn't and that was that.

An hour later I was at Mary's house. I didn't talk about what happened, I just hung out and went home around ten.

As I reflect back on what happened, I believe my father was in a blackout that day, and that was the reason why our confrontation was never brought up again. I wish now that I could have understood all of that back then, because that particular incident caused me many years of emotional pain.

I never went back to East High.

A week or so later, my father stopped drinking for good. He finally accepted his alcoholism and went back to the 12-Step Program. This time it was different. He really changed! He had a more positive attitude and a better outlook on life. He appeared to have the hope he'd never had before.

One day, with help from his good friend Kenny G. from the program, my father started a halfway house for alcoholics and drug addicts. He called it the "Maverick House." He was asked in an interview by a local news station, why Maverick House? He said it was because he looked at all alcoholics and addicts as mavericks, and his job was to bring them back to the herd when they strayed too far out.

It was early 1967 and Maverick House took off with great success. It was full its first week and stayed full until it closed its doors in October of 1981, when the property that Maverick House was sitting on was recalled and construction was started on the new freeways the land had been intended for.

I was fifteen when Maverick House first opened and I thought I knew it all. You couldn't tell me anything. I was working at the Desert Sky Motel on East Van Buren. My job description included room service, busboy and part time dishwasher. I was good at my job, when I was there. The problem was, I would call in sick three or four times a month, so I wasn't very dependable. My job was getting in the way of my drug use. Oh, I made attempts to control it. I would tell myself things like, "Slow down, you've got to work tomorrow," or "I need to stop at a certain time." I always meant it when I said it, but throughout the course of the night, I would always blow it. I hated not being in control. Of course, I now know that it was part of the progression of my disease.

Chapter Fourteen

A Rendezvous in the Desert

I kept my mouth shut. I knew I was standing
on thin ice, and I was starting to feel it
crack beneath my feet.

My Aunt Betty was going through another divorce, and during this time she came to live with us. Soon after she moved in, she offered to teach me how to drive, if my parents would agree to sign for my permit. They did so, because they thought to use it as a bargaining chip in an attempt to get me to change. And, of course, I agreed to do all the things they requested of me.

We got up early on Thursday morning, and before 9:00 I had my driver's permit. I drove my parents' Ford Falcon station wagon home. I was scared at first, but after a mile or two, I began to feel like a pro. By the time we arrived home, the long way of course, I had pretty much mastered it. I continued to practice for an hour a day, and it wasn't long before I was ready to get my driver's license. Based on our agreement that I'd change, there was some talk about buying me a used car.

I did everything that was asked of me for the first week. I helped clean the house, hung up clothes for my mother, and helped take care of my sisters Lynn and Penny so she could get some much needed rest. I was starting to feel better about myself, and my parents were beginning to trust me again. Well, my mother was anyway. When it came to my father and me, I was always suspect in his eyes.

I felt that I deserved their trust. I was finally on track and doing well the past four days, and that was a long time in my book.

It was Friday night, the start of the weekend, and I got ready to go out. My plan was to go over to Mary's house. I thought I'd see what the night would bring. When I walked into Mary's living room, I saw Leonard, Tooter and Denny. Leonard was sitting on the couch next to a girl he introduced as Bonnie. He had his arm around her.

Bonnie reminded me of a bulldog, because her bottom lip stuck out further than her top lip, which caused one hell of an under bite. I wouldn't have called her ugly, just different. But I knew that when Leonard got horny, he'd have sex with a snake if you held its head.

They were all discussing what to do for the night and they invited me into the conversation. "Have any ideas?" Denny asked.

"No, not really." I sat down on the couch next to Bonnie.

"If we only had some wheels," Tooter said and when he did, my mind was already there. Having just learned to drive in the past few weeks I had an idea.

"Denny, is your brother Richard home?" I asked.

"I think so, why?" he wanted to know.

I smiled and asked him to call home and find out. When he called, his brother Roger answered. "Is Rich home? Good, put him on." Denny waited about 30 seconds, then he said, "Wait a minute, John wants to talk to you." He handed me the phone.

I said, "Richard, do you have any plans for the night? Good. Wanna hang out with us? I have a plan, it could be fun. Okay, meet me at the corner by my house. Cool, see you in a few." I handed the phone back to Denny; he unwrapped himself from the cord and hung up. My plan was, Richard had a license and I had a permit. My brother Steve, who was in Stokes Canyon, CA, in his second year at the seminary, had a red and white, two door, 1955 Plymouth sitting in the backyard of my parent's house. It had been sitting there for months; no one really used it. I had behaved myself all week, and Richard was willing to teach me some nighttime driving before I applied for my license the following week. Plus the car needed to blow out some of that carbon built up (from sitting so long). Everybody would win, if my parents would just allow it.

We had it all worked out when we walked through the back door. My father was in his chair drinking a cup of coffee and watching television, and my mother was feeding Penny at the kitchen table. Penny had food all over her face and on the floor around her, and she was playing with what was left on her tray. She was a mess!

I presented the idea to my mother first. I talked fast. I wanted to convince her what a great idea it was before she invited my father into it.

At first, my father said no, but she convinced him by using the same arguments that we had presented to her. Richard just stood there not saying a word. My father finally gave in to the pressure my mother was putting on him. "You can use the car, but you have to be home by midnight." he said. I thanked him, and my mother handed me the keys and five dollars for gas.

We walked around to the back yard, where the car was parked under a tree. It was a mess. I took out a rag from the backseat and started to wipe it down. We hopped in and I started it up. Richard said I should let it warm up for about three or four minutes. I looked at my watch and gave it five. We pulled out onto Van Buren and headed for Mary's house to pick up the rest of the gang. Five minutes later I had a carload, so I threw the keys to Richard. Leonard, Bonnie, Denny and I jumped into the backseat, and Richard drove. Mary rode in the middle, between Richard and Tooter.

With no clue about where we wanted to go, we drove up and down Van Buren for a while, but that got old quick. Tooter suggested we cruise Central. When we hit Central Avenue, there were cars everywhere. I had heard it was a popular place on weekends, but I had no idea how crowded it could get. It was almost like a parking lot. There was every kind of car you could imagine going both ways.

We pulled into Bob's Big Boy around 8:30. We had to drive around two or three times before we found a stall to park in. I read the menu on the lighted sign that hung on the wall in front of us, Hamburger, fries and a Coke, for seventy-nine cents. That's what I wanted. Everyone was ready so Richard flagged down the waitress. She roller skated over and asked us for our order. She came back in about fifteen minutes with a tray, which she hooked up to the driver's side front window. She then asked if we needed more ketchup for our fries. We told her no. The bill came to $6.27 with tax and a $1.00 tip. We all pooled our money together and paid with exact change, and then Richard passed out the food.

As we were eating, Tooter was talking about this old haunted church he had heard about. He said he thought it was somewhere around Tatum and Thunderbird Road.

"That's where we should go," Denny blurted out. "You know, we could buy some beer and party with the ghosts."

Tooter came back with, "Way to go Den, that's a great idea."

Everyone else thought so, too—except one. OL' bulldog face Bonnie, who started to cry. Even Leonard, who gets freaked out listening to ghost stories, thought it was a good idea. Bonnie protested by saying, "I've got a real bad feeling about this. Please don't go!"

Denny's response was, "Shut up, you big baby. We're not taking you home. You're going, too!"

We stopped at a store and picked up a case of Coors along the way. Bonnie continued to cry and Denny, Mary, Tooter and Richard continued teasing her, which made her cry even more. "No mercy," I thought. "Glad it's not me." Leonard, who still had his arm around Bonnie's neck, told everyone to just shut up. He then tried to reason with her. She wouldn't have any of it. I was thinking, "What a bitch! She needs to accept it, shut up, and go along for the ride." But Leonard had a one-track mind and he was not giving up. She continued crying as we drove up and down Thunderbird Road looking for the church. Thunderbird Road was a dirt road back then, and with all the dust that we were kicking up and her crying, I was becoming more and more agitated. Then Tooter asked if he could drive. Richard pulled over and handed him the keys. Tooter had a lead foot and was told several times to slow down. I was worried he would lose control in the dirt.

We looked everywhere for the church but we just couldn't find it. Then Richard suggested that we look on Cactus Road. Tooter drove up and down Cactus Road for a while, each time going faster and faster. We told him several more times to slow down. Even with the brights on it was hard to see. Bonnie never stopped crying and she became more vocal about it. Tooter continued driving faster and faster, and I was getting more pissed off at both of them.

Tooter drove east on Cactus at sixty-five or seventy miles an hour. The next thing we knew, the road ended at Tatum and there was about a two foot embankment along the opposite side of Tatum Road. We hit that embankment at about sixty miles an hour. The car flipped three or four times and finally landed on its top. Being packed so tightly into the back seat must have acted as protection, because only one of us was really hurt. And can you guess who that was? Yep! Of course, it was Bonnie!

Everyone in the front seat climbed out after Richard kicked out the windshield. I was dazed at first. And then I heard Bonnie screaming, "My face, I hurt my face!" She then turned to Denny and asked, "Does my lip look fat?" I thought that Denny was definitely the wrong person for her to ask.

He took one look at her and said, "They look even to me now, bitch, now let's get the fuck out of here!"

Richard stuck his head into the car and screamed, "Hurry up and get out, the motor's on fire and it's spreading fast!" It didn't take long for us to scramble out of the car after that. We met outside the car. The fire was out of control so we started to run. We ran about four or five hundred yards before the car exploded and parts of it went everywhere! And then it wasn't dark anymore. I was sure you could see it burning for miles. Over the years, I have often wondered how anybody could have survived that accident.

We must have walked two miles before we saw any signs of life. Mary pointed at a car that was coming toward us. When they got close enough, we waved them down. When the car pulled up, there were several girls inside, all wearing just their nighties. Tooter or Denny said he thought he died and went to heaven, or something to that effect.

The girl riding shotgun cracked the window about an inch. She said, "We saw the fire out in the desert and we were driving out to see what it was." I told her that it was our car and we were trying to get back to town to get help. Then one of the girls from the backseat asked us if we knew about a haunted church that was supposed to be out here somewhere. Richard and I looked at each other while Leonard explained to her that that's what brought us out here in the first place.

I noticed Leonard was no longer holding Bonnie's hand, and I knew why. Ol' Len had his eyes on the ladies in their nighties.

I asked if they could help us get back into town. At first they said no, but they must have thought about it and decided to help us. They told us that we could ride on the hood and trunk area of their car and that they would drive slowly so we wouldn't fall off. They offered Mary a ride inside because she was a girl. That's when Bonnie cried out and said, "What about me? I'm a girl too!" At first they didn't believe her, but she protested so much they finally gave in and let her ride in the car along with Mary.

They brought us back to the store we where we'd bought the beer earlier. We thanked them and they left. The reality of what had happened started to hit me; it was about 5:00 in the morning, and I knew I was in trouble, big time!

When I walked into my house an hour later, my parents were really angry. They told me they were up half the night worrying. They were out of control as they screamed at me. I stood there looking down at the floor. I had blown it again. "So I messed up, what else is new?" After about ten minutes, they were calm enough for me to let them know what had happened.

When I explained, I left out a few details, like the fact that we had beer with us. (We never got a chance to drink it anyway, so why bother mentioning it? I had heard the beer cans exploding as we ran from the car.) I also left out the fact that Tooter had been the one driving. I thought that would probably get them going again, and quite frankly, I didn't want to hear it.

When there was a lull in the conversation, I announced that I was going to bed. I left it up to them to tell my brother what happened to his car. After all, they had some responsibility here. They were the ones who had let me use it. I thought that since he was studying to be a priest, he needed to learn forgiveness anyway.

My father's ride showed up shortly after I had gone to bed. At work that morning, my father took a break and drove over to the scene of our accident. The car was still burning when he arrived, and a sheriff was there doing an investigation, trying to put together what had happened. My father introduced himself and explained, as best he could, what had taken place from the information I had given him earlier that morning. The officer wrote up the report based on the information given to him by my father, and then he called a tow truck to take the wreckage away.

When my father came home that evening, I was on my way out. He called me into the kitchen where both my parents were sitting at the table. He then proceeded to tell both my mother and me that he had seen the car and talked to the investigating officer. "After looking at the car and the condition it was in, I just don't know how the hell somebody didn't die." Then he turned to my mother and said, "Rosie, we almost had a funeral to go to. He must have an angel on his shoulder. If you had seen that car too, you would have wondered how they lived through it." I just kept my month shut. I knew I was standing on thin ice, and I was starting to feel it crack beneath my feet.

There was never any mention of the beer. There must have been evidence because of the way the cans exploded, but it was never brought up.

I found out several days later that the church we were looking for was about fifteen hundred feet from the crash.

My brother came home to visit two months later. Nothing was said about the accident, at least to me. He used my parent's car to get around.

Chapter Fifteen

It's A Bird, It's a Plane. No, It's My Car!

"Do you want to be right or happy?"

By this time, my father was working with recovering alcoholics and addicts, providing a place for them to live. He was also very involved in his own 12-Step Recovery program. My father was committed, not only to his own recovery, but for others as well. He would go out of his way to help as long as they wanted the help. I remember that he had a saying; "If you want help and are willing to do your part, I will go to hell with you—but not *for* you." Then he would ask, "Do we understand each other?" At which time they would either stay and get involved in the program or they would walk out.

Through time, I finally came to believe his commitment to his recovery, and helping other suffering alcoholics and addicts helped keep his commitment strong.

However, when it came to me, he didn't know what to do. His guilt got in the way. He knew I was just like him. When he felt guilty, I sensed it, so I would use that guilt when I needed it.

He would often have friends in his 12-Step program talk with me. One of them was Black Wally. When Wally talked, you couldn't help but listen. However, I had just turned sixteen, and although he would make perfect sense, I wasn't ready to listen. I do have to say, Wally was persistent and in the many years I knew him, he was always there. He never gave up and when I did get clean and sober some seven years later, he played a major role.

Getting high was more important to me at the time than anything my father said. I remember many times going to the Maverick House when I was under the influence to ask my father for money so I could continue to party. Father would tell me I was no different from anyone else who came there under the influence. Then he would tell me to leave or he would call the police and have me arrested. Then he'd follow me out to the street and give me money. The next time I saw him he would tell me not to do it again. I would feel bad because I knew how it embarrassed him, but when I ran out of money, I'd do it again. My mother was just as bad. She gave me money just about every day because she didn't want me to be without. I took the money because at my age and immature thinking, life was all about me. It wasn't that I didn't care—I did. However, all I thought about was getting high, and that was the only thing that really mattered to me. When I would feel bad about how I was treating others, it was usually short lived. All I had to do was "get high" and the feelings would go away. How cool was that? It worked every time.

One day my mother asked me to start being more responsible with my life. I remember telling her, "I have too much time on my hands and it would help if I had a job. But since I have no transportation it would be hard to find one." I knew I was manipulating her, but I didn't care. All during my little speech I was giving her a look that said, "I can't do this by myself."

As I looked up into her eyes, she patted me on the head and said, "Let me talk to your father." I batted my eyes at her and smiled. I knew I had her, and two days later I was the proud owner of a green two door 1952 Ford. It was fifteen years old and it looked like a Sherman Tank. I loved it!

I felt some guilt over how I had obtained my car, so I went out of my way to look for a job with every intention of paying them back. However, I never changed my way of living to accommodate my job search. I was still hanging out until one or two in the morning raising hell and getting loaded, so it was hard to take my job search too seriously. And, of course, it didn't take long before I was getting up as if I was going out to look for a job and ending up at Mary's house sleeping on her couch until one or two in the afternoon. Each day a repeat of the day before, always telling myself that tomorrow would be different.

I'd had my car for eight months when some friends—Roger, Rodney, and Tommy—and I drove up to South Mountain. We were all drinking, and I was drunk. We parked at one of the ramadas about three quarters of the way up the mountain and, without realizing it, I had parked very close to the edge. All four of us got out of the car and walked a tenth of a mile, or so, further up the mountain. We sat at one of the cement picnic tables to finish the case of beer we had brought up with us. We were there for about an hour when Rodney announced he needed to get home. Roger volunteered to go back and get the car. The rest of us continued to drink as we waited. It didn't seem like Roger was gone very long when all of a sudden there was a loud crash over the side of the mountain. It looked like a car had gone off the mountain below us and found its fate a little over half way down. It was smashed up against what looked like a big boulder. When it hit, whatever kind of car it was became unrecognizable. I was laughing when I turned to Tommy and said, "I'd hate to be the owner of that pile of crap." Tommy and Rodney laughed.

We were laughing when Roger came running up, completely out of breath. He was bent over with both hands on his knees, gasping for air when he screamed out, "Did you see that car go off the mountain?" He was still fighting to breathe.

"Yeah, why?" I asked.

"That was your car!"

"What!" I yelled.

"That was your car," he said again. "When I got into the car I put my foot on the clutch. The car started to roll, and as close as it was to the edge, I couldn't stop it. So I jumped out, and it went over the side."

I was angry, but I knew Roger was only fifteen. I shouldn't have let him be the one to get the car in the first place.

We walked down the mountain and called Roger's brother, Richard, to come and get us from the horse stables at the foot of the mountain.

My parents didn't ask what happened to my car until almost a week later. I told them, "Someone stole it from in front of Mary's house about a week ago. You don't have to worry, because I called the cops and reported it." They said okay and it was never mentioned again.

Chapter Sixteen

Car Wash

He said, "Okay." But Tooter was just like me; he came from a dysfunctional family, and he was used to getting his way by wearing you down. "Okay" really meant that it was time to regroup and approach it in a different manner. He just didn't take "no" for an answer.

It was almost a year after Tooter rolled my brother's car in the desert that I let it slip to my parents that he was the one driving the car that day. We were sitting at the kitchen table one afternoon. I was eating leftovers from the night before and my father was drinking a cup of coffee, waiting for his partner from SRP to pick him up for his 3:00 shift. My mother was drinking her Mountain Dew and smoking a cigarette when the secret I had been hiding from them came out. My father's only comment was that it was "water under the bridge now."

A week later my father co-signed on a 1962 Ford Fairlane for me but before he signed he made me promise that I wouldn't let anyone drive it. "And especially not your friend Tooter," he said. I agreed.

I loved being mobile again. It made my life less complicated, and I didn't have to depend on others to get around. However, I didn't have my car very long before I went back on my word and let Tooter drive. One afternoon Tooter and I were over at Mary's house and we were drinking. When we started to run low on beer, Tooter asked if he could drive my car to Mac and Marge's to get more. "Tooter," I said, "I promised my dad I would never let you drive one of my cars again."

He said, "Okay." But Tooter was just like me; he came from a dysfunctional family, and he was used to getting his way by wearing you down. "Okay" really meant that it was time to regroup and approach it in a different manner. He just didn't take "no" for an answer.

Mary and I were playing around and it was beginning to become sexual. We needed to be alone. So I let my judgment lapse and threw Tooter the keys with the understanding that he would just go to Mac and Marge's and back here.

"Thanks, Ol' buddy!" he told me as he walked out the door, grinning from ear to ear.

Mary and I were just coming out of the bedroom when Tooter came running up to the house. He was all wet. "John!" He was staring down at the ground. "John, I got some bad news, Ol' buddy." That was what Tooter called people either when he wanted something, or when he had done something really bad and he was feeling guilty.

"What happened?" I asked him.

"Oh John, you're not going to believe me when I tell you what happened."

"What!" I yelled out.

"Oh John, Ol' Buddy, I'm so sorry." He was now shaking his head, continuing to stare down at the ground. "I was driving down Van Buren and I had my right blinker on to turn at 37th Street. I must have turned the corner too fast, I drove right through the fence and into the swimming pool at the Vagabond Motel."

I was in shock; I couldn't believe what I was hearing. "This just can't be happening," I thought.

With head still down, he handed me the keys. Then he said, "I remembered to turn it off."

"Thanks," I said, as if it mattered.

Mary, Tooter and I trotted down to the corner without saying a word. When we got there, all I could see was my car submerged in about five feet of water. I was told there were people in the pool when it happened. They were able to get out in time when they heard the car coming through the fence.

I turned to Tooter and said, "You're an amazing guy. I don't know how you do it. You always come out smelling like a rose and never hurting anyone."

He looked at me, with eyes full of pain, and announced, "I've got to go now." He walked down 37th Street toward Crocket School.

I stayed while the police investigated what happened.

When all was said and done, my father didn't speak to me for almost a week, and I had to pay $200.00 for the fence.

And Tooter never asked if he could drive any of my cars again.

Chapter Seventeen

Love, Dysfunctional Style

My blackouts were always an adventure!
They happened so often, I started to look forward to them.

A friend's sister introduced me to a new girl in our neighborhood. Her name was Glenna Ramsey, and I thought she was the most beautiful girl I had ever seen in my sixteen years of living. She was tall and thin, and she had long, soft red hair that flowed down past her waist. She was only fifteen, but she acted much older. At first, I didn't feel I had a chance with her, but she seemed to like me and we spent a lot of time together. We spent so much time together that I started pulling back from my other friends.

I was walking her home one evening around ten. We were walking on the canal bank holding hands. We stopped about halfway, I turned to face her and we kissed. One thing led to another and we made love. It was incredible; I was in love!

I stopped sniffing glue the day I met Glenna. I didn't want her to know. I did, however, continue to drink. She didn't seem to mind. As a matter of fact, she drank too. She not only drank, she could probably match me any day of the week, hands down. She liked Sloe Gin and she drank a lot of it. I thought she was wonderful. In my eyes she was the perfect woman.

Glenna's mother was a devout Pentecostal, and was very active in her church. She was very clear about how she felt and had no problem expressing it. Glenna's behavior troubled her and it created major conflicts between them. Glenna was drifting away from the church, and her mother knew I was partly responsible. I told her I had nothing to do with it and that maybe she needed to back off of her a little and not to be so hard on her. Her mother was not a bad person; she loved her daughter and wanted what was best for her. However, Glenna thought very differently.

I was beginning to experience blackouts from all the alcohol I was drinking. I'd had a few in the past, but nothing like what I was experiencing now. They were happening more frequently, and they were lasting longer. I used to joke about it saying, "My blackouts are always an adventure."

I remember one time waking up as I was flying through Mary's screen door. I stood up, trying to make some sense of what had just happened. I remember thinking, "Do I really want to know?" My next thought was, "No!" So I left, and to this day I still don't know.

Glenna and I were spending even more time together, and it wasn't long before she became pregnant. Well, she was only fifteen, and I was sixteen. Needless to say, our parents were livid! I wanted to do the right thing and marry her, but my parents tried to discourage me. They asked me, "How the hell are you going to support a wife and a baby when you can't even take care of yourself?"

When I went to Glenna's house her mother said, "You need to do what is right and not let this baby live in sin."

Glenna and I were mixed up. We both loved our parents and didn't want to disappoint them, but we also loved each other, and those feelings could not be denied. We decided to marry in spite of how it made our parents feel. I would find a job, stop drinking and using drugs, and become more responsible. That was my plan, but where was I going to gain all of this control over my life that I had never seemed to have before?

The answer had to be love. I loved her and all I wanted was to be with her. When I was with her, I really didn't think about anything else, so doing it for love made perfect sense to me.

My parents finally signed a permission slip for us to be married. It was January 20, 1968 when we became husband and wife. We were married in front of a judge in Sonoita, Mexico. We had friends and some family with us: there was Glenna's older sister, Bernice, Mary Brown (Bernice's daughter), and Jack, who was Mary's friend and who stood as best man at the ceremony.

Mary was a year younger than Glenna and was just as pretty. Jack really liked her. They went out a few times together, but they just couldn't seem to make it work.

On our way back from Mexico, we were tired. Glenna, Mary and I were in the backseat. I sat in the middle between the two girls, Glenna was asleep to my left. We had a blanket draped over our laps. Bernice was asleep in the passenger side of the front seat and Jack was driving. I was tired so I laid my head back and was dozing off.

As I lay there, I was thinking about some of the changes I needed to make. All of a sudden I felt this hand on my right inner thigh and it was rubbing me gently. I sat there with eyes closed thinking about my new wife and how gentle she was with me. "Oh how I love her," I thought. Then I realized it was not Glenna but her cousin Mary. I looked at her and she looked back out of the corner of her eye and smiled. I just sat there, half afraid we'd be caught and yet knowing that excited me more. She made it very clear that day that if there was anything I needed, she would be around, with the emphasis on *anything!* So much for commitment. I whispered to her that I loved my wife and that it was nice of her to offer, but no thanks. She smiled and stopped what she was doing. I closed my eyes and went to sleep.

When Jack pulled into my driveway, I shook Glenna to wake her up. He let us out, and we both unloaded his car and went inside. My parents were talking at the kitchen table when we walked in. "How was your trip?" my mother asked. Glenna told her it was wonderful and then told her about being married by the judge.

My mother listened, while my father handed me an envelope with $50.00 in it and said, "Being newlyweds you should have some privacy. This should get you a motel for a couple of nights."

I thanked him, and we left to go find a room.

As we passed the Sand's, Glenna read the marquee, $17.50 a night, Sunday through Thursday. I made a U-turn and we pulled in. "Room 214," the clerk told us, when he handed me the key.

I thanked him and drove around the side closest to the room.

We spent two glorious days together. They will stay in my memory forever. I loved my wife and I never wanted those two days to end. But like everything that's great, it was short-lived.

We moved in with my parents, and we took over Steve's old room. This wasn't the best situation to be in; we had very little privacy. But it was a place to live until we could get on our feet. I found a job at the new K-mart store in Scottsdale. I worked in the Garden Department and if there was a job to be done in that department, I did it. I ran the cash register, sold, and watered plants, and unloaded trucks. I was bringing home $68.00 a week after taxes, and it wasn't long before Glenna and I were able to move out of my parent's house.

Glenna found a three-bedroom apartment on Polk Street. It was a four-plex and it was across the street from Mary's house. It was almost as big as the house my parents lived in. It had three large bedrooms, a kitchen, dining room, living room and two bathrooms. The rent was $35.00 a month plus tax and we paid the utilities. In 1968, a dollar went a long way. We could fill a shopping cart with groceries and staples for about $25.00 back then. It seemed that things were really working out for Glenna and me. When I drank, it was on the weekends and I rarely got drunk. I was no longer sniffing glue or using other drugs. Yes, life was good and our love continued to get better. I was truly happy.

I worked hard at my job and everyone liked me. After being there several months I became friends with a co-worker named Luis who worked in the Garden Department on weekends and in Housewares three days a week.

One day I was standing outside getting ready to unload a truck when Luis came out on his break to smoke a cigarette. He offered me one. I took it, then he took out his lighter and lit it. I thanked him and headed back to the forklift I had left running about four feet away.

"You look tired," he said.

"I am," I told him. "I was up half the night with my wife. She wasn't feeling well."

He then asked me if I needed help. I thought he meant unloading the truck I was ready to start on, so I told him yes. "I'll be right back," he said and went out to his car. He came back with five little white pills with a cross-inscribed on one side. He told me to take three now and two more in three hours. I asked him what they were. He told me they were "White Crosses."

"What are they for?" I asked.

"They're a mild form of speed. You know, not the hard stuff. This is the kind truck drivers or college students use to stay up all night. You know, nothing major."

Well, all I heard out of that whole conversation was "mild form of speed," and what that meant to me was it was nothing more than taking an aspirin, so I took them and because they were so small I took all five at the same time.

Forty-five minutes later, they kicked in. I unloaded two trucks that day by myself and probably could have done more. I loved how they made me feel. I went to see Luis the next day in housewares. I asked him to see me when he went out on break. It was 11:15 when Luis walked into the Garden Department to find me. I was watering the trees that I'd unloaded the day before. "What can I do for you?" he asked when he saw me.

I told him how much I had enjoyed the crosses I had taken the day before, and how they had made me feel.

"I thought you'd like 'em." He said with a big smile.

"If they don't hurt you I'm interested in getting more," I told him.

"How many you want?" He explained that a rack of ten crosses rolled up in foil was $2.00, ten racks were $20.00 and a jar of a thousand was $200.00.

I bought two racks and took five more. Again, I kicked butt that day. I had a little trouble sleeping that night, so I was really tired the next day. I took seven more and ran circles around everyone. What was this new drug that made you feel so good and yet couldn't hurt you? This discovery was revolutionary. There was no other way to explain it. Even my boss told me to slow down.

During a break the following day, Luis took one look at me and asked if I was all right. He said I looked pale and asked me if I was drinking enough water. He then told me that if I didn't stay hydrated while taking speed it could cause problems. He told me what those problems were, and then he apologized for forgetting to tell me.

I took his suggestion and forced myself to drink some water and he was right. I did feel much better. I didn't take any more until the following day, when I was so tired that I didn't want to get out of bed. I could have slept a couple of days. "Luis didn't tell me about this part. I guess he forgot that, too," I thought.

I took my last eight crosses to get myself through the rest of the day.

I needed to find a solution to this new problem I had encountered. I guess I needed to buy more—that was what made the most sense to me—so I started to buy ten racks at a time.

That weekend I discovered even more about this new wonder drug I was taking. I learned that I could drink more. Over the weekend I drank a lot of beer and I didn't seem to get as drunk as I had in the past, drinking the same amount. Even Glenna commented on how much I drank. Of course, I didn't mention the white crosses. I knew she wouldn't understand anyway. Back then I was ahead of my time...I had already developed the attitude "don't ask, don't tell" way before the military did, and I learned early in life that you only told people what they needed to hear, and when it came to my life, I decided what they needed to hear.

It wasn't long before I was taking about a rack a day and drinking more. I didn't drink as often, but when I did, my tolerance was much higher.

I was coming home from work one day and at the light on Van Buren and 40th Street, I saw Denny walking in the same direction I was going. I stopped and he jumped into the passenger seat. I asked him how he was doing, and he told me he just had an argument with his father about his drinking and making no effort to do something with his life. "He called me a bum. I'm no bum!" he said almost yelling. Denny asked me about the empty room in our new apartment. "If you'll let me stay there, I'll get a job and pay you rent."

Glenna and I talked about it later that night, and Denny moved in the next day with the understanding that he would follow through with work and rent.

Well, we knew within the first week of his stay that we had made a mistake. He sat around drinking and sniffing glue all day. He never attempted to look for work and what made it worse, Tooter would come over almost everyday and join him. Glenna expressed concern at first, but it didn't take long before concern turned into frustration and then to anger. She would ask me to talk with him. I tried several times and each time I did he would threaten to tell Glenna all the things I was doing behind her back, so I'd back off of him and do nothing. This would only make Glenna more angry and upset.

The pressure from my wife and the no-win situation that Denny put me in created an enormous amount of stress on me. It was on my mind constantly. Every night when I came home from work, Glenna would start in on the things that Denny did or did not do. I felt divided. I loved my wife and didn't want to fight with her. She had every right to be angry, but I didn't want to get caught, so I continued to do nothing.

Well, what I have learned since, but didn't know then, was that when a problem exists and we do nothing, nothing changes and the problem takes on a life of its own. It gets worse. It finally came down to "him or me," so I had to decide. Enough was enough and I told him he had to move; I gave him a week. He told me he would tell. I told him I didn't care. I had taken away his defense. He was angry at first but he got over it. He moved out toward the end of the week and he never did tell Glenna.

It wasn't long after Denny moved out that Glenna had a miscarriage and lost the baby. It was a very emotional time. She went through a bout with depression, and had it not been for her mother and sister to help take care of her, she might not have gotten through it as well as she did. Glenna's mother was like an emotional rock, and the longer I knew her the more I listened to and respected her. She was a very wise soul. She was always clear about her beliefs, and although Glenna and her mother fought, I knew they loved each other.

My using was getting worse...and I was losing more control. I was even caught sniffing glue once when Denny lived there. Glenna was so angry she threatened to leave me. I begged her not to go. I somehow convinced her that it was my first time and that I would never do it again. She believed me. She could see I was drinking more, and on several occasions she expressed some concern. We were arguing more, and she believed my use of alcohol was partly to blame.

I don't know how I did it, but I managed to convince her that the neighborhood was the problem and that we just needed to move. We found a small apartment on 28th Street. It was a small back apartment that sat over a garage. It had a large bedroom with a small kitchen, living room, and a bathroom. There was a front porch with a swing for two and two lawn chairs. I thought it would be nice to sit outside and enjoy the evenings.

Glenna, with her knack for decorating, turned our house into a home in no time. I was always proud of her talent. When friends came over, I didn't have the embarrassment I used to feel when I lived with my parents. When I was growing up, house cleaning was not a priority. I used to tell my friends to wait outside or I'd go outside and meet them so they didn't have to come inside. I always hated doing that. The sad thing was that I never gave my wife the credit she deserved. Life was still all about me and getting high. She went out of her way to please me. She always had the house clean before I came home, if I came home at all. Dinner was always ready and she was a great cook. She even went as far as to ask me what she needed to change, because she thought that if she was a better wife, things would work out between us. In other words, she thought it was her fault, and I let her think it. How self-centered was that?

Let's face it, drugs were more important then those I loved. Even then, I knew what I was doing, but I didn't care enough to change. As long as she felt responsible for my behaviors, I never had to change, and that worked for me.

One evening after dinner, we sat outside to relax on our porch when Glenna told me she was pregnant again. I was happy at first, but soon became frightened. This meant I would have to be more responsible, maybe even slow down my drinking and whatever else I was doing. Again, it was all about me! I know she was thinking pretty much the same thing, and that made me angry. I wasn't ready to stop. So, over the next few months I started to emotionally distance myself. This made her try harder to make our relationship work. It also created an excuse for me to come and go as I pleased. One of the many regrets I've carried through the years has been in remembering all the pain that I would see in Glenna's eyes, knowing that I was the cause of it.

One early evening after a very frustrating day at work, I stopped at the Circle-K on the way home and bought some beer. I pulled into my driveway around 6:15. I had taken several white crosses throughout the day mixed with the four beers I had just downed right out of the six-pack. I was starting to catch a buzz and was feeling on edge. Every little thing seemed to irritate me.

Glenna had cooked a delicious dinner that night and had it on the table when I walked in. Steak, potatoes, corn on the cob and dinner rolls hot from the oven. She was taking butter out of its wrapper and putting it on a dish.

I told her how good it all looked, and I sat down. She thanked me and sat down across from me. I finished my beer half-way through the meal and Glenna asked me if I wanted another one. I told her that I did, so she took one from the refrigerator, opened it with the church key she had sitting on the counter, then put it on the table in front of me. She bent over to kiss me and when she did, she knocked over my beer.

I went off! I don't know why, I just did. I backhanded her across the face with my left hand. She looked shocked! She stood there holding her face and I watched as her eyes filled with her tears. I felt so ashamed, but at the same time, even more enraged. I lost it. I went nuts. I started throwing the food and dishes against the wall. I couldn't stop! She ran out of the house holding her face and crying as I destroyed the rest of the house. I passed out on the swing on the porch.

Whack!!! "What the fuck!" I yelled out. I was dazed. It felt like someone had hit me on top of my head with a pipe or maybe a flash-light. I sat up, holding my head where I had been hit and saw my psychotic brother-in-law, Ted, standing over me with a very large gun. He had this vacant look in his eyes. As I looked into those eyes, I could see that there was nobody home, and that scared me. He pulled back the hammer slowly. I heard the clicks, there were four of them. He had the gun pointed at my head. Everything slowed down, and I watched as if we were moving in slow motion. Ted was a nut, I had always known it, so I had just done my best to stay out of his way.

It had always intrigued me how things could go from bad to worse with no effort at all, and this was definitely one of those times! I just knew I was a dead man when he said, "Why shouldn't I shoot you after what you done to my baby sister?" in his crazy hillbilly accent.

I found out later that after I hit Glenna, she ran out of the house and down the stairs to the landlady's house. She invited Glenna in to use the phone and Glenna called her sister, who rushed over and picked her up. She took Glenna over to her house, where Ted heard the story. It made him angry, so he took it upon himself to take care of the situation the only way he knew how, with violence!

When a person who appears to be more unstable than you are is standing over you with a Colt .45 long (as he identified it), and is aiming it at your head, what do you do? You're right. Pray! And pray I did! I prayed what I'm sure every addict prays when his life is in danger and he sees no way out. I prayed... "God get me out of this situation and I promise you, I'll never do it again," and I meant it. But, as I have said, even though I really meant it, I had crossed that line of no return and my behaviors were now controlling me. So my promise, though sincere, didn't last long.

But right then I started to talk fast, even faster than I had when I was facing that giant officer on Van Buren a few years back. I just kept talking. I told him I loved my wife and that I didn't know what got into me and that I'd never do anything to harm her and that it wouldn't happen again and that... I don't even remember what all I said, I just didn't want to die!

I must have been convincing because he backed off. He smacked me on top of my head with his gun again and said, "It had better not."

I said, "Okay."

He then backed off the porch, turned and ran down the stairs. He was gone as quickly as he had come.

I have to tell you that this was the *only* time I ever hit my wife, and I have always regretted it. I am truly sorry.

The very nature of the disease of addiction is that it begins to speak for us rather than using our collective intelligence. Addiction seizes control of all of our behaviors and enslaves us to do its bidding. It not only enslaves us, but those whom we love as well. My addiction was holding those I loved the most hostage and no one was safe. I apologized to Glenna and she came home the following day. Glenna and I fought so often about my drinking and acting out behaviors that the landlord finally told us we had to move.

We moved into a one-room cabin converted from a former farm labor camp. We called them "The Candle Light Apartments," because the electricity was always out and we had to frequently use candles. The cabin consisted of a single twenty foot by twenty foot room with a stove, refrigerator and a sink in one corner. A bed, dresser, and bed stand were in another corner, with a small area to put a table and chairs in still another corner. The roof was flat and I wasn't sure if it was even fastened down. There was a community bathroom and showers just outside our cabin, so we didn't have far to walk. At any given time, there was no guarantee that the toilets would even work. However, I thought it was a "smokin' deal" for $13.00 a month. Glenna, on the other hand, didn't feel the same way.

The people who lived there were just as colorful as the place itself. I already knew most of them from the neighborhood. There were Ted and Ida, who had been married for a month without telling anyone. (When I went to school with Ted in the seventh grade, I never thought he'd marry because of his popularity with the girls.) They lived across the courtyard. Next to them was Marty, Ida's sister, then Sam and George, Ida and Marty's brothers. Going around the courtyard were Johnny and Jimmy, brothers who lived with their father in one cabin, and their mother who lived with her boyfriend in the cabin next door to them. Their mother would go back and forth between cabins, depending on how she felt or who she wanted to be with for the evening. We used to sit out in courtyard and drink and make bets on who she would be with that evening.

Most everyone who lived there drank, and some used drugs, but mostly we were all dysfunctional in our relationships. When Ted drank too much he would beat up Ida. Marty had a different man in her cabin almost every night. Sam had a girlfriend who would sleep around on him, and George was involved with Wanda, who would fight with him about his drinking. Yes, this certainly was a colorful place, and Glenna and I were becoming a part of it all.

It's amazing how people will invite you into their world as long as you are willing to fit in and not try to change anything. I was willing, but I couldn't convince Glenna to come along. She hated it there. When I came home from work, I'd eat, then go outside into the courtyard and drink. Some didn't work and would be out in the courtyard all day long. Everyone would pool their money and someone would do a beer run. If you used anything other than alcohol, you were on your own. The women who lived there supported each other and they invited Glenna into the fold.

When Ted and Ida would fight and it became physical, she would end up in the emergency room at the County Hospital with some fabrication about how she fell down the stairs or some other bullshit story. She went there so often with several broken bones, cuts and contusions they must have known the truth. If she wasn't hurt enough to be in the hospital, the women would clean her up. It reminded me of Arnie and Joy, the couple who lived across the street from us on Roosevelt, and how Dot, Joy and my mother would take care of each other. I guess dysfunction never changes.

I used to watch Sam, George and Marty cry when Ida was being beaten and they would do nothing. Yet they all had reputations for being scrappers. Everyone feared them, even the girls. I asked George one day why they allowed their sister to be beaten by Ted. I knew that any one of them could kick his ass. He told me that they were taught by their mother that when you are married, family doesn't get involved unless invited. He looked sad when he spoke. "Ida knows that and she's never asked." That made perfect sense to me but it didn't sit well with Glenna. She didn't understand.

Glenna hated our apartment so much that I would often find her at her mother's house down the street when I got home.

One rainy Sunday, the wind was blowing hard. Glenna and I had just gone to bed. It was around eleven or so when all hell broke loose! It sounded like our cabin was coming apart. I looked up and watched as our roof rose up from the walls of the cabin about a foot and then came back down with one hell of a crash. It sounded like an explosion. Well that was it for Glenna, the last straw! She told me that night that if I didn't get more serious about moving soon she would be moving in with her mother. I felt I had no choice if I was going to stay married, so we started looking the following day when I got home from work.

I let my parents know we were looking and asked them to keep their eyes open. On Thursday with still no prospects, we stopped by the Maverick House. My father and Harry were in the office talking. Harry asked us if we would like a cup of coffee. I took him up on his offer, but Glenna declined. I had known for a while that the state had plans to build more freeways in Maricopa County to support its growth and that the highway department was buying up all the properties in its path. It would be several years before they would start construction so these buildings sat empty. My father had a friend at the highway department, and he would rent some of these structures to my father for recovery houses. Because Maverick House was non-profit, the rent was very low. He rented three houses on 14th Avenue and Lathum. His plan was to put a men and women's drug program across from each other, and the other house he offered to Glenna and me if we wanted it. He gave us the key so we could drive out there and look at it. When we got there, Glenna took one look at it and fell in love.

It was a white house with turquoise trim. There were three bedrooms, a living room, dining room, large kitchen and two inside bathrooms with plumbing that actually worked. We moved in the following weekend, and it didn't take long before she turned it into a home again.

I'll say it again; I loved my wife. However, I was so far into my addiction by this time that, even though I would tell myself not to, I would end up doing things that created friction in my marriage. She couldn't trust me. I would lie for no reason and then get mad at myself for doing it. I had no defense. I didn't understand it myself. She would tell me, "Don't lie to me, I know when you're doing it." Or, "Don't give me any more of your empty promises John, because I'm sick of them!"

This was also a time in my life when I was drinking more in bars. I was seventeen, almost eighteen years old, but because of what I was putting my body through, I looked much older.

Mac and Marge's had a six-ounce draft for ten cents. I drank there three to four times a week, usually on my way home from work. On those nights I would often come home at one-thirty or two o'clock in the morning and there were some nights that I didn't come home at all. Glenna continued to go out of her way to try and make our marriage work. She would plead with me, get mad at me, even try to be a better wife hoping things would change, and I would continue to do as I pleased without any regard for her feelings. Sometimes I would come home bloody from fighting or some type of accident. She would clean me up and beg me to stop drinking. She was still unaware of the drugs I was doing. There were times I couldn't tell you what happened because I didn't know. I blacked out so often that I'd wake up in a different bar from the one I started out in. Sometimes I woke up at someone else's house, or at home wondering how I got there. No matter how bad it got, I wouldn't talk about it. I didn't want others to know how bad I was getting.

One evening after work, I stopped at the bar. Roy and his crew were there; Jimmy, Bobby and Willie. Roy's presence and mannerisms always reminded me of Dan Blocker, the actor who played "Hoss" on the old television show "Bonanza."

Roy was talking to this lady he'd invited over to their table. I sat with them shooting the bull with the rest of the boys while Roy continued his conversation with Brenda, his new friend. Marge brought over another round and Bobby paid for them. Brenda was telling Roy that she was here to meet her two friends. They were already fifteen minutes late, and she was wondering if she was even at the right bar. "I thought they said 38th Street and Van Buren, but maybe they said 32nd or 33rd Street, I can't remember," she was telling Roy, who was already offering to go over to the "Serendipity Bar" with her.

I excused myself to go to the bathroom. When I came out I sat at the bar. Roy was helping Brenda put on her coat, and then they both walked out the door. I thought to myself, "I hope he has money, because she don't look cheap." At the bar, I talked with Mike and his wife Lori. Lori and her friend were trying to guess the ages of those in the bar. Marge was playing along whenever she wasn't waiting on people. Mike and I were talking about the new 1969 Ford Mustangs and how cool they looked. He was thinking about getting one.

Mike was a painter by trade and owned his own business. He was going to trade in his 1963 Rambler. "I could get maybe $300.00 on a trade-in," he was telling me. I was half listening when I overheard Lori's friend ask Marge how old she thought I looked. Being almost eighteen, I thought I was in trouble. Mike and Lori already knew how old I was; Lori was looking sideways at me. I think they must have been thinking the same thing. I held my breath. Marge looked hard at me and studied my face.

"This is it," I thought. I was trying to look older. "I'd guess about thirty-five." She put her right hand on her chin and closed one eye. "Yeah, at least thirty-five."

At first, I was relieved because I didn't want to be caught, but then I became concerned. "Do I look that rough?" I wondered.

Lori smiled at first, then started laughing. "Thirty-five sounds right to me."

I looked at her, refusing to confirm or deny. I should have felt good about getting away with it, but it only made me feel more out of control, and that was something I didn't want to face.

Chapter Eighteen

God, Get Me Out of This One, "Again"

"The real test is not avoiding sticky situations,
but getting out of sticky situations you're in."
A thousand paths to comfort.
-- *David Baird*

One afternoon, after a big fight with my wife, I started drinking. I couldn't tell you how much I drank, only that it was enough for me to black out.

A month earlier I had bought a jet black 1964 Ford Station Wagon from Bobby, a man who lived at the Maverick House. Bobby bought cars to work on and sell. He gave me a good deal and this Ford was cherry.

I remember sitting at the kitchen table, still arguing with Glenna, and then the next thing I knew I was waking up, driving my car, with a girl that I didn't recognize sitting next to me, and she was rubbing the inside of my right thigh. My mind was in a fog, a state that was becoming more familiar to me. "Who is she and how did she get here?" came to mind as I tried to clear up my confusion.

"Look out!" she screamed as she put her arm out to brace herself. I looked up just in time to see the back end of a yellow station wagon, which I was about to hit. The driver of the station wagon was waiting for traffic to clear so that he could turn left into one of the driveways at the Ramada Inn. As he was waiting for the last car to go by, I plowed into the back of him at forty miles an hour.

I hit him hard, no brakes. The girl I was with flew up against the front window, but didn't break it. She fell back into the front seat. I hit the steering wheel hard with my chest and fell back into the seat next to her. "Damn, that hurt." I was even more confused.

She screamed, "YOU ASSHOLE!!!"

When I looked over my steering wheel, I saw the crumpled black metal of what was once the hood and fenders of the "cherry" Ford station wagon, which I had owned maybe thirty days. Hell, I still owed $50.00 on it! Forty feet in front of me to my left was what looked like a yellow station wagon with maybe four people in it. The car was in the middle of the two lanes he had been trying to cross. He was almost facing in the wrong direction. I saw movement, but not much at first. I couldn't tell if anyone was hurt.

"What now?" I thought. I was mad at first at them for being in my way, but somehow I knew that wasn't going to work. Logic set in; I was drunk with a girl, and I had no idea who she was. There was no doubt in my mind that I was going to jail this time. I started to pray and I prayed hard. I was in a no-win situation again. "God, please get me out of this situation again and I promise I will be good!" And do you know how much God loved me?

The next thing I saw was all four doors of the station wagon flying open, and from the driver's side my brother Richard jumped out, followed by Roger riding shotgun, then Gary and Reighley from the backseat. When they ran over to my car, they realized it was me. "Way to go, bro," Richard said with this shocked look on his face. "What a dumb shit! You are in so much trouble!" The car I had just hit was my parent's Ford Falcon station wagon, which my brother and his friends were using. I was sure glad to see them.

"Who's the babe?" Roger asked. I ignored him.

Then Gary, realizing the seriousness of my situation, offered some suggestions. "Hey, why don't we push your car into the parking lot?"

My car was totaled and it wouldn't start. Hell, I was completely at their mercy. "Let me get out and help," I offered.

Richard started his car and pulled it into the lot next to mine. He then got back out and assessed the damage. Not bad, a taillight and lens out, bumper bent a little. "You lucky bastard!..." Then he looked at my car and said, "Maybe you're not so lucky."

Roger suggested that we get the hell of there before the cops came.

"Good idea," Gary said.

We all piled into the Falcon and Richard took Ol' what's-her-name home. She was angry. I didn't know what to say to her, so I said nothing. She was riding between my brother and me, and she was explaining to my brother that she thought I was a real chump and that she didn't know I was married. When we got to her house, I let her out. She didn't even offer me a kiss for the wonderful time I had shown her. She just walked away without saying a word.

"Way to go," Reighley offered.

I looked sideways at him, and then they took me home.

Of course, Glenna was upset because I wrecked the car, but was relieved that I wasn't hurt in the hit and run accident I told her I was in. She was happy that my brother and his friends just happened to come along and give me a ride home.

Chapter Nineteen

Empty Promises

I learned that there was no bottom to a bottomless pit. Life just continues to get worse when you're using drugs, no matter how low you sink.

I knew my relationship was in trouble. I had been sensing even before my last car accident that things weren't the same. The pressure that I imposed on us with my chemical use was, to say the least, overwhelming. The problems continued to escalate and my life was spinning out of control. I found myself doing things I said I'd never do. I had reached a new dimension in my addiction.

My father used to tell me, "If you continue to use, eventually you will hit bottom." Well, I learned that wasn't entirely true. What I discovered was that there was no such thing as "bottom" in a bottomless pit. If you're still drinking or using it will always take you down to another level.

I was without transportation, so I asked my father if I could use the Falcon. He said it needed a new light and lens in the right taillight. "Someone must have backed into it in a parking lot or something. Repair it and you can use it." I thought that was the least I could do. I took the keys and left.

At work the following day Larry, a co-worker, asked me if I played pool. I told him that I wasn't very good at it, but that I could play. He invited me to meet him at the "Golden Eight Ball" in Tempe. We were on our second game of eight ball when Randy Richardson, my old friend, walked in. We talked for a while about things we had done when we hung out as kids. We laughed as we shared old stories that we remembered together. I introduced him to Larry. They shook hands and then Larry announced he had to go. He said something about being in trouble with his old lady for being late.

"See you tomorrow at work," he said as he put one hand up over his head, his way of saying goodbye.

Randy and I talked more about our past and then he asked me if I got high. I told him that I did. He then asked me if I wanted to. He reached into his shirt pocket and pulled out what looked like a joint. I was somewhat disappointed. I really didn't care for marijuana, never had. It made me paranoid. "I'll smoke it with him, for old times sake, but I'd rather drink," I thought. I wondered what kind it was. Not exactly an expert on the subject of marijuana I knew of maybe one or two kinds and the only reason I knew that was because all my brothers smoked it and I considered them experts.

"What kind?" I asked, wondering if he even knew. "Sinsemilla, Panama Red, or just plain old dirt weed?" I was hoping for dirt weed because the other stuff really messed me up.

"Better," he said.

"Better?" I repeated, being inquisitive.

"Better, because it's laced with Angel Dust." I'd heard about Angel Dust, but I really didn't know much about it. "Oh well, no time like the present to learn," I thought. We were outside, and his car was parked in the side parking lot. Randy told me to get in. He then took that joint out of his pocket and fired it up.

I must have blacked out immediately because the next thing I knew, I was home and Glenna was leading me into the bathroom. She told me to sit down on the toilet after closing the lid. As I backed into the toilet to sit with Glenna holding my arm to support me, I saw myself in the mirror. My face looked like five pounds of raw hamburger. "What the hell!" I yelled. I hadn't even been aware that I was hurt. I couldn't feel it, and I didn't have a clue what had happened. I wondered what happened to Randy. Was he with me? And if so, did he survive?

"What happened?" I yelled out.

"You tell me, I wasn't there." I could tell she was angry, but even more than that, she was beyond angry. It was more like controlled disgust. She took a hand towel and poured peroxide on it, then she started to dab the cuts on my face. She tried to be gentle, but I could sense that she wanted to push it into my face. I believe that, in that moment, it took every ounce of emotional strength she had to hold back from hurting me. She wanted me to feel as much pain as she was feeling, but somehow she knew that if she let go, she would lose all control.

I had put her through a living hell, and this was one of those times in which I had to look at my behavior. Our relationship had changed because I was completely oblivious to her feelings. I didn't see it coming. This was my fault and there was no one to blame but me.

It's funny how events in our lives come full circle. I had grown up watching my mother go through this very thing with my father, and I had always said to myself that I wouldn't be like him. Well, I am my father's son. At that moment I realized that I was just like him, and I hated it.

I wanted to hold Glenna and tell her how sorry I was. I wanted to tell her that I would stop drinking, because now I could see what it was doing to us. But, somehow, I knew it wouldn't do any good. I'd told her this countless times before and was convinced she would see it as another "empty promise." No, this time I had to show her.

I stopped drinking and drugging that night. I was in my second week of sobriety before I started to see some changes in Glenna's behavior. She wasn't as uptight. I was spending more time at home and enjoying my time there. I felt good about my life. We were working things out. I wasn't lying to her and I didn't have to hide anything from her. Oh, I still never told her about all the drugs I'd done, but I didn't have to now that I had stopped. She was beginning to trust me more, thank God. I hated being suspect all the time. Yeah, life was good again.

Glenna and I were sitting on the couch watching the news one evening. The closeness I was feeling was something that I hadn't felt in a very long time. It reminded me of those times I used to walk her home along the canal bank at night when we were courting. Glenna was the most important thing in my life and I didn't want to lose her. Why did things have to change? Why was my life so out of control? I still loved her, and when she had become angry with me that night a few weeks previously, I had felt complete terror over the thought of losing her.

As we watched TV, she laid her head on my shoulder. I had my right arm around her. She lifted her head to face me and looked into my eyes. And then she spoke, "Johnny, thank you. These two weeks have been all I've ever wanted. I love you!" She put her head back on my shoulder and we held each other close. I was elated. If this was what I had been missing, I was an idiot for waiting so long. We went to bed after the news and made love until three in the morning. We fell asleep in each other's arms.

When I awoke the next day, I was walking on air. I felt like we were the only two people on earth. I couldn't wait to be with her again, and why I would trade any of this happiness for getting high was beyond my comprehension. I simply had no answer.

Chapter Twenty

Free for the lovin'

"Don't pick up anything you can't
put down!"
-- Cecil Rachael
Bank Robber
1907-1981

The following day I was stopped at a red light on my way home from work when Randy pulled up next to me. He honked to get my attention. He wanted me to pull into the parking lot of Bob's Big Boy on the other side of the light. He pulled ahead of me and I followed him into the parking lot. He asked me how I'd been and expressed concern about me leaving after I smoked that joint at the pool hall a few weeks back. Well, that answered my question about what had happened to him that night.

Before I even had the chance to answer, he was asking me if I wanted to get high. He pulled out the joint he had in his shirt pocket.

"Same stuff?" I asked.

"Yeah."

"*What are you thinking?*" I heard this voice say in my head. "You just spent two glorious weeks with your wife. Think about it." The voice was pleading with me. I said, "Randy, I'd love to, but I'd better not." Damn, that was hard to say. The voice continued, "Don't do it, John." It knew I was wavering.

"All right John, I guess I'll smoke it by myself," he said, then turned and headed for his car. "But you know how good this stuff is." He reached for his door handle looking back at me.

I was struggling; I loved my wife, and when I was with her that was all I wanted, but I missed being high. Why was I so conflicted?

"*Don't do it!*" the voice was yelling at me. Even with all this going on in my head, I was already calling Randy back. "Wait a minute," I said. He stopped and turned to look at me. I was already justifying smoking it in my head. Maybe I'll just smoke a little bit. I'll stay high for a few hours, then go home and spend time with my wife as if nothing happened. "Best of both worlds," I thought. He was waiting impatiently for me to tell him what I was going to do. "Okay, let's do it!" I told him, and I jumped into his car.

"I need to make a stop up the road," he told me as he started the car. To our right was the National Guard Armory. He was telling a story his father had told him about when his father worked there. I wasn't paying too much attention because I couldn't get my mind off Glenna. I was having second thoughts, but I didn't know how to tell him. I was already committed.

He turned right on 28th street, going North, and then he turned right again into a driveway. A man with a heavy beard and long brown hair, wearing a black leather vest as a shirt, was standing with one foot outside holding the screen door open, waiting for us to come

"What's up?" he asked Randy as they shook hands. Randy nodded and the man smiled. He was missing a tooth on the bottom in the front. Randy introduced us. His name was Jimmy. We followed him into his living room. It was decorated in "Early American Drug Addict." Four bean bag chairs in four different colors, a couch with holes in the arms and wood showing where the stuffing used to be, and a bookshelf with an old black and white TV sitting on the top of it. The TV had a set of rabbit ears with one of the extended ears missing and a straightened metal coat hanger in its place.

Jimmy invited us to sit. He walked down the hall and into what looked like a back bedroom. I watched him as he walked past a motorcycle he had sitting in the middle of the room. Jimmy reached up with both hands and took down a wooden box from a shelf high above his head. He walked back up the hallway and sat down on the couch, then he put both knees together and placed the box on his lap. When he opened the lid, I noticed it had what looked like a dragon carved into the top. He reached in and pulled out a joint just like the one Randy had in his shirt pocket. He handed it to me and told me to fire it up. Randy handed me his Zippo lighter. I lit it and took a long drag off of it, then handed it to Jimmy. He did the same. I watched him hand it to Randy. He took a few hits, then it came back to me. I took a few more hits. I went into hypo-speed, I was moving in slow motion. I saw trails that followed every movement. It went back to Randy and when he handed it back to me, I reached for it. After a few more hits, I was gone.

The next thing I remember was sitting across from Randy in a bar. Randy had his hand on a pitcher of beer offering to fill the empty glass that was in front of me. "Do you need a fill-up?" I heard him say.

I realized I was staring at him and I was confused. "How did I get here?" I wondered. I didn't remember leaving Jimmy's house.

"Earth to John! Do-you-need-a-fill-up?" Randy shouted.

"Where are we?" I asked. He filled up my glass. Then he told me we were at a bar that he drank at in Scottsdale. Randy said he knew the bartender; although she knew his age, as long as he was cool, she let him and his friends drink.

I didn't much care. My mind was on Glenna. I felt so far away. I had this scared feeling that I'd already lost her. "Randy, what time is it?" I was frantic! I had lost all track of time. I was still going in and out and I wanted it to stop. I felt out of control in this muddled state and I hated it. I wanted so desperately to get home. Something was wrong; I could feel it.

As I got up to leave, Randy told me to chill out. I sat back down and drank my beer, trying to calm myself down. The next thing I knew, I was waking up in a car I had never seen before. It was daytime and I knew I was in trouble. Glenna must be livid about now.

I tried to pull my thoughts together, but it was difficult. I needed to get my bearings, but I didn't recognize my surroundings. I read the sign above an entrance to another part of the park. "Griffith Park Zoo." Griffith Park Zoo, I mouthed the words. Where the hell is Griffith Park Zoo? I was trying to recall what had happened, trying to make some sense of it, but I couldn't. My mind was a complete blur. I noticed that I only had a pair of Levis on. I looked in the car for the rest of my clothes, but they where nowhere in sight. Then my mind went back to the car I woke up in. "Whose is it?" I wondered. It was a tan Olds model ninety-eight. It didn't look like whoever owned it took care of it very well because the interior was ripped up. I knew it was an early 60's but not sure of the year.

There was a man sitting on a bench not far from where I was parked, reading a book. Rand was the author, something about a fountainhead if I recall. "Sir, do you have the time?" I asked him. "11:00," he said without looking up. "Do you have a cigarette?" Again, without looking up, he said he didn't smoke. I almost called him an asshole because he had a burning cigarette in his hand when he said it. I just walked away. I was really mad at myself. "Why do I continue to use?" I thought, hoping that it would be different this time. It never was. Who was I kidding anyway? Here it was the next day. "I am in so much trouble. How am I ever going to explain this to Glenna?" I thought. I could just see the look of hurt and disappointment in her eyes. "Damn it, John, how could you do it again?"

I saw a young couple holding hands and walking toward me. "Can you spare a cigarette?" I asked. The girl reached into her hip huggers and pulled a pack of non-filtered Camels out of her back pocket. She popped one up; I reached for it and put it into the left side of my month. "Got a light?" I asked.

The guy she was with handed me a book of matches. "Do you want me to smoke it for you too?" He was laughing when he said it.

I smiled. Good, a friendly face I thought. "Maybe you can tell me where I am. I don't recognize anything and I've never heard of

Griffith Park Zoo." My voice was bordering on panic. It was quivering and I wanted to cry.

When he looked at me, he looked concerned. "Do you even know what state you're in?" he asked.

"Arizona," I told him. They both looked at each other and laughed. They must have thought I was kidding.

"Do you have any more of that stuff you're smoking? I'd like to try some of it." The girl laughed.

I must have looked scared, because when they saw I wasn't laughing they stopped. "You're serious, you really don't know, do you?" They already knew my answer. They each grabbed an arm, walked me to the nearest bench and sat me down between them. "I'm Ken and this is Carla. You're in Los Angeles, California in Griffith Park."

In a panic I asked, "What day is this?"

"Damn, you really are lost? It's Thursday," Ken said.

I couldn't believe what I was hearing! The last thing I remembered was three days ago! How could I have lost three whole days? I was disgusted with myself. How am I ever going to explain this? I didn't want to lose her, but she would never understand. I felt hopeless and I had a bad feeling down in the pit of my stomach. I made the decision not to call her. She needed to move on without me.

Ken wore low cut bell-bottom jeans, sandals and a flowered long-sleeve button-up shirt. He had stringy blonde hair down past his shoulders. Carla wore brown corduroy hip hugger pants, sandals, and a tie-dyed red and brown t-shirt that was too small for her. It stopped just above her navel and with her hip hugger pants as low as they were, I could see most of her lower abdomen. She had long, black straight hair that stopped just below her waist, and she was hot!

They were what I considered Hippies. At least that's what they would have been on Van Buren Street. Most of my friends called themselves cowboys, though most of them couldn't ride a horse. However, they were cowboys just the same.

Ken and Carla talked off to the side while I was thinking about my next move. I thought about hitchhiking back to Phoenix, but I wasn't ready to face Glenna just yet.

Carla smiled and said, "We could make room for you at our place. I mean, we're not the only ones who live there but I'm sure they'll understand."

"Yeah, come on, we'd love to have you," Ken said with a big grin.

There wasn't much to think about. "Sure, thanks." I felt relieved.

"Bitchin!" they both said at the same time. I guess that was their way of saying we were all in agreement.

I walked beside my new friends, heading for the parking lot. As we walked I told them my situation, leaving very little out. Carla stopped and hugged me. Ken patted me on the back. In the parking lot, three spaces from the car I was in, was a blue and white VW bus. Ken opened the side door, reached in and pulled out a white t-shirt. When I started to put it on, he suggested that I use it first to wipe down the car I had found myself in for prints, just in case it was stolen or used in a crime.

"Good idea," I said and opened the door on the driver's side and started wiping. I walked back to the van and Ken handed me a pair of black thongs. I was glad to have them. My feet were sensitive because of my birth defects and surgeries as a kid. I never went barefoot.

Ken drove, Carla rode shotgun and I sat in the back on a rolled up sleeping bag. I had no clue where I was. All I knew was that we drove about thirty-five minutes before we pulled into an old abandoned apartment complex. There were eight units in all. The one on the end had no roof. "It doesn't have electricity or running water, but it's home for about eighteen of us." Ken explained. "If we need water we go next door to the Texaco and use theirs. We've hooked a couple of hoses together that we run over to use. Lonny works there and has worked it out with the owner. We use candles for light."

"What does all this cost you?" I asked.

"Not a dime," Ken said.

I thought, "Hell, I've lived in the Candlelight Apartments. I could live here—no problem!"

We pulled up in front of the first unit. As we got out, people were walking up to the bus to greet us. I was still talking with Carla. "How do you take care of your needs, like eating and such?" I really wanted to know. I was truly impressed!

"Some work, some don't. We all chip in where we can, and everyone contributes in their own way. In the end it all comes together." People were all around us now, waiting for Ken and Carla to introduce us.

I was introduced first to Harley, and Bobbie, the girl he was with. "They called him Harley because he rides a Harley-Davidson motorcycle." I was told that he was a construction worker who happened to have called in sick that day. Harley looked like a biker. He had a full beard, and greasy long brown hair down to his shoulders. He wore a black leather vest as a shirt. I thought this must be a biker thing.

Now, Bobbie got my attention. She was beautiful and the closest thing to an angel I've ever seen. She was about 6'-2" tall and 130 pounds. She had shoulder length, platinum hair with a band of flowers that she wore like a crown. She was wearing hip hugger Levi bell bottoms and a light blue halter-top. She was barefoot. Her toenails were painted a bright red, the same color as her fingernails, and the paint was beginning to chip. Her skin was evenly tanned a golden brown, and with her dark green eyes and platinum hair against her golden body, I couldn't keep my eyes off of her. Next to Glenna, she was by far the most beautiful woman I had ever been around. I was introduced to more people that day, but none I remember like Bobbie.

I was taken to unit number two. Bobbie walked beside me while Carla led. With Bobbie towering over me about seven inches, I couldn't help feeling very short next to her. Carla opened the door and walked in. Bobbie and I followed, with Bobbie going in first. Habit I guess, that old cowboy mannerism instilled in me. Inside there was an old couch with one arm missing most of the stuffing, a coffee table in front of the couch, and an end table set up next to the arm with the stuffing gone. There was a military green colored sleeping bag, rolled but not tied, on the opposite end of the couch. Sitting almost in the middle of the coffee table was a candle with three wicks. "Barry used to sleep here, but he moved back to Arizona to live with his grandparents. Gary and Gloria are in that room, and Terry and Mary are in there." Carla pointed to the two rooms down the hall. "If you need to use the bathroom, go outside in the back or walk over to the gas station for now. We'll get you more clothes later." Carla looked at Bobbie and wanted to know if she had anything else to add. She just smiled, putting her hands in her back pockets, and then they walked out together.

I found a book of matches sitting on the end table, so I lit the three wicks of the candle, then sat on the couch and watched the shadows of the flames dance on the wall behind it. I must have been tired because I fell asleep right away. "Are you hungry?" I heard someone say as they were shaking me, trying to wake me up. "Are you hungry?" the voice repeated. I looked up and saw this girl standing over me holding a plate of food. "Sorry, Carla sent this plate of food. She thought you might be hungry," she said.

I was hungry! I couldn't remember the last time I had eaten. "Thanks," I said and took the plate from her. It looked like stew with very little meat in it, but it smelled great.

"Carla uses just enough meat to give it flavor," she told me. I smiled.

"My name is Terri, and I stay in the room at the end of the hallway with my roommate, Mary." I had assumed that Terry was a man but was delighted to learn that Terri and Mary were both girls.

"I'm John," I told her.

"I know. Ken and Carla told me what happened, and I'm sorry." She sat down next to me on the couch and when she did, I was able to see how pretty she was; not as beautiful as Bobbie, but pretty nonetheless. She wore cutoffs and a tie-dyed pink and green halter-top. Her body was also tanned. She put her right foot on the table in front of her and spread out her arms along the back of the couch to relax. She looked seventeen, maybe eighteen. I couldn't tell. She told me that she and her roommate mowed lawns. "We don't do too bad. Keeps us in groceries," she said. I was finished eating so I put my plate on the table and turned to face her. I wanted to ask her if they were lesbians. I'd heard about gay women, but I'd never met one. I didn't have to wonder long, because she was very open about her sexuality and talked freely.

"I go both ways. We both do." I didn't know what to say, so I just smiled. She smiled back. I'll admit I was aroused. I thought that if Mary was as pretty as Terri, I had died and was now in heaven! That's when the door opened and in walked Gary, Gloria, and Mary. Terri introduced us. "This is Gary. He works construction with Harley. Did you meet Harley yet?" She paused for a second, then continued when I told her I had. "This is Gloria, she's in there with Gary and this is Mary."

Gary shook my hand and Gloria said, "Hi." Gary told me that if I ever needed anything, just knock. I thanked them, then he and Gloria went into their room and closed the door.

Mary sat down Indian style on the floor on the other side of the table. She was every bit as pretty as Terri. She was wearing almost the same attire as her roommate, only her cutoffs were shorter. "Do you get high?" she asked.

"Why, what do you have in mind?" I asked her.

"Acid. You know, LSD?" She looked at Terri and smiled.

"I've heard of it, but I've never tried it—but I'd like to," I told her.

They looked at each other, and then Terri stood up and headed for her room. She came out with a flat brown leather bag.

"Is that it?" I said. I'd never seen it before.

"Yeah, I have over a hundred hits in here. We sell it at concerts and parks when we need extra money, a dollar a hit. Not bad huh?" She opened it up and inside were five 8 x 11 sheets of what looked like newsprint paper. On each page were twenty pictures of Woody WoodPecker. There were five rolls of four Woodys, all of them in the same pose. On each, Woody had a small discoloration where a tiny drop of L.S.D. had been dropped. Mary told me it was blotter acid and each Woody was a hit. Terri tore off two hits and handed them to Mary. She tore off two more and handed them to me. The last two she tore off and kept for herself.

"Put them both in your mouth and chew on the paper. You'll start feeling it in about fifteen or twenty minutes," Mary was telling me. Terri was already chewing on hers. Then Mary put hers in her mouth and started to chew. I sat there between both girls, with my head resting against the back of the couch. We were watching the three-wicked candle with its dancing flames and the shadows it produced on the wall behind it. It was quiet and I felt so relaxed I couldn't tell you how long we sat there. I thought I heard Mary in the distance. "WOW!" I could hear them both laughing. I turned toward Terri who was now playing with the flames on the candle with the fingers of her left hand. "She must be left-handed," I remember thinking. While she played, one of the flames went out.

The room now appeared to be brighter. I could see with incredible clarity. Mary got up and walked toward the door. She looked back at me and said, "Come with me," and reached for my hand. I put my hand out and asked where we were going. She guided me outside, with Terri following behind. It was like I was walking through a tunnel. The lights from the gas station were extremely bright with colors pulsating in and out of them. Things appeared so far away, yet so close at the same time. I couldn't explain it. I felt like I was on the edge of losing it, but then again in full control.

The next thing I realized I was on my back, on the grass, looking up at the sky. I heard one of the girls say, "There's the Big Dipper." I couldn't tell who said it or even if they pointed when they did.

Time jumped ahead again and I heard Harley say, "Are you alright back there?" as the wind blew against my face. I realized that I was now on the back of Harley's bike, with no idea how I had gotten there, and that we were traveling very fast down the highway. "Not so tight, I can't breath," he yelled. I loosened my grip.

"Where are we?" I yelled out, confused.

"Pacific Coast Highway. Isn't it awesome? Look at that ocean, smell that air."

Hell, I was still tripping hard. We were moving so fast it was like a blur, and moving that fast got me sick. I was trying not to puke, telling myself that if I did, he would be pissed. The rum-drum sound of the motor, mixed with the sound of the waves breaking along the beach, didn't help. And where were Terri and Mary anyway? I was extremely confused. It was then I realized that I wasn't blacking out like I did on alcohol or angel dust, but more like moving in and out of awareness.

It was still dark outside, so I asked Harley what time it was. He screamed out that he didn't have a clue. I remembered pulling into a parking lot and him saying, "I'll be right back." Then he walked away. The next thing I remembered, after the parking lot, was waking up on the couch using the sleeping bag as a pillow, my jaw feeling like it was going to fall off. It hurt clear into my ears and all of my teeth hurt.

I stayed there almost three weeks, and it did help keep my mind occupied, but I still loved my wife and wanted to get back to Phoenix and check things out. It was May of 1969 and I had just turned eighteen a few months back. I felt as if I'd been gone forever. I had been invited to stay there as long as I wanted, and for that I was grateful, but I was ready to go. I said goodbye to everyone the night before I left. Harley said he'd give me a ride to the truck stop about a mile and a half up the road in the morning. I made a sign from the flap of a cardboard box and a black grease pen that simply read: "Phoenix." I folded it in half and put it into an old canvas bag along with two shirts and some fruit that Bobbie had given me for my trip home. On his way to work Harley dropped me off at the truck stop. We had left at 4:00 a.m. and it was just getting light enough to see without the headlight when we pulled into the parking lot. When I got off the bike, he got off with me. He gave me a hug and said, "If you're ever back this way again, remember you have a home." He backed up and smiled, then jumped back on his bike and left, heading in the direction of his work.

I walked up to the truck stop coffee shop. I had no money, so I sat outside on a bench facing the door, then took my sign out and sat it on my lap. I wasn't there long when I heard, "Phoenix, I'm going to Phoenix." I looked up and saw a tall, slightly overweight gentleman. He was probably 6'-4" tall, with a beard, but no mustache. "The name's Jackie," he said as he reached out his hand to shake mine.

"Hi, I'm John," I said, noticing how much bigger his hand was than mine.

"So you're going to Phoenix, huh?" Jackie said.

"Yeah, I live there, trying to get home," I said. When I stood up next to him, I realized he was almost a foot taller than me.

"Well, I'm going to Phoenix, and if you don't mind this old fart talking your ear off, I'll take you." He was laughing, something he probably did often because he looked like he had a natural smile on his face.

Jackie was true to his word. He was still talking when he let me out in the parking lot of the Roadrunner truck stop in Phoenix. I thanked him and went inside to call someone to come and get me with the quarter I bummed off of him to make the call and get me a cup of coffee while I waited. "Nickel for a tip. Perfect," I thought.

My family was relieved to know I was still alive. Richard and Roger picked me up. Richard was upset with me for putting my parents through a living hell, worrying about me. "A phone call would have been nice," he told me.

"I'm sorry, I never even thought about calling." Nothing more was said about it on the ride home. When I explained what had happened to my parents, leaving the part out about my blackout of course, they dropped the subject too.

Over the next few weeks I helped my parents pack up our house on 40th Street. They were moving back to their house in Tempe. I made it a point to stay clean, and off of all chemicals during this time.

The rest of my family were already living in Tempe, so I stayed at the old house with only a couch, blankets, an old black and white TV and enough essentials to keep me sustained for a day or so. We were pretty much out and only needed to move a few more things, and then clean it up.

That night at about eight o'clock, I was watching TV when I heard a knock at the back door. It was Glenna. She said she was back living with her mother. It was hard for me to look at her, so I avoided eye contact. I was ashamed about what had happened and about all of the empty promises I'd given her. Instead of telling her my hopes of starting over again, I acted angry. "What are you doing here?" I said.

"I thought maybe we could talk," she said in such a low voice I could hardly hear her speak. She was looking down at the ground; she had been crying, and shc didn't want me to know. This made me angrier. I felt guilty enough and this was making it harder on me.

"Hey look," I said. "I'm a big boy now and I'm tired of people telling me how to live my life. I'm capable of thinking for myself." I was starting to lose control and I now realized I was yelling. "You know what?" I screamed.

"What?" she said in almost a whisper.

"I don't want to be married anymore!!"

I looked into her eyes and I watched them fill with frozen tears. I had hurt her completely this time and I knew it. She turned away from me, held her head high, and walked out the door without saying another word. I will never forget the turmoil I felt at that moment. I wanted to run after her, hold her in my arms and wipe the tears from her eyes. I was sorry, I wanted those two weeks we spent together before my last escapade. Yes, I wanted it all back, but instead I let her walk away. I tried to justify it in my mind that it just didn't matter, but in the end, I knew I was lying to myself. I let the most wonderful part of my life walk away from me. I couldn't turn it off in my mind; my thoughts kept racing. I was trying to convince myself of something I knew was bullshit and I just wasn't doing a very good job of it.

"Let sleeping dogs lie," I kept saying over and over to myself. It was then that I heard another knock at the door. I was hoping, with all my heart, that it was Glenna again. I would tell her I was sorry this time.

I loved Glenna, I always have, but what I didn't know was how to make our relationship work. It was at this time in my life that I discovered that being in love and loving someone were two different things.

I reached for the door handle and pulled it open and, to my surprise, it was not Glenna standing there, but Mary Brown, her cousin. "I just left Glenna and she told me what happened, so I thought you might need a friend," Mary told me. She stepped into the living room; she was wearing a tight, blue, see-through dress. She looked hot! My heart was beating so hard it took my breath away. She walked up to me and looked deep into my eyes; I was intoxicated from the smell of her perfume. I became lightheaded, she pulled me in to her and we kissed. She announced, "I'm here to help you get through this. I told you I'd be here when you needed me, didn't I?" This was the only time that Mary and I were together and when she left at 4:00 a.m., I broke down and cried.

Chapter Twenty-One

My Very Best Friend

I should have asked, but I didn't.
Something bad was about to happen,
but I tried to ignore it.

My marriage was over. I had nobody to answer to. I hadn't heard from Glenna in over six weeks, and even though we weren't divorced, with all my chemical use, she was nothing more to me than a fleeting thought.

One day, around one o'clock in the afternoon, I left work early and went over to Mac and Marge's. I was sitting at a table by myself, with my back to the front door, drinking, when I heard, "How are you doing, John?" I turned around and saw Johnny, a friend I had met six weeks earlier at a gas station I had worked at for a few weeks when I came back from California. (I went in one night under the influence during a graveyard shift and was fired.) I had just finished my glass of beer and was ready to start on a fresh one when he invited himself to sit down.

Johnny was crazy. He reminded me of my psychotic brother-in-law. He was about as hillbilly as they come. Hillbillies really believe the concept of "an eye for an eye," so I didn't want to offend him for fear that something crazy would happen. He'd come out here from Ohio about a year before, and he was already talking about getting some money together and moving back. Even when he smiled, he was scary.

Johnny was pounding down the beers and I tried to keep up. I think I did pretty well, but if we had been having a contest, he would have won hands down.

"I'm thinking of robbing the gas station and leaving for Ohio," Johnny said.

I didn't want to hear this, but I thought, "How can I tell him without making him angry?"

He continued, "You know that asshole who works the graveyard shift?"

"Yeah, you mean Jack," I said.

Johnny continued, "I don't like him anyway. I'll just walk up to him and put a bullet in his worthless fucking brain, then take the evening shift's money before he puts it in the safe. Then I'll jump into my car and drive away. Nobody will ever know." I couldn't tell if that was the alcohol talking or if he really meant it. I did realize however, that by telling me his plan he had put me in a very awkward situation. I tried to change the subject, but he continued. "This ain't the first time I killed someone, you know. I killed this fucker one time for hurting my baby sister. Beat him in the head from behind with a baseball bat. I warned him but he didn't listen. Fucker had it coming."

I thought to myself, "If he remembers this conversation in the morning, I'm a dead man!"

"Buried that son-of-a-bitch in the woods by my daddy's farm so deep they'll never find him!"

I thought, "This is that hillbilly justice I was thinking about earlier." Again, I tried to talk about something else.

"How's work going?" I asked him.

"Let's not talk about that damn place." He slapped me on the back and said, "Let's get fucked up instead."

"What do you have in mind? I'm almost out of money," I told him, hoping he'd leave me alone.

"Well," he scooted his chair closer to the table. "I was drinking with a friend of mine down the street at the Wagg Inn, but he made me angry, so I left. When I walked by this place, I was thirsty. So I came in, looked around, and saw my very best friend in the whole wide world."

I thought, "Just great! Now I'm his very best friend. I hope he remembers that when he sobers up."

He looked around, and then in a lowered voice he asked me, "Do you still get high?"

"Every now and then," I told him. When I was still working at the gas station I would often be high when he would relieve me at seven o'clock in the morning.

"I can score in South Phoenix where I live, but I need a ride." He even told me he'd pay for everything, including gas if I needed it.

I had my parent's Falcon outside, and had I known what was in store for me that night, I would have told him, "No!" As it was, though, twenty minutes later I was pulling into a trailer park on Central Avenue in Phoenix.

"I live there." He pointed to an old, faded brown and white trailer that looked like it had seen better days. "Belongs to my aunt. She lives there too." I didn't say anything. "Pull over there," he directed. "Wait right here." He jumped out and walked over to the trailer two doors down from his. It was the same kind and the same color, but it looked to be in worse shape than the one that Johnny had pointed out as his aunt's.

"What a dump," I said under my breath.

Johnny knocked and waited. Finally a tall, slightly overweight black man, who was naked from the waist up, opened the door. His belly hung over his Levis, and he had the top button of his pants opened to make it easier for him to breathe.

"What's up, Bro?" I heard him ask Johnny as they gave each other a high five. "Is he cool?" He pointed to the car I was in.

"One of my best friends next to you," I heard Johnny say. He let Johnny in, looked back at me and smiled; then he closed the door.

While I waited I turned on the radio and sang along with Eddie Arnold, "Turn the world around the other way." I loved that song; I thought about Glenna every time I heard it.

"Later," I heard Johnny say as he walked toward the car.

I found myself turning the song off before he reached the passenger door.

He had three racks of white crosses. "Here," he handed me a rack and split the second one with me. "Now let's party!" he yelled out. He took five crosses and I did the same.

We drove to a bar on Central called "The 49er."

"This is where I do most of my drinking," he told me. That wasn't hard to figure out, just by the way we were greeted. They obviously knew him, and my gut was telling me that something wasn't right. The atmosphere felt very tense.

The bartender put up his hand to stop us as soon as we walked through the door. He said to Johnny, "Before you sit down, I want you to understand something."

"I know," Johnny was defensively trying to play it down.

"No, you don't know!" the bartender screamed at him. "If we have another repeat of what happened last week, I will eighty-six you for good, understand?" He was nose to nose with Johnny.

"Yeah, yeah, yeah! No problem!" Again Johnny tried to play it down. The bartender walked off. I should have asked, but I didn't. My drug addict intuition was telling me that something bad was about to happen, but I chose to ignore it.

We sat at the table along the east wall. We were there for about forty-five minutes; the beers kept coming and I was drunk. Johnny decided to play the same song ("Momma Tried," by Merle Haggard) over and over again on the jukebox. The more he drank, the louder he sang along. There were five gentlemen, all dressed up in cowboy attire, sitting around a nearby table. I overheard one say he was getting tired of the song, and his friends were starting to agree with him. I suggested to Johnny that maybe he needed to cool it on the song. "Fuck 'em" he said.

That made me angry. "Look man, I'm too drunk to fight anyone right now, so cool it!" He told me he would and I thanked him.

I then excused myself to go to the restroom. I was standing at the urinal when I heard Johnny's song come on again. "Damn it!" I yelled. That bad feeling was back. On my way back to the table, I saw the bartender come running out from behind the bar and jump between Johnny and one of the cowboys. He was telling

Johnny to just leave. I thought that sounded like a very good idea. Johnny was maybe 5'-11" and weighed 155 pounds or so, and he was taller and weighed more than I did at the time. There were five of them and the smallest one was six feet tall and weighed at least 200 pounds.

Let's face it; the odds were against us, so I was relieved when Johnny decided to listen to the bartender. We walked out into the parking lot and found the car. I opened my door, then climbed in. Johnny hesitated at first, and then climbed in beside me. I could see he wanted to go back. I pulled out of the parking lot and turned right onto Central heading south. I needed to get him home before he got me killed. He turned to me and said, "They called me a wussy. God I hate that, I'm no wussy!" He wanted to go back, but I took a stand and said no.

We were sitting at a light when the five cowboys from the bar pulled up along side of us. They were driving a mid-sixties white Caddie convertible with the top down. "Hey, look over there." The driver was pointing at us. "A couple of wussies."

Before I knew it, Johnny was out of the car and it was on. I saw two of them running toward me. They jerked open my car door, pulled me out and proceeded to kick my ass. I was so drunk I couldn't even defend myself. As I lay on the ground with one on top of me punching me in the face, I looked over and saw Johnny with the other three and I have to tell you, he didn't look like he was doing too badly. He was kicking, biting and scratching; he didn't seem to give a damn.

All of a sudden, they jumped back into their Caddie and took off, squealing their tires, heading down Central toward Baseline Road.

I was overjoyed to see them go. I needed to lick my wounds and get home. I didn't care. There were more of them than me and I clearly understood those odds.

But not Johnny. He was really pissed. He helped me up and then told me to get in, that he was driving. He jammed it into first and let out the clutch. I didn't even have time to close my door before we were fishtailing in their direction. The chase was on! They were sitting in the left turn lane at Baseline when Johnny plowed into their car at about twenty miles an hour. He pushed them half way into the street, against the red… and the same two guys proceeded to beat my ass even harder this time. I just wanted to go home. "God, help me," I prayed.

The right side of my face and my right ear were throbbing, but, at the same time, they were kind of numb, too. I was back on the ground again, being kicked repeatedly by a size twelve cowboy boot. That's when I got another glimpse of Johnny with the other three; he had one by the hair, he was biting another on the side of his neck and the one being bitten was screaming to get him off, while the other one had Johnny by both legs almost in a horizontal position, trying to pull him off of his friend as Johnny bucked. I had to laugh, Johnny sure was mad, no question about it!

Again, they all jumped back into their Caddie and completed their left turn, heading east on Baseline.

Johnny helped me get up. "You alright?" he asked.

"Mostly pride," I told him. "Good, then get back in the car and let's get some more of that cowboy ass," he said, racing for the car again.

"I can't believe it! I guess he's one of those guys you have to kill to stop him," I thought as I opened my door to get in.

"I'm not sure I want anymore of that cowboy ass," I told him, trying to make him laugh, hoping he'd back off some. I don't think he even heard me.

He turned, making the left on two wheels, heading East with speeds climbing from eighty to a hundred miles an hour, weaving in and out of traffic, trying to catch up with them. He was on a mission, and I think he was willing to get us both killed to accomplish it. We blew the light at 7th Street. No sign of them. Made the light at 16th Street, just as it turned yellow, with still no sign of them.

"Maybe they turned somewhere," I said.

Johnny spotted them on the other side of the light at 32nd Street. "The light's fucking red!" I yelled out, bracing myself.

Cars slammed on their brakes to keep from hitting us. He was so fixated on the Caddie that I don't think he realized what had just happened.

"You're going to get us killed," I was more angry now than scared. I was riding with a frigging mad man and I just knew I was sucking in borrowed air.

He caught up with them and rammed their car from behind. All I could do was hang on.

The three in the back seat were looking back at us. The one in the middle screamed, "He's still coming! He's fucking crazy!" I recognized panic on their faces. Pulling up to 40th Street, I watched them put on their blinker. The lens was broken and it showed the white bulb.

"That was dumb telling us which way they were going," I thought. Then I realized they were probably scared and weren't thinking at all.

When they made the left on 40th Street, they were going too fast and the car went up on two wheels. That was when Johnny T-boned them at about forty miles an hour. The Caddie started to just flip over onto its side, but we hit them so hard that it ended up rolling five or six times before it landed on its wheels in the middle of a field.

There were cowboys and debris everywhere. Our car stalled. Johnny was trying to get out of the car because he still wanted more. "Johnny! Look man—nobody's moving! You won, okay?" I was so angry I was yelling at him. It took a minute before Johnny came to his senses. He looked bewildered, and then he tried to start the car.

A tow truck driver drove up and jumped out of his truck, "You need to stop right there, I just called the police and they'll be here soon." He looked scared.

"I'm going to jail this time," I thought. I started to pray. What else could I do? I wasn't sure He'd even listen, but I had to try. "God, I know I keep promising, but I really mean it this time, please!" We sat there waiting for the police to show. Hell, it was a long time coming and I knew it. How many chances does one person get, anyway?

Then I heard, "Jack, you asshole! Come here and give us a push before the cops get here." I was shocked! They knew each other, and when Jack realized that it was Johnny driving the car, he jumped in his truck and helped us out. He was able to get us started, and then Johnny drove as fast as he could to the freeway. He turned left entering the freeway and drove home. When he pulled up in front of his aunt's trailer, he jumped out and thanked me for a fun afternoon. He staggered up to the trailer, opened the door and walked in.

I felt so relieved—I thanked God for getting me this far. Now if I could only get home... I got out of the car and assessed the damage; it was a mess. As I drove through the trailer park I could hear a loud knocking in the motor. As bad as the car and I looked, it's a wonder I didn't get arrested on the way home. I pulled into the driveway and gratefully turned off the engine for the very last time, as it turned out. It was no surprise to me that it never started again.

"What happened to the car?" my father asked me when I woke up the next morning.

Of course I lied. "The brakes went out and I hit a small wall on 7th Street and Southern. I'm sorry, I should have called, but it was late and I was careful driving home." I don't think he believed me, but the car was insured and I was told later that it worked out pretty well for my father.

I checked the newspaper and listened to the news for about a week to see if anyone had died in the accident with the cowboys, but I never heard anything.

Johnny's aunt called me three months later. She said that Johnny had shot and killed someone he knew at the gas station he was working at, and then he took some money and left the state. The F.B.I. found him two weeks later at his daddy's farm in Ohio. They tried to arrest him for felony murder; there was a shoot out and Johnny was killed.

Chapter Twenty-Two

Normal Dysfunction

"In a dysfunctional family, we develop
a high tolerance for inappropriate behaviors.
As a result we don't see the signs or
signals until it becomes of crisis proportion.
When a crisis happens, we all pull together
and we get through it. During the crisis,
communication seems to improve,
but when the crisis is over, we return back to
normal dysfunction."
-- *Claudia Black.*

I was now living with my parents in Tempe, so I had to use some discretion when I went out on the town. I'd either stay overnight at wherever I happened to be drinking, or I would come home late, after everyone had gone to bed. I mostly hung out on Van Buren Street, because the people who lived there were the ones I knew best. I slept at Mary's a few nights a week, on her couch. Her father always referred to me as "The Bum." There were times that I wondered if he even remembered my real name.

I was drinking with Mary at Mac and Marge's one afternoon. Billy was there with his father, drinking beer and playing bumper pool. He was telling me about his new job at the Ford dealership. He worked in the truck shop at night and he loved it.

"Do they need any more help?" I asked him. He told me he had heard that they were looking for someone else. I told him I was interested and he told me where to apply. I was hired the following week to work the same shift as Billy—8:00 p.m. to 4:00 a.m., with Sundays and Mondays off. My first week there was spent learning the job, and I have to tell you I really liked working there. I liked the people I was working with and I was learning a trade. Again, I was feeling better about myself and it was nice having a paycheck.

The shop would close at 2:00 a.m. late Saturday night\Sunday morning. We'd work six hours and get paid for eight. Billy or I would be the last to leave on Sunday mornings and we'd take turns locking up. Billy and I worked so well together that we decided to share a room at the Rock Haven Motel, which was an old rundown motel on 51st Avenue. It was a perfect location for us because it was in walking distance from work.

Billy didn't use drugs. He only drank, which enabled me to do better. I would drink, with the occasional drug slip now and then.

I was doing so well that even my father took notice, and in my third month of working and living on my own, he co-signed for me to buy a car from the used car department at the dealership where I was working. It was a 1964 Ford Galaxy, two tone, tan and white with a tan interior. The seats and headliner were made of a thick woven cloth. The car looked like it had just come off the showroom floor, and I was proud to drive it. It appeared that my life was finally coming together; a good job, new wheels, a new place to live and a new outlook on life.

One evening, while repairing a tire that required me to break down the rim on a large transporter, I noticed Ted, my boss, standing at his office window watching me work. When I finished repairing the tire and was putting it on the truck, I heard my name. It was my boss calling me. "John, come into my office when you're done putting on that tire, would you, please?"

When I was finished, I walked over and knocked on his door. He was busy working on a stack of papers on his desk. He stopped what he was doing and invited me to sit down on the leather couch in front of him. "I've been watching you work. You did a good job changing that tire. I'm impressed." I thanked him, and he went on to say, "As a matter of fact, you did such a good job, how would you like to take over that area? You would be responsible for all the tire repairs on the trucks that come in. Of course, there would be a small raise in it for you. Does fifty cents more an hour sound good to you?"

"Fifty cents is great!" I told him. I felt elated that he had even noticed my work, but to offer me a promotion was astounding! I was filled with an incredible sense of accomplishment. I walked out of his office after thanking him again and went over to where Billy was working. I told him what had happened; I had to share the good news with somebody!

"B.F.D." he told me in a loud voice. He was upset.

"What?" I said, thinking that he must have misunderstood.

"You heard me. Big Fucking Deal!"

I was taken aback because I thought we were better friends than that. The truth was it hurt my feelings, so I just walked away, wondering what his problem was.

It was Saturday evening and my turn to lock up. It was around 1:15 a.m. when I tried to talk with Billy again, but he pretty much ignored all of my attempts to try and communicate with him. He was angry for whatever reason, and I wasn't about to let him piss on my parade. Not tonight anyway. So I gave up.

At two o'clock I let everyone out of the gate, including Billy, who was one of the first to leave. Then I walked around to make sure that everything was in place before I let myself out and locked the gate behind me.

I felt so good about my promotion that I decided to drive out to Tempe and sleep on my parent's couch. This way I could share my good news with my family in the morning. Besides, with Billy mad at me I really didn't want to be around him. So I walked out to my car, which was the only one left in the parking lot. I climbed in, put the key in the ignition, turned it, and nothing happened. I tried it three more times, each time with the same result. "Damn it!" I howled, as I slapped the steering wheel with the palm of my hand. "I can't believe this." I sat there wondering what to do next. "Maybe it's my battery," I thought. I got out and popped the hood.

The only light I had was from the light pole that I was lucky enough to have parked next to when I arrived at work. It wasn't the brightest light, but it was enough to see that the positive cable connected to the battery was corroded. I reopened the gate, walked over to the Coke machine and bought a six-ounce bottle of Coke. (I had learned from working there that the acid in the coke would clean the corrosion from the battery cable.) I almost bought another bottle, because I wasn't sure that one would be enough, but I couldn't find another dime. I opened the Coke with the opener on the front of the machine and headed back to my car.

I poured a couple of ounces on the corroded cable. Where it had no insulation, it started to bubble, and then it turned a turquoise green. I took out my pocket knife, opened it, and used it to scrap off as much of the corrosion as I could. "Looks good," I thought, then poured the rest of the bottle on as added protection against the corrosion. It produced a little more green, but not much. I climbed in again, turned on the ignition, and still nothing. "Shit-shit-shit!" I was frustrated.

Again, I sat there wondering what to do next. Then it came to me. Behind the truck shop where I worked, in several rows, were probably 500 new and used cars. I would take the battery out of one of the used cars and put it into my car, and then on Tuesday when I returned to work, I'd buy a battery from our parts department and replace the one I took. Problem solved. It was a hassle, but by 3:15 I was on my way to Tempe.

It was 11:00 in the morning when I woke up to my sister, Penny, yelling at my mother that she didn't want to take a nap.

"Get in your room right now!" My mother was yelling at her from the kitchen, where my parents were sitting at the table. Penny ran off to her room crying. She slammed her door, mumbling something I couldn't understand. When I walked into the kitchen, my mother asked me if I was hungry. I told her that I wasn't.

Then I said to them, "Guess what happened to me last night at work!" I was so excited!

"Don't tell me you lost your job," my father said, looking down at his coffee cup.

"No," I said. I was a little hurt.

"What then?" my mother asked, but she didn't listen to my answer. Instead she started talking over me to my father about some bill that needed to be paid.

It was as if I wasn't even there. I was crushed. I looked at them in disbelief. I felt wounded. Funny, I had thought I'd gotten over that, but I left myself open for it again. I had thought they'd be proud of me. I heard a familiar voice in my mind say, "That's what you get for thinking! Let's face it John, no matter what you do, it won't matter. They just can't see it." I was so hurt that I told myself I would never try to please them again. I walked out without saying a word.

On my drive home, all I could do was think about what had happened with my parents, and the more I thought about it the more hurt I felt. I started to cry. I tried to control it but the more I tried, the less control I seemed to have over it. I knew now that my parents still had the power to hurt me.

At this time, once again, I transferred that pain into anger and that anger into destructive behavior, which only made my acting out worse. It was a huge cycle that never seemed to end with me.

I once heard Claudia Black, who wrote the book, *It Could Never Happen To Me*, about adult children of alcoholics say, "In a dysfunctional family we develop a high tolerance for inappropriate behaviors. As a result we don't see the signs and signals until it becomes of crisis proportion. When a crisis happens, we all pull together and we get through it. During this crisis, communication seems to improve, but when the crisis is over, we return back to normal dysfunction." (Not an exact quote.)

When I walked into the room I shared with Billy, he wasn't home. I didn't see him all that day. I figured he must have stayed with his father over the weekend. It was obvious that he was upset over the other night and didn't want to be around me, so screw him too. I was building a resentment list and I really didn't care who was on it.

Billy came walking in at around 9:30 Monday morning, while I was still sleeping. He woke me up and said he'd been at work and that our boss had sent him over to get me. He said that Ted needed to talk with me. He still appeared to be mad and I tried to find out why, but he walked away from me, refusing to talk. He was walking back to his car when I hollered out, "Tell Ted I'll be there in twenty minutes." Billy jumped into his car and pulled out, throwing dirt and gravel everywhere as he fishtailed out of our driveway.

I wondered what Ted wanted. Maybe he needed me to work a Monday through Friday shift. Weekends off, that'd be cool. Twenty minutes later, I was walking into Ted's office.

"Sit down," he told me, pointing to the leather couch. He was chewing on the end of his cigar, which I knew was something he did when he was stressed.

"John, I want to ask you about a battery that was discovered missing from one of the cars out back."

I told him what had happened at the end of Saturday's shift and my plans to replace it on Tuesday when I came to work.

He sat there, inertly listening to me speak. When I was done, he set down his pen, then he looked right at me and said, "As far as the company is concerned, you stole that battery and I don't believe you had any intention of replacing it." At first I thought he was joking, but it didn't take long for me to figure out that he wasn't.

"Ted, I'm sorry you think that, but I meant what I said. I wasn't stealing that battery." I was trying really hard to convince him. I didn't want to lose my job, but it didn't seem to matter what I said, he wasn't hearing me.

He nervously moved papers around on his desk, as if he was saying to me, "We're done." Finally, he said, "I need your keys." I handed them to him, he gave me my last paycheck, and then he asked me to leave. I was devastated; I didn't want to believe it. I walked out of his office, past the truck bays toward my locker to clean it out. I had a lump in my throat and felt like I might start crying again, but I fought back the tears. I thought, "How could things be going so well one minute and then all fall apart like this the next?"

I found an empty box by the drums of oil that were sitting up against the wall. I then went over to my locker and put everything but my shop uniforms in it. Richie came over to say goodbye. He then told me, "I don't know if you know this or not, but your pal Billy has been in Ted's office all morning, and I'll bet he has a lot to do with you cleaning out your locker. You know, Billy wanted to be the tire man and when you told him you got the position instead of him, he was really upset."

Now things made sense. I was wondering why my check had already been made out. They already had plans to let me go before I ever walked into Ted's office. "Fucking Billy, what an asshole! That's what I get for trusting the wrong person." I felt betrayed, again. "I guess you can't trust anyone," I thought. I thanked Richie for telling me. We shook hands, and then I walked out to my car, put the box into the trunk and left.

As I drove away from my job for the last time, I was thinking about what a loser I was. Twenty minutes later, I was sitting in Mac and Marge's drinking a beer and feeling sorry for myself. I couldn't stop thinking about what had happened; the more I drank, the madder I became, I couldn't turn it off in my head. My intentions were to get fucked up, and that's just what I did.

Mary was there helping Marge serve drinks on the floor. I bought a rack of white crosses from Christopher, who was sitting at the table closest to the back entrance. He was a truck driver and I knew he'd have some. I took five with my beer and put the rest in my shirt pocket. There was a Hispanic man sitting at the bar, and he kept looking my way. It didn't take long for me to say something to him. I felt like shit and I needed someone to take it out on.

"What the hell are you looking at?!" He ignored me, so I said it again, only louder this time.

He responded with, "Look man, I don't want any trouble. Besides you're drunk." I really didn't care. I wanted someone to feel as bad as me and I chose him. I invited him outside several times and when I did, he kept telling me he didn't want any trouble or that I was too drunk. I wouldn't let up.

Even Mary suggested that I back off. She told me to go over to her house and sleep on her couch, but I wouldn't listen. I told her, "I don't remember bringing my mommy with me." That made her angry. She glared at me with piercing, angry eyes, and then she walked away.

The man watched as Mary walked away, and then he looked up at me again. That was it. I pointed to the back door and this time he said, "Okay, you asked for it!" He stood up and headed for the back door. I climbed off the stool and followed him. Behind us was most of the bar. Hell, there was going to be a fight and they wanted to see who would win. I couldn't blame them.

Well, all I can say is that if they had any money on that fight, I hope they didn't put it on me, because by the time I reached the door I was starting to realize just how drunk I was. I could hardly stand up, much less defend myself. I was beginning to think that maybe my mouth had written a check that my ass couldn't cash, but it was too late to back down now.

I made it outside and walked to the alley, then put my fists up. I swung out with my right, and the guy stepped back to avoid my punch. When he did, it threw me off balance and I started to fall forward. To avoid landing on my face, I grabbed on to a telephone pole to keep from hitting the ground. My fall was perceived as an aggressive move, so he proceeded to kick my ass. I couldn't even fight back; all I could do was to hang on to that pole. He beat me like I'd never been beaten before. He hit me so hard, I bet he even broke a bone or two in his hands. When he realized I wasn't fighting back he stopped hitting me. He looked at me with disgust and just walked away. I let go of the pole and fell the rest of the way to the ground.

I watched him walk away through very painful, swollen, slit eyes, and when he stopped by his 1965 Chevy Impala he turned around and looked back at me with contempt. Then he jumped in and drove away. Probably a good thing too. I was beginning to catch my breath. Mary helped me up and walked me back to her house around the corner. When we got there she cleaned me up. When all was said and done I hadn't come out too bad; a black eye, sore teeth, a fat lip and fractured pride. All I could think about was losing my job and the beating I had just taken. I fell asleep on Mary's couch around 11:00 that night.

I woke up the following day with Mary's father sitting across from me in a chair, smoking a Camel cigarette and sipping on a cup of coffee. "Bobby, those non-filtered cigarettes are going to kill you some day," I said. I stretched, and then pulled back from the pain.

"Shut up, you bum. Don't you have a home?" He was joking but trying to act serious.

"I'm not really sure," I said. It hurt to talk. My whole head hurt, but mostly my face. I was looking down at the ground and thinking about how Billy had betrayed me.

"Got anything for pain?" I asked him. I started to wonder why God had let me survive such a beating. I really hated myself and, at this point, I assumed that God hated me, too.

Bobby walked over to his suitcase and pulled out a bottle of aspirins. "Here, ya bum. I'm counting how many you take so you can pay me back when you get a job." He was laughing as he threw them at me. He just assumed I wasn't working because he had never known me to work.

I asked him if he was just getting into town. I already knew the answer. "Yeah, 'bout an hour ago." He had been gone for over a month. He told me he'd only be here for the next three days. "Driving to Maine next, be gone another month," he said. Then he asked me if I wanted a cup of coffee.

"Don't think I could drink it," I told him as I touched my lip where it was split open. When I touched it, I flinched.

We spent the next fifteen minutes or so talking about my job, how I had enjoyed working there, and its demise. He listened to my story, and he really seemed to care. He thought about what I had said, and then he spoke. "John, I know you're angry. What happened to you may not be right, but it happened and now you need to find a way to get through the anger and not let it hold you back." He just didn't understand, I thought, but it was nice to talk with someone about it anyway. I thanked him for listening. "You're welcome," he said. I smiled. "Now get out of my house. This isn't a motel." I thanked him again and I left. It was 7:00 a.m., a bit earlier than I was used to. I walked to the bar parking lot, to my car, which was the only one there. I jumped in and drove to my parents' house in Tempe.

Chapter Twenty-Three

My Trip Down The Mountain

The Pleasantries of The Incredible Mulla Nasrudin
From the short story: The Reason -- Idries Shah
The Mulla went to see a rich man.
"Give me some money,"
"Why?"
"I want to buy…an elephant"
"If you have no money,
you can't afford an elephant."
"I came here," said Nasrudin,
"to get money, not advice."

A few days after I was fired, Leonard called me to see what I was doing. During our conversation it came out that I was no longer working. "Are you looking for another job?" he asked me. I told him that I was. He then told me about a bookkeeper he knew who had been in a bad car accident and had lost his driver's license. He was looking to hire a driver to get him around.

"I'm interested," I told him. I was excited and said I'd be right over to get him.

"Pick me up at my mom's. I'll be waiting," he replied.

When I pulled up he was waiting outside for me. Fifteen minutes later I was sitting in front of an Old Spanish style apartment complex in which the front office doubled as a bookkeeping office.

Ira—the man that Leonard had told me about—owned both the business and the housing.

Ira was about six feet tall, maybe fifty years old. He had thinning brown hair with a small amount of gray around his ears. I sat in one of the two chairs he had sitting in front of his desk and Leonard sat in the other one. "Tell me about yourself," he said. I told him enough to get me the job, leaving as much out as I could without making it look like I was trying to cover something up.

"I like you" he told me, "and if you want the job, its yours. I'll pay you $2.00 an hour."

"Thank you!" I said and stuck out my hand to shake his, closing the deal. "When can I start?"

"How does eight tomorrow morning sound to you?" he wanted to know.

"I'll be here at seven," I said. I was happy to get the job.

"Eight is fine," he laughed, shaking my hand again.

For the next five months I was Ira's driver. It wasn't a bad job, not too complicated, and I enjoyed it. As a matter of fact, it would have been the perfect job if it weren't for a minor issue...Ira was gay. Now I had no problem with that. I figured, "to each his own," But he was always trying to convert me. One night after several attempts on his part to get me to have sex with him, I got angry. We were drinking and I was drunk, which didn't help my mood. He wouldn't let up, so I hit him in the mouth and then quit. I drove to my parent's house and passed out on their couch.

The following morning he called, begging me to come back. "I won't bother you again" he promised me.

"You don't pay me enough for this bullshit. I just don't know." I was hustling him now, hoping for a raise.

"I'll give you a quarter raise. Now will you do it?" he sounded desperate.

I didn't want to answer too quickly, so I said, "I don't know. I need to think about it."

"Please John, I need you. I have to be at the Salt River Canyon Inn by six tomorrow morning and I need you to drive me, so let me know today." Ira had an account at the Salt River Canyon Inn, at the bottom of the Salt River Canyon, between Globe and Show Low, Arizona. The Inn was owned by a gangster-looking Italian named Ed, who was from New York. Ed portrayed the gangster image right down to the 1911 Colt .45 semi-automatic he carried in his belt. I had known for a while that Ira was afraid of him.

"For twenty-five cents more I'll come back and drive for you, if you leave me alone," I told him when I called him back an hour later.

"Deal," he said. He sounded relieved. "I'd like to leave tonight around six. We'll be there a few days, so why don't you bring a few friends?" I could tell he felt better now that I was back on board. He continued talking. He was telling me about how Ed messed up his books so badly that it would take him a few days to straighten them out. I knew the Inn wasn't open this time of year, and the last time I stayed up there I had my own cabin. I had enjoyed the solitude.

"See you tonight," I told him and hung up. I asked my brother Richard and his friend Roger to go with me. We arrived at Ira's office at 5:45 p.m. Ira knew both of them so no introductions were in order. We loaded up Ira's 1961 Caddie and left for the Salt River Canyon Inn. We arrived at the Inn at around 10:30 that night, after a stop in Apache Junction to eat.

When we pulled into the Inn, Ed was outside with his gun drawn. "Put that thing away," Ira barked, using us as an excuse.

"Someone tried to start a fire around my gas pumps and I chased them away." He looked like a person who'd been up for days. He had a crazed look in his eyes and he was acting very strange. I felt uneasy. Ed continued, "Just two nights ago, they were shooting at my employees. I think somebody's trying to scare me off my land." He was becoming more agitated and with that .45 in his hand I was nervous. "They don't know who they're fucking with. I'm like a bulldog. I swear to God I'll kill their asses and then throw them in the river." He pointed in the direction of the Salt River, just south of the Inn. I could tell by the wild look in his eyes that there wasn't anyone home—Ed's mind had gone bye-bye.

We all looked at each other and I could tell I wasn't the only one with these feelings. "We've been driving for several hours and we're tired," Ira told Ed. I could see that Ira was uncomfortable and wanted to get away, but Ed wouldn't let up.

"Yeah, they don't know who they're fucking with," he said again. "I believe in that old street justice like we have back East."

I had to know, so I asked him what he meant.

Roger looked at me as if to say, "Shut up." Ed went on.

"We don't believe in calling the police. If we have a problem with someone we call our friends, and take care of it. Now that's justice. Police only get in the way. Fuck 'em."

Richard leaned over and said in my ear, "Thanks, Bro. We're fucking dead now. He's been breathing way too many gas fumes from those pumps." He straightened up quickly so Ed couldn't see him.

"I can't let you sleep in the cabins. Too dangerous. I'd feel bad if something happened. You can all sleep in the restaurant where we can all be together. Be fun, like a sleep out." He reminded me of General Patton giving orders to his men.

"No sleep out I've ever been on," I said under my breath as Ed walked into the restaurant. I was pretty freaked out.

Roger called us into a huddle. "One of us needs to stay awake at all times. I'll take the first shift." I agreed with him.

We unloaded the car and went into the lobby. I dropped all that I was carrying in a corner by the cash register. Richard and Roger did the same, and we all turned to Ed, who was standing there with another man.

He told us, "This is Jimmy, our cook and maintenance man. He'll cook you something to eat. Just tell him what you want."

Jimmy put up his hand to say hi. I introduced myself first, and we went around until we'd all told Jimmy our names. He then walked back to the kitchen and yelled, "Orders, taking orders."

When I finished looking at the menu I said, "Two eggs, sunny side up, hash browns, two strips of bacon and toast."

"The toaster and bread are behind the counter. Help yourself with the toast, I'll make the rest," he yelled back from the order window.

"I'll take the same, only scrambled," Roger said.

Then Richard followed with, "Eggs over easy, hash browns, and ham if you have it." Ira wasn't hungry. He was too freaked out and wanted to start working on the books. Roger went behind the counter and started making toast for everyone.

We all sat down to eat at a large booth at the back of the dining room. "It sounds like it's been crazy around here," I said to Jimmy.

"Yeah, just like Ed told you, there have been fires, gun shots in the middle of the night, and phone calls with no one on the other the end of the line. It's real crazy alright." Then Jimmy leaned into the table and waved us into a huddle. "There's something else," he waved us in even closer. "When all this stuff was happening, Ed was by himself. I've never seen anyone, I only know what he's told me. Kinda freaky, huh?" The hair on the back of my neck stood up.

"It just doesn't feel right," Roger was saying. "I've got a bad feeling." My brother wasn't saying anything; he just listened.

"I don't know, things just don't add up. I've been here two weeks and I have to tell you, it feels much longer," Jimmy's voice was so low I had to strain my ears to hear him. I was tired so I asked Jimmy where I could lie down. I walked into the lobby and laid down on a red leather couch, using one of the arms for a pillow, and fell asleep immediately. It was just past midnight.

I was awakened by the sounds of Ed and Ira arguing from Ed's office next to the lobby. Ira was trying to explain to Ed that there were missing receipts and that he couldn't complete the work without them. Ed was screaming at Ira, telling him that he didn't know where they were and that he couldn't understand why he needed them anyway. I looked at the clock on the wall above the register and saw that it was 7:00. Roger was asleep on the other end of the couch, sitting in an upright position, his left hand holding up his head. Richard was asleep in the booth we'd eaten in the night before and Jimmy was awake sitting at the counter sipping a cup of coffee. He invited me to get my own cup and join him. "Want to go to the river for a swim later?" Jimmy asked. I said okay. He told me to invite my brother and his friend along and that he'd bring the booze. We would leave at 9:30.

"Sounds good to me, I'll let everyone know." As he left to go to his cabin, I woke Richard and Roger up and told them about the river. Richard said he'd like to be anywhere but here, with Ed around. Roger agreed.

Roger then offered to cook for everyone. I told Ira about our plans. "Just be careful," he said, "I don't want you guys to get hurt." I assured him we wouldn't. We waited for Jimmy to come back from his cabin. When he walked in he had two six packs of Budweiser and a fifth of Ten High whiskey.

"Let's party!" he yelled. As he came through the lobby, we followed. We borrowed the Ford truck that belonged to the property.

None of us had bathing suits, so the plan was to swim with our pants on, but when we got to the river I just swam in my underwear. I would have gone full nude, but the bridge over the river carried the only traffic through the canyon and I was modest.

It was starting to get warm and I was thirsty, so I asked Jimmy for one of the cold Buds he had in the cooler in the bed of the truck. I opened it with the church key that was on the key ring of the truck. I slammed it down and opened another one. "Damn, you must be thirsty," Jimmy said. He was wide-eyed and laughing. "I'd give you another one, but I'm afraid when I hand it to you, I'll pull back a stump," he was cracking up.

"You're on a fuckin' roll, aren't ya?" I said, keeping it going. He smiled. Richard and Roger were starting on their first. They were laughing at Jimmy and me as we went back and forth with each other. "Give me a pull on that whiskey," I said. Jimmy handed it to me. I opened it and took a long drink.

"Hey! That ain't water—slow down!" He reached for it and I let it go. He held it up to measure how much was gone. "Damn! Save some for the fishes." He said as he saw the amount I had drunk.

"I am a fish!" I said.

"Oh, well that explains it then!" I could tell Jimmy felt better being away from the Inn for a while.

We swam and drank for the better part of the day. Around three o'clock we ran out of alcohol, so we pooled our money together to get more. I had drunk half of Jimmy's fifth and four beers. I was drunk, and he wasn't much better, as he had drunk the other half of that fifth and three beers himself.

Now I might have been drunk, but I wasn't ready to stop drinking yet, and with the money we pulled together, $25.00 in all, we didn't have to. Jimmy and I headed for Show Low to buy more. On our way up Highway 60 it was already starting to get dark, so Jimmy turned on the headlights. "Ah, shit!" he yelled out.

"What?"

"We only have one headlight, so let's get what we've come for and get back down the mountain."

In town we turned in to the first liquor store we saw. "Give us two cases of Budweiser and two fifths of Ten High," Jimmy said to the clerk.

"A party?" the clerk asked.

"Something like that," Jimmy told him.

Then the clerk looked at us and said, "Sorry to give you the bad news, but with the Rodeo in town this weekend, there's nothing left, and it is unlikely you'll find it anywhere else."

We looked at each other and then back at him. He took a bottle off the shelf to show us.

"Got plenty of this, all you want." He showed us a bottle of Thunderbird wine.

"If that's what you have, that's what we want." Jimmy said. We bought all that he had left on the shelf; twelve bottles in all, at $1.29 a pint. We bought snacks with the money we had left over, saving $4.00 for gas to get back on.

In the truck I took out four bottles, so we'd have a little something to drink on the way home. I took two and gave the other two to Jimmy as we pulled out of the Show Low liquor store and into the full service gas station across the street to put our last $4.00 into Ed's 1953 red Ford pick-up truck. It was already dusk, and Jimmy knew that it got dark early here in the canyon. He expressed concern about the burned-out driver's side headlight. "It gets so dark here you can't see your hand in front of you, and the other headlight is as old as the truck, and I'm afraid it's not as bright as it used to be," he said with a worried look.

Jimmy knew we were taking a chance driving up here, but we had been drinking most of the day, and we were drunk. We ran out of alcohol around 3:00 p.m., and we weren't finished partying yet, so we exercised one of the only two options we thought we had: continue to swim in the Salt River with nothing to drink, or drive up highway 60 to Show Low and buy more. We chose option two.

Jimmy pulled up to the pump where the attendant was waiting. "$4.00 regular, please." Jimmy told him. As he pumped the gas, the other attendant washed the windshield.

"I noticed your driver's side headlight is out. We can replace it for another $5.00," the attendant told Jimmy when he finished washing the glass. A good deal no doubt, but we had no more money because we had spent it all at the liquor store.

"No thanks," Jimmy said as he started the truck. I sensed he was none too happy about driving down the mountain with only one headlight, but what else could we do?

We left town, heading back in the same direction we'd come. As we passed the Show Low city limits, I opened my first pint of wine. I put the bottle up to my lips and tilted my head back. I took in almost three quarters of the bottle before I needed a breath.

I'd had my first beer at ten o'clock that morning and had been drinking most of the day, so I had no business drinking this wine like I was drinking a soda on a hot day, but I didn't care. Two minutes later I killed the pint. I turned to Jimmy and said, "That's some good shit!." He just looked at me.

I dropped the empty bottle to the floor of the cab and opened another pint. I put it up to my mouth and took a long drink, and then I screwed the cap back on.

I could feel the wind blowing up against my arm as it hung out the passenger side window as we entered the canyon, starting our descent.

The next thing I remember, I was waking up. I felt like I was floating in mid-air, like the initial drop on a roller coaster.

I looked toward Jimmy, but he wasn't there. I instantly thought, "We must be going off the mountain! Jimmy must have jumped out before we became airborne!"

I was so drunk, I didn't even think about the possibility that I could be killed. It never even crossed my mind. My only thought was, "I better hang on to this bottle [Which I had hanging out of the window in my right hand.], because I'm going to need a drink when this ride is over."

Well, I did hang on, with every ounce of strength I could muster. Besides, I couldn't have pulled my arm in anyway, because it kept hitting the trees and bushes on the mountainside as I continued my solo descent downward. I couldn't see them in the darkness, but I could feel them just the same.

My only objective was to hang on to that bottle. I was determined to have that drink when that ride ended, and that was as complicated a thought as I could put together at the time.

I must have lost consciousness, because the next thing I knew, I wasn't flying anymore, and I couldn't see a thing. The darkness was so thick I felt smothered by it. The truck was on its right side, and my arm, still holding the bottle, was pinned underneath it. We had hit with such force that only my nose hit the windshield and punched a hole clean through the glass with no other breaks or cracks. As I lay there on my side, my arm started to throb, and through my drunken haze I began to realize how serious my situation was.

I had just gone over the Salt River Canyon as we entered it from the Show Low side at its highest point. The locals referred to this gorge as the "Mini-Grand Canyon," and I knew deep down inside that I had come down a long way.

I wasn't sure how badly I was hurt, but I knew something serious was wrong. I didn't know what had happened to Jimmy. Hell, I didn't even know if anyone had seen me go over the side. I was in trouble, and I knew it.

Somewhere I had heard that when we are close to death our lives start to flash before us. However, it wasn't a flash of light that caught my attention at this instant in time, it was the abyss of complete darkness. It's weird how blindness in the dark triggers awareness in the mind. As the gears in my head began gathering a raging momentum from the lethargy of a drunken stupor, I found myself at war in my mind. Crisis has a way of sobering the thinking process. It was at this time that I went back and assessed the battlefield.

I felt scared and completely alone. I didn't know how badly I was hurt or if I was going to die. My life was flashing before me as I lay in complete darkness. I couldn't tell you how long I lay there on my side, reflecting on my life, but it seemed like a very long time before I heard what sounded like moaning just outside the driver's side window. I turned my head toward the noise and through strained eyes I thought I could see the outline of a person. "Who's there?" I asked, not sure whether or not the night was playing tricks on me.

"Fuck, who do you think it is?" It was Jimmy sitting on a rock just outside the driver's side door, and I was sure glad to see him.

"Are you all right?" I asked.

"I think so. What happened?" he asked me. He appeared to be confused.

"I'm not sure," I told him. "We must have gone off the mountain. I thought you jumped out. I didn't see you on the way down."

I could feel that there was no blood getting to my arm, and I was in a lot of pain. I felt claustrophobic, and I was bordering on panic.

Jimmy said, "I'm not sure what happened. I just woke up outside the truck here." He sounded like he was starting to come out of his fog. He then asked me if I was okay.

"My fucking arm is killing me. It's under the truck and I can't get it out!" I said. I kept fighting with myself, trying not to lose it. Maybe I needed a drink to control this horror I was feeling in my head. "You know all the wine that we bought?" I asked him.

"Yeah." He must have stood up because he sounded closer.

"Try and find a bottle. I need a drink!" I was feeling light-headed and my arm was hurting badly. I couldn't help thinking of an amputee experiencing phantom pain. All I knew was that maybe a drink would make it feel better. Jimmy took out his Zippo, lit it and for the first time we could see each other. He didn't have a mark on him; I couldn't believe it.

When he saw me, though, he almost lost it. He was scared. "Fuck, John, are you okay? You really look messed up."

"I'd be fine if I could have something to drink, now look will ya?" I was moving quickly into hysteria, and I was finding it harder to maintain control.

Jimmy backed out of the truck to look around. He was gone for what seemed like an eternity, until finally he came back to the truck. "I can't find even one bottle. I've looked everywhere," he was apologizing; it was obvious he felt bad.

"That's okay," I told him. My only hope was the bottle I had in my hand.

We talked while we waited, hoping for a rescue. I must have looked pretty bad because Jimmy kept asking me if I was all right. If I had to guess, I believe he must have thought I might die and he was feeling responsible. My arm stopped hurting some time later, and then it went numb. "Look, I can see lights," I heard Jimmy scream. "They're almost here." He lit his lighter to give them a location. I could hear voices. I couldn't make out what they were saying, but I heard them. Jimmy yelled out, "H-E-L-L-P!"

"There they are!" I heard someone yell as several people ran toward the truck. There were five of them, Jimmy told me.

"Is anyone hurt?" I heard one of the officers ask Jimmy.

"I'm okay, but I think my friend is hurt pretty bad. The truck's on his arm." Jimmy sounded like he was hyperventilating.

Two men ran over to the truck. One shone a light in on me, and then he asked how badly I was hurt. He bent over, with one knee in the driver's seat, as he assessed my injuries.

"I feel fine except for my arm. It went completely numb about a half hour ago. I can't feel my fingers."

He went out to talk to his friends. They were talking about what they needed to do to get me free. He and his partner walked around the truck several times, and then walked back over to talk with the others to discuss how they would do it. "Tom, John, Bob and

I will try to lift the truck enough for Carlos to pull him free," I heard one say. They all agreed; everyone moved into position. "Now, on the count of three. Ready now, one," I could feel the truck rock, "Two," I heard the sound of heavy breathing. I glanced at Carlos; he looked scared. "Three." I heard grunting.

I could feel the weight lift off my arm when they lifted the truck maybe three inches, just enough for Carlos to pull me out. When they pulled me from the truck I still had the bottle in my hand. I was still hoping for that long anticipated drink that I so deserved. So you can understand my disappointment when I discovered that the bottle was broken and had long since spilled its contents onto the ground beneath the truck. I wanted to cry.

John, the officer who had spoken to me inside the truck, looked at my arm and said, "I'm not a doctor, but it looks like you may have a broken arm, and you've taken most of the skin off of it as well. Must have been from hitting those trees and bushes on the way down."

The blood was flowing back into my arm now, and I was beginning to feel the pain—man did it hurt! John and Carlos put a sling on my arm, and then they laid me in the rescue basket and strapped me in. I was pulled up to the road and loaded into an ambulance. They transported me to Apache County Hospital on Highway 60. The doctor that saw me was a small man in his early sixties, with thinning white hair that he combed way over to the right side of his head in an attempt to hide his baldness on top. I wondered if he knew that this hair thing wasn't working. Bald is bald and you can't hide that very well. I wanted to tell him, but I decided not to.

The doctor took x-rays and gave me a quick exam. As I laid on the gurney waiting for him to return, my body felt like a massive toothache all over. I laid there for forty-five minutes before the doctor walked in with the x-rays in his hands. "Well son," he held up one of the films and looked at it nervously, then continued, "You have a broken arm. Broke in two places. Here," he pointed to it on the x-ray, "and here. Your nose is also broken. Now there's not much I can do with all the skin loss." I just listened. "You're going to be hurting in the morning, if you're not already. I can't give you anything for pain.

You've had too much to drink and I'm afraid it will kill you. We'll give you aspirin, and that should help. I'm sorry, that's all we can do." He stood up and walked out without another word.

The nurse came in to clean me up. "I called your friends at the number you gave me, and they're on their way here," she told me as she scrubbed my wounds and bandaged what she could. She then put a make-shift sling on my arm. When she was finished with me, I discovered that Ira, Richard and Roger had been waiting just outside my room.

"You look messed up," Roger said when he walked through the door. I looked at him.

"I called mom and told her what happened and I let her know you were okay. You know, that you're alive and all. She wanted you to call her when you could," My brother announced when he walked through the door. He was standing between Ira and Roger. I never realized just how short he was until that moment, as he stood in the middle, sandwiched between them.

Ira just stood there. He wasn't saying anything. He looked concerned, but at the same time he looked angry. I couldn't tell. I broke the ice. "I guess you're pissed and I don't blame you." I was trying to get a handle on how angry he was and if I still had a job.

"I'm not angry with you. I was more scared you were hurt really bad or were killed, and I couldn't live with that." Ira looked like he might cry.

"How angry is Ed about his truck?" I asked. Ira told me that Ed was really mad and that he pressed charges on Jimmy.

"Jimmy is now property of the Globe Police Department and is a guest in their jail."

"Ed's a real asshole!" I was angry when I said it. Richard and Roger sided with me. Ira didn't disagree, he just didn't respond. "Am I in trouble too?" I asked.

"Ed only pressed charges on Jimmy because he was the one who took the truck in the first place," Ira was explaining as we headed for the Caddie out in the parking lot of the hospital. I crawled into the back seat with my brother.

There wasn't a part of my body that didn't hurt on our drive back to the Canyon Inn. As we drove, Ira explained to me what had happened, which he had learned from one of the officers investigating the accident scene. "It was reported by several truck drivers who watched you go off the mountain that when you passed the Show Low city limits and were getting ready to enter the canyon, whoever was driving was weaving and driving at a high rate of speed, and that your truck was going at least a 100 mph when it went off the mountain. One trucker reported there was no driver, or at least that's what it looked like at the time you went off."

Roger looked back at me and said, "I think I know what happened."

"What?" I asked.

"He passed out, then slid down to the floor, and by doing so, hit the gas pedal and floored it," Roger offered.

"That makes sense. I was already passed out and when I woke up in mid-air, I looked over and didn't see him. As a matter of fact, I thought he had jumped out before we went off."

"And the rest is history, as they say in the movies," Richard said, while Roger laughed.

Ira went on to say that the investigating officer had told him that if we hadn't been going as fast as we had been, we probably would have been killed. "Just ten miles slower and you would have hit a very large drainpipe sticking out of the mountain." I shuddered at the thought. He also said that this was the first time he'd ever seen speed save someone's life.

Then Richard told me that I wasn't the only one who'd had an exciting day.

"Why, what happened?" I couldn't imagine what could be more exciting than going off Salt River Canyon at 100 mph in the dead of night.

Richard then told me that someone was shooting at them from the bridge. "It happened shortly after you guys left," he went on to say.

"Yeah, and I know who was doing the shooting" Roger blurted out. "It was Ed. I saw him standing by his car with the door open." Roger was slowing down the Caddie for an upcoming curve.

I looked at Ira, and I couldn't help feeling bad for him. He looked so scared I felt sorry for him. If he ever had to defend himself, I'm afraid he'd faint. No, Ira was definitely not a fighter.

We drove in silence the last ten minutes. When we pulled into the Canyon Inn parking lot Ira turned to us and said, "It's time to go. Let's go in and get our things. We'll meet in the lobby in ten minutes. John," he turned to face me. "I'm going to tell Ed that you're too hurt and that I need to get you back to Phoenix, okay?"

"Sounds good to me. Hell, I'll even cry if need be, I don't give a shit." I was ready to go. We met back in the lobby ten minutes later. Roger had packed up my things. Ed came out to say goodbye and to tell me how sorry he was that I was hurt. When he said it he sounded hollow. I thanked him and we left.

I never saw Jimmy again, and through the years I have often wondered what had happened to him as a result this incident.

A few months later I received a call from Ira. He told me that the Salt River Canyon Inn had burned down and that Ed had collected a large sum of money from an insurance policy that he'd taken out at the time of purchase. Then he moved back East.

For over a month I stayed close to home. I needed to heal from all my injuries. I think the most painful part was not the broken bones, as one might think, but the layers of skin that were taken off. I would never want anyone to endure that kind of pain. Because it took so long to heal, Ira was forced to find another driver, so I never went back to work for him.

Chapter Twenty-Four

Betrayal

Loneliness...
Looking into eyes that don't look back---
Believing that you're no one's favorite friend---
Depending on drugs---
Seldom hearing someone else's footsteps---
Not being able to really explain the emptiness you feel---
Having a great deal to give, and no one to bestow your gift upon---
Wanting to belong, then to discover that
you're not really wanted---
-- *Unknown*

About a month after my accident my parents asked to speak with me. We all sat down at the kitchen table and my mother said, "John, your father and I have been talking with Steve and we thought that, since you're not working, it would be nice if you guys could spend some time together." My father didn't say anything, he just sat there drinking his coffee.

I sensed they were becoming more concerned about my drinking since my accident. And since they didn't know how to talk with me about it, they had asked my brother if he could help. "What do you have in mind?" I asked.

"We talked to your brother and he told us it was summer break at the seminary. We thought maybe you would enjoy getting away from Phoenix and spending some time there. You just might like it. So what do you think?" she asked.

I thought about it and decided to go. Who knew? Maybe I would enjoy it. What could it hurt? I really had thought that I had been doing okay over the past month. I hadn't used alcohol or drugs in that time so—from where I was sitting—it looked to me like I was cured. But I agreed to go because I could see that it would help them feel better. Two days later, I had a one-way ticket to Los Angeles.

When I arrived at the airport in L.A., my brother was there to meet me. We half hugged each other and exchanged greetings. I was sure he knew everything that had been happening with me, because he and my mother talked on the phone every day. In the parking lot we made our way to a green, two-toned VW bus that belonged to the seminary.

When we drove out of the airport parking lot, Steve told me that the seminary where he lived was in Stokes Canyon. I had no idea where that was. I had only been to California once and that was under bizarre circumstances. I told him okay and let him know it didn't mean very much to me, because I had no clue where I was. As we drove, I could see the ocean to my left. It was beautiful and somehow familiar. It rather looked like the area where I had stayed with Ken and Carla. My mind wandered off to the time I had spent with them. "I'd love to see them again," I thought. "Where are we?" I asked Steve.

He said, "Malibu, why?"

"Just looks familiar is all." He explained that we were driving up Pacific Coast Highway and that it would take us all the way to where we were going. "I knew it," I thought. "I've been on this road before. The store we just passed was the same one we were at the night I rode on the back of Harley's bike when I was tripping on acid." I missed my California hippie friends and at times felt sorry that I'd left. Ah well, I had, and that was that.

It was quiet so Steve turned on the radio. It was playing "He Ain't Heavy, He's My Brother," by the Hollies. I started to ask Steve what the song was all about, but changed my mind.

"See those houses up there?" He pointed to several houses that over looked the ocean.

"Yeah, they're really nice," I said.

"A lot of money up there. C.E.O.s of large corporations, movie stars, lawyers, doctors, anyone with a seven figure income. You'll see some of them at Mass on Sunday. They come to worship at our services." I thought that was very cool. Then he pointed to other stuff along the way, just making chit-chat. This was his way of avoiding conversation with me. It was at this time that I realized that my brother had just as much trouble talking with me as my parents did. It wasn't that they didn't try—they did. It was me. I think I made it difficult for people to talk about what was going on with me.

When we pulled up to the gate of the seminary, Steve talked into a black box off the side of the gate. It reminded me of ordering food at a drive-thru burger joint. He identified himself, and the gate swung open. When we drove inside, I saw heaven. It was the most beautiful place I had ever seen in my eighteen years of life. It was breathtaking! There were rolling green hills, and a river wound its way through the middle of the property. There were bridges in several places to cross over to the other side, and paths that led in many different directions. It was what I had always pictured paradise to look like. I could literally *feel* the beauty of it.

It was getting dark and we were losing light, so Steve told me he would show me around the following day.

We pulled up to the church, jumped out of the bus ,and went inside. When we walked through the doors, Steve put the first two fingers of his right hand into a silver bowl just inside the door that held holy water. He then made the sign of the cross, reciting, "In the name of the Father, the Son, and the Holy Ghost. Amen." It was a ritual I'd seen many times by Catholics when they entered church. Well, I may have been baptized Catholic, but I wasn't a practicing one so I walked past him. I wasn't sure, but I thought I heard him say a little prayer for me; it sounded like, "Forgive him, Father," or something to that effect.

We walked through the cathedral and into a room at the back where there were two men, both wearing black robes, sitting on a red leather couch watching television. Steve introduced them to me as Roland and James. James was a brother in the order and Roland was studying to be a priest, just as Steve was.

James was holding a magazine with a picture of Janice Joplin on the cover. When he showed it to us he said, "She's a Goddess. She has a beautiful voice, and they say she'll take the music industry by storm." It was mid 1969, and I had never heard of her until then. James turned out to be right. She did take the industry by storm. Every time I'd hear Janice on the radio after that, I would think of James, right up until she died from an overdose in 1970.

My brother took me to a room where the priests prepared for Mass. There were several robes hanging up, a rack with three bottles of wine and a bottle of grape juice, and a cabinet that held various supplies needed for the holy sacrament. Next to the cabinet was a door that led to an office. Steve knocked.

"Come in," a voice commanded from the other side. Steve opened the door and walked in, and I followed. Sitting behind a large oak desk was an older priest. He looked to be well over sixty.

Steve said, "This is my brother John. You know, the one I told you about."

The priest reached over his desk and shook my hand. He said, "Hi John, I'm Father Hymes, and I'm in charge here. I'm sure you'll find our place accommodating. Please feel free to come in and talk with me whenever you'd like. My door is always open." I thanked him and looked at Steve.

"I'll show him to his room. Thank you, Father," Steve said. I thanked him again, and then we left. We climbed back in the van, and then drove up to a big house that stood beyond the church. Steve explained that this was where the priests lived. It looked like a mansion! On the other side of it was another building—the dorm—that was hard to see because the house was so large. "That's where you'll be staying. You'll be there by yourself tonight, but there are two guys joining the order tomorrow. I've already met them. You'll like them. " He told me their names were Reggie and Phil, and then he explained that they'd both been here before and knew what to do.

He put me on the third floor in room seven. Then he told me if I needed anything at all to just walk along the side of the big house. He explained that it was the quickest way to his dorm; then almost as an afterthought, he told me to be careful of the pool. I told him that if I needed him I'd come over and get him. After he left, I took a quick shower, pulled a pair of pants on, walked over to the TV room on the third floor and turned on the television. I was the only one there and it was kind of scary. In truth, I was afraid to be by myself. Being alone triggered my abandonment issues, and I was very uncomfortable.

Television news was different somehow when watched in a monastery. It seemed more violent. They were talking about finding dead bodies on the beach and riots. "This stuff wouldn't happen in Phoenix," I thought when I turned off the TV to go to bed. I was tired and fell asleep immediately.

The following morning I was awakened by someone kicking the side of my bed. I opened my eyes and saw a very tall black man, with the biggest hair I had ever seen. He had a large comb buried so deeply in it that all you could see were the ends sticking out. He was wearing a flowery long sleeved shirt that buttoned up the front, hip hugger bell-bottoms and sandals. When he saw me looking up at him he said, "Hey, you gonna sleep all day?" He was with another guy who was dressed in a white t-shirt, Levis, and sandals. They were talking about getting a pail of water to help me get the sleep out of my eyes or something to that effect.

"You guys must be Reggie and Phil," I said to them when I sat up in bed.

"I'm Reggie," the black guy said.

"And I'm Phil," the white guy announced.

And then, in concert, they said, "And we're your new roommates."

"Well, at least they have a sense of humor," I thought. I had been half expecting a couple of nerds.

Reggie threw a bag of potato chips on my bed and Phil handed me a Coke in a six ounce bottle. "We brought you breakfast in bed, but don't expect this every morning," Phil said as they both laughed.

"These guys are cool," I thought. I was starting to like being there already.

I got out of bed, went into the bathroom to brush my teeth, and then went down to the second floor TV room where Reggie and Phil were waiting for me. Phil asked me to sit down. When he did, I started to wonder what was happening. Then he explained, "Steve shared your story, and when we were sure you were coming, we all had a meeting. It was decided that Reggie and I would spend time with you. I hope you're not angry. It would be an honor for us." Reggie agreed.

Neither of them were much older than I was, and they both seemed to be real enough. "Okay," I told them. I was willing to see where things would go from here. After all, I knew my life wasn't going well, and I didn't have a better plan of my own. I would be happy if my life was just a little better, so what did I have to lose? "As far as I'm concerned, you guys are calling the shots," I said with resignation.

They looked at each other, and then Reggie said, "Cool." They stood up and gave each other a high five. My brother had put me in their hands, and as I got to know them it became clear to me that they both felt honored to have this opportunity. From that day on, I spent most of my time with them, only seeing my brother in passing a time or two, right up until the time I left three weeks later. I learned from talking with them that Phil was from Seattle and Reggie was from San Francisco. They both were against drugs and they both had experience working with inner city kids doing drug prevention.

On my third day there, Reggie, Phil, and I were in the main dining room when Father Hymes walked in. "Reggie," he nodded. "Phil," he nodded again. Then he looked at me and said, "John, would you come to my office when you're done eating, please. I'd like to speak with you for a moment." I told him I'd be there in a few minutes. He nodded a third time, then turned and walked away. Phil told me that they'd wait for me in the TV room.

I walked through the room where the robes were hung and I knocked on Father Hymes door. "Come in," he said. I went into his office and stood in front of one of the two chairs in front of his desk.

I waited for an invitation to sit. "Please sit," he waved his hand in a backward motion over his head, as if to say, "Pick one." I sat down in the one closest to the door.

"I called you in to get to know you better," he began. "Sounds like you've had some problems, and I want to know how I can help." He got up, walked around my chair and stood behind me, looking down at the top of my head. He started rubbing my shoulders. I felt uncomfortable. Then he moved down to the middle of my back. I didn't like him touching me that way. I found myself wanting to pull away from him. I was confused. I didn't know what to do. I didn't want to offend him, but I couldn't help it. I couldn't take it anymore. I felt my skin crawling.

I quickly jumped up and walked over to the door. I wanted to run, but I controlled myself. I turned to face him and said, "Thank you for your concern, I really appreciate it. If I feel like talking, I'll let you know." I couldn't get out of there fast enough. I felt dirty and I hated it. I reached for the door handle and pulled the door toward me. I was half way out the door when I looked back at him standing there smiling as if nothing had happened. I ran to the TV room where Reggie and Phil were. I must have looked upset because Reggie asked me what was wrong.

"Let's go," I yelled. "I'll tell you later." We walked out together. When we reached the house where the priest's lived, Phil asked me again what happened. I told him that I didn't want to talk about it. I saw concern on both of their faces, but I wasn't ready yet. We walked the rest of the way in silence. When we walked through the door of our dorm, I told them I needed to be alone for a while. I went to my room and laid down on my bed. I laid there with my hands folded behind my head, thinking about what had just happened. It had brought back memories of Steve, my brother's friend, who had molested me when I was nine. I felt angry. For a while, I was that kid again. My shame and feelings of hopelessness came back. I wanted to crawl inside myself and die. I felt exhausted and I must have fallen asleep.

I was awakened by someone kicking the side of my bed again. "Hey, you gonna sleep all day?" This sounded very familiar. I opened my eyes and saw Reggie and Phil standing almost in the same position as they had been when I first met them a few days back. Phil was holding a six pack of Budweiser and Reggie was handing me a "church key." "We know what will make you feel better. Dinner in bed, but don't get used to it. People will start talking," Phil said.

I laughed as I climbed out of bed.

"Hate to see a good friend down." Phil announced. "Nothing like an ice cold beer to bring friends closer together." He held up his beer in a toast to friendship, "To good friends!" he said.

I sat on the edge of my bed, while Reggie and Phil sat on the bed across from me. I looked at them and said, "I thought you guys were against drugs and getting high." Having spent time in 12-Step meetings because my father asked me to attend as a condition for him giving me money or a place to live, I had been taught that alcohol was a drug. Well, that wasn't their understanding, and who was I to argue with them? They were the authorities on the subject, having worked in prevention programs, or at least that's what I believed. I downed the rest of my beer as we talked.

Reggie opened up another one and handed it to me. "We're against drugs; they steal your happiness and put you on the road to destruction. Just drink. You can't get in trouble with alcohol." I could see as Reggie talked that he really believed what he was saying to me, and Phil co-signed everything Reggie was saying, so who was I to question them?

As I sat there listening, I struggled with whether or not to tell them what had happened with Father Hymes. I didn't want to cause them problems when I left to go back to Phoenix. I followed them down to the pantry. Reggie opened the two refrigerators and showed me that they were well stocked with beer. There was every kind you could think of, and I was told that I could help myself as long as I acted responsible.

We then walked outside to a sitting area where there were four lawn chairs and a concrete bench surrounding a fountain. Coming out of the fountain was an angel in flight. Out of its mouth flowed a stream of water that ran down into a small round pond which had fish swimming in it. The pond looked like it needed cleaning. The water was dark and it looked like there was green algae covering the concrete bottom of the pool. I sat in one of the lawn chairs and used the edge of the pond as a foot rest. Reggie handed me another beer. I was beginning to think they were trying to get me drunk so that maybe I would talk about whatever was obviously bothering me.

They both sat on the edge of the pond facing me, with Phil to my left and Reggie to my right. We sat there in silence for the longest time. I was still fighting the thoughts of telling them what had happened with Father Hymes. I needed to talk about it, but I was afraid I'd cause problems. I guess the need to talk about it was greater than my fear of starting problems, because I started talking, and when I did, it all came out. I even told them what had happened with my brother's friend when I was nine.

They sat there and listened. I felt better just talking about it. I explained to them that I hadn't let it get that far with Father Hymes because of how I had handled it. I also told them that it had taken me back to age nine and feelings of being dirty, ashamed, and worthless. Then I asked them how someone in his position could take advantage of those he should be helping. I felt so betrayed. Phil took a deep breath and let it out slowly. Then he leaned forward, reached out his right hand, and touched my knee. I wanted to flinch, but I controlled it. He looked into my eyes as he spoke, "John, I can understand how you must feel. I can't understand how someone like that could hurt people either. I don't think there is any worse feeling than the betrayal of someone you thought you could trust. I'm sorry for that, but please understand that not everyone is like this. You did the right thing by talking about it."

Reggie touched me on my shoulder and said, "I'm proud of you for talking about it." He then told me, "Phil and I already knew about Father Hymes' history; we were warned by others who had been here before. I had no idea he would try anything with you. I'm sure Phil feels the same way or we would have told you, but I guess we were wrong and I'm sorry."

I let them know I understood, and then Phil said, "We'll just watch each other's back," and we all agreed.

"Now lets party!" I said as I toasted my beer in the air. Reggie and Phil did the same. We drank until two a.m., and then I crawled up to my room and passed out. I avoided Father Hymes as much as I could, although there were a few close calls. He seemed to be everywhere. Reggie and Phil would run interference for me when they could, but even though they did the best they could, they couldn't be with me all the time.

On Wednesday of the following week, I was told that Father Hymes would be gone for a few days. He would be going to another parish in downtown L.A., and he'd be gone until Friday or Saturday. When he left I felt an enormous relief. I was able to roam the grounds as I pleased. I wanted time by myself to sort things out, and with him gone I finally had the freedom to do so. It would also give Reggie and Phil some well needed time to themselves. They had spent so much time with me in the last week that they hadn't even had the time to settle in. They had become true and loyal friends through all of this, and I was grateful.

I spent most of the day and part of the evening walking the grounds. I was deeply touched by its beauty. It was around 1:30 that afternoon and I was sitting in one of the gazebos. Surrounded by all that glorious beauty, I sat there reflecting on the past few years of my life. When had things changed? How could I have done those things? Could I have done better? I was filled with questions, most of which I had no answers for. However, all of my problems had a common theme; alcohol and drugs. I hated the way I behaved when I was under the influence. I was always telling myself to stop or not use as much, but in the end, I would always end up in the same place…in trouble! I must have sat there for several hours thinking about my life and the people in it.

The day slowly turned into evening as I walked back to my dorm. I thought about Father Hymes and what had happened in his office. I wondered how many people who had put their trust in him had also been betrayed. What had happened to their faith? How did they deal with it?

I'm sure I wasn't the first person to ever be betrayed in that way. Even Reggie said he'd done it before. Besides, he was too good, too slick. It was obvious that he'd had a lot of practice. He moved with such skill—a true predator. The way he continued to look at me, I could feel his eyes watching me. I was afraid to be alone. I couldn't trust him, because I wasn't sure how far he would take it. I remembered that day in his office. The hair stood up on the back of my neck and chills ran up and down my spine when I thought about it. I had been nothing more than a lamb in a trap, and he had moved like a tiger, slowly coming up from behind, premeditating every step, ready to pounce. I was very thankful I had been able to get out of there before he'd had the *chance* to pounce!

I looked at my watch as I headed back to the dorm. It read 7:30, and it was dark as I entered the back area of the house where the priest's lived, taking the short cut to my dorm. The lights in the back weren't on, and I didn't want to fall or step in the pool, and being half-blind from my injury as a kid didn't help, so I walked very slowly and deliberately.

"I've been sitting out here thinking about you," I heard a voice in the darkness say.

I stopped in my tracks as I felt panic set in. "That sounded like Father Hymes, but it can't be," I thought. My heart was pounding against my chest so hard that I felt like I was having a heart attack. I tasted blood in the back of my throat. I wanted to ignore him, not wanting to believe he was there. I thought for a brief second that maybe my mind was playing tricks on me, but then he spoke again.

"You miss me?" he asked, then he reached up and grabbed my left arm in an attempt to pull me into him. I tried to fight him off, but I was weak with fear. I felt like a deer in the headlights of a car. "Don't fight it, you know you want to try it." He spun me around and when he did, he tried to kiss me. I turned my face to avoid his kiss. He was laughing and wouldn't stop.

"This guy's crazy!" I thought. I believed my life was in danger. His laugh wasn't a funny laugh—it was an insane one. I could both hear and feel the insanity in that laugh. I was more afraid than ever. I thought that if I didn't get away now, I could possibly be one of those people they find dead on Santa Monica Beach. This thought turned my fear to anger and I started to fight. I fought with all I had in me. I hit him as hard as I could with my fist on the side of his head. I heard the sound of a hollow thud, and his glasses dropped and hit the concrete deck. I felt his arm tightening around my waist.

"Quit fighting, you know you want to try it," he said again. "Stop fighting!" He tried to kiss me again. I started kicking, punching and biting; I was determined to survive. I broke free and ran toward my dorm. I didn't remember entering the building or climbing the two flights of stairs to my room. I just remember being there. I lay down on my bed and curled up into a ball. Within a short time, I fell asleep. I woke up at six the following morning fully dressed. Reggie and Phil were still sleeping when I turned on the television in the TV room on the second floor. I didn't want to be alone, and knowing they were both nearby helped.

Phil walked in around 8:30, wearing the cut offs he had gone to bed in the night before. When he looked at me, he could tell something was wrong. When I started to tell him that Father Hymes was back, Reggie strolled in. Phil turned down the TV and I let them know what had happened. "Shit!" Reggie yelled out, then punched the small pillow he was hugging as I spoke. "What an asshole!" he screamed, punching the pillow again. Then he threw it across the room. Phil agreed with him, but he was more level-headed, trying to work out a solution to the problem at hand. Phil told me I needed to move into a room on the second floor, and that one or both of them would stay with me at all times. I moved that day. Reggie and Phil stayed true to their word and never left my side. I pretty much stayed drunk the rest of my time there. I would often see him staring at me from a distance, but I never talked with Father Hymes again.

Toby A., a friend of my father's, came to see my brother and me. He said he was there to see his wife and was heading back to Phoenix in two days. He asked me if I wanted to catch a ride with him. Both Reggie and Phil were getting ready to go to school, and it was time for me to go. I was tired of looking over my shoulder everywhere I went and I needed to get on with my life. Toby was an alcoholic, sometimes in recovery and sometimes not. I always enjoyed being around him because he was a funny guy. He had a "what the hell" attitude and really didn't give a damn about how people felt about him. I admired that about him.

Two days later, when he pulled up to my dorm at 9:00 in the morning, I was standing outside with my bags packed, talking with Reggie, Phil and my brother. Toby said hello to Steve as he opened the trunk of his 1969 Ford Mustang and put my bags inside. He loved his new car, which his wife had bought for him three months earlier. It was red with white leather seats. Toby and his wife had an interesting relationship. She loved him but she couldn't live with him, so she was happy with his visits three or four times a year.

Steve introduced Reggie and Phil to Toby and then I said goodbye, shaking my brother's hand. He told me to stay in touch. I told him I would. Phil extended his hand, shaking mine, and then pulled me into a hug telling me he'd miss me. I turned to Reggie next and as I put my hand out, he put his arms around me and gave me a bear hug. "I'll see you soon little brother. Don't forget about us." I thought I could see tears in his eyes. I told him I wouldn't. I smiled and he smiled back.

"Are you ready to go back to Phoenix?" Toby asked. I told him I was. "Good, you drive, I don't have a driver's license," He threw me the keys. I jumped in, waved one more time, and drove off.

"Are you in a hurry to get back?" he asked me.

"I'm on your time, nothing pressing on my end," I told him.

"Good, slow down then," he started laughing. We left the L.A. city limits at 11:30 that morning and didn't pull into the Maverick House until 3:00 the following afternoon. We must have stopped for pie and coffee five times, and if Toby liked the waitress, he would hit on her. He got laid twice on the way back.

When I did get clean and sober several years later, I lived with Toby for almost a year, and in that time I'll bet he slept with thirty different women. I came to realize that Toby had a sex addiction that he couldn't face, which would always bring him back to his drinking. When they found him dead in a motel room six months after I had moved out, I was not surprised to hear he had been drinking.

When we arrived at the Maverick House, I called my brother Richard to come and pick me up. I thanked Toby for the ride and Richard took me home to Tempe.

Richard Carter: Passed Away in December of 2005
He was Three Years Sober at the time of his passing.

I spent the next week looking for a job. One day, feeling somewhat discouraged, I decided to visit the old neighborhood. I parked in front of Mary's house. When I knocked, she told me to come in. I walked through the living room and into the kitchen where she was washing dishes. "Back from California, I see." She turned her head around and looked at me.

"Yeah," I told her.

She then let me in on the latest gossip around the neighborhood. She said that Ted and Ida had moved in across the street from her, and that Ida had really fixed up the place and how nice it looked. She finished washing the dishes and was drying her hands when she asked me if I wanted to go over and visit them. I said okay. She took off her apron and hung it over a chair to dry, and then we walked out the front door and over to their house.

I knocked hard about four times before Ted finally opened the door. He was getting ready for work. He was a cook at the "Big Apple" across the street. Ida was feeding little Teddy, their son. "The house looks great," I told Ida.

"There's beer in the fridge." Ted said, as he reached in and handed me one. Ida threw me an opener. "Leave me some for when I get off of work," Ted said. Then he turned toward Ida and his son, kissed them both and said goodbye. He needed to be there at 11:00 to prep for the lunch crowd.

Ida put little Teddy down for a nap and joined Mary and me at the kitchen table. She started telling us about the newest drama that was happening in their love-hate relationship. As I've said before, on our worst day, Glenna and I never had problems such as these. After an hour of listening to Ida vent, Mary and I walked over to Mac and Marge's. On the way, Mary asked me why I listened to Ida complaining about her relationship all the time. She informed me that I was about the only one who would any more. Everyone else had given up on her long before.

I thought about it before I answered. Just before we walked through the back door of the bar, I turned to her and said, "I think I listen to her because when she's finished she looks like she feels better. Nothing really changes, but she feels better."

Mary looked up at me and said, "Sometimes things are just the way they are and you learn to live with it." She reached for the door handle and we both walked in together.

Chapter Twenty-Five

There's Bliss in This Blackout!

To those who understand me, thank you.
To those who tried to understand me, thank you.
To those who couldn't understand me, thank you.
To those who helped me understand, thank you.
I needed what all of you gave me, thank you.
-- *A former addict*

Mary and I were at Mac and Marge's, sitting at the table closest to the front door. I ordered a draft and Mary ordered a Coke. We were talking about this and that, you know, chit chat about nothing at all when Randy walked in looking for me. I invited him over to the table and then ordered him a beer. It wasn't long before the conversation turned to getting high. "It's been awhile," I told him.

"Good" he said, "I think you'll really enjoy this then." He reached into his front pocket and pulled out a joint.

I turned toward Mary and saw that she looked angry. "What?" I asked her with a hint of irritation in my voice.

"Nothing!" she said angrily, and then she stood up, glared at me, and left without another word.

Randy asked me what her problem was. I told him that I didn't know, although I knew she didn't like or trust him, because she thought he was responsible for my drug use. We went outside to his car and jumped into the front seat. Randy pulled out the joint and fired it up. He took a few hits and passed it over to me.

As Randy pulled out of the parking lot going east, I took several hits and then handed the joint back to him. We continued to pass it back and forth until it was almost gone. When I handed it back to Randy for the last time it felt like I was moving in slow motion. I remember Randy turning left into Papago Park, and then I must have blacked out, because the next thing I knew I was waking up naked on thick green carpet in the living room of someone's trailer.

"Hey, anybody here!" I yelled out. There was no answer, so I called out again. In looking around, I noticed that the front door was open but the screen door was closed. I went on a quest in search of my clothes. I looked in every room with no success. All that was there were women's clothes. I thought that was a good sign, and then I laughed out loud. I was concerned, and wondered what to do next. I couldn't leave without my clothes. I sat on the couch with a small pillow in my lap trying to cover what I could. As I sat there, I wondered what I would say to the person that lived there if they came back. I was there for the longest time, and as I sat there, my thoughts began attacking me. My fear was about not knowing how I had wound up there. Maybe I had done something wrong or offensive, and I wondered if that's why they weren't there, or—worse yet—maybe they'd called the police. I was very apprehensive and I wanted to leave. I wasn't sure what to do next, but I knew I had to do something. When I walked into the bathroom, trying to cover myself as best I could with the pillow, I looked behind the door and there I found a pink housecoat hanging on a hook. On the floor next to the bathtub, under the towel rack, was a matching pair of house slippers. Both the housecoat and the slippers had a feather-like material that covered the button area of the housecoat and top area of the house slippers. I put the housecoat on. "Good fit, little short in the arms, but oh well." I looked in the mirror, and then turned completely around to see how I looked. "Not bad." I said under my breath. I put the slippers on and walked out of the bathroom.

I took a deep breath and looked around one more time; still nobody. I headed for the door. I could see no other way. I walked out to the street. There was a gas station on the other side. I looked around to get my bearings, running north and south was a street sign that read, "Stapley." I looked up at the sign, at the street that ran east and west, and it read "McKellips Road." "Good, now I know where I am." I was in Mesa, and my parent's house was two streets north of McKellips on 68th Street in Tempe. A straight shot going west, five miles or so.

I took another breath, and then, as I had done so many times before, I began to pray. I figured I had nothing to lose. I mean He was probably up there laughing his butt off about now anyway. I was sure I looked like a complete idiot. "God, here I am again. Please help me. Pleeeease!" Now let me tell you how much God truly loved me. It appeared as if He was bound and determined to get me through all of this and, once again, he sent one of his Angels to pull me out of another seemingly hopeless situation. As I stood alongside McKellips Road, I stuck out my thumb, and when I did, a white 1963 Chevy pick-up swerved across two lanes of highway and stopped in front of me. The driver looked at me and said, "Get in." With a great deal of humiliation I climbed in and slammed the door. He let out the clutch without saying a word, going in the direction of my home.

I really felt the need to explain, but when I opened my mouth to try, it was as if he already knew what I was about to say. He turned his head toward me and said, "No need to explain kid, I've been there." He then asked me where I lived, and I gave him directions. No words could express how grateful I felt at that moment. He didn't say another word until we pulled into my driveway ten minutes later. He let me out, wished me good luck, and then he backed out of the driveway and continued on his way.

I opened the back door and stepped into the kitchen where my mother and her friend, Marie, were at the kitchen table drinking coffee. When Marie saw me, she almost dropped her cup. She continued to stare as I walked through on my way to my bedroom, my sole intention being to change into something more appropriate as quickly as possible. My mother, on the other hand, acted as if nothing was wrong. She asked me if she could make me something to eat. I wanted to tell her that eating was the last thing on my mind right now, but instead I told her no. Actually, I was too embarrassed to ever show my face again in the presence of her friend.

Richard and Roger were in the living room watching television and when I passed by, Roger looked up at me and asked, "John, is there something you're not telling us?"

"Go to hell," I told him in passing.

He laughed and went back to his TV program.

Once in my room, I changed as quickly as I could into my own clothes. Then I put the housecoat and slippers into a paper bag and threw them in the trashcan in the alley. Two weeks later, a small package was sent from Mesa, AZ. I opened it and found my wallet inside, with a note enclosed that read simply, "Thank you."

Chapter Twenty-Six

My First Born

Kid in the Park
Lonely little question mark
on a bench in the park:
See the people passing by?
See the airplane in the sky?
See the bird flying home before dark?
Homes just around the corner there...
But not really anywhere.
-- *Langston Hughes*

My eldest daughter, Diane Renee, was born on January 5, 1970. Glenna's mother called me at my parents' house to let me know. She said that it was a girl and that Glenna was at the County Hospital.

For the previous several months I'd been avoiding Glenna as much as I could because of how I still felt. I loved her and it was painful to be around her, but now that our daughter was born, I wanted to be with her even more. I was torn; I wanted her back, and I wanted my freedom. What was I going to do? I wasn't even sure she'd have me back. I was afraid that if I asked her she would tell me no, so seeing her again was going to be hard for me. I was feeling extremely anxious about the whole situation, so I asked my mother's friend Marie to go with me for moral support.

When we arrived at the hospital that evening, Glenna was holding our daughter, which was one of the most beautiful things I can ever remember seeing. Glenna had this glow about her that only a new mother could have. My heart was pounding out of control. I wanted to hold her and let her know how much I still loved her. I wanted to say I'd straighten out my life and make things work. Well, that's what I wanted to do, but instead I acted just the opposite. I was indifferent and distant, as if our daughter was no big deal. I watched Glenna's eyes fight back the tears. I behaved like an immature jerk. I could see the pain on her face. She stared at me in disbelief. I was angry with myself, but I directed my anger toward her. I knew she didn't understand why I did what I did, and to tell you the truth, neither did I. I had a beautiful wife and a new daughter right here. All I needed to do was grow up, but I guess I just wasn't ready.

Somewhere deep inside I realized I had nothing to offer her. I didn't want anyone to know I was still having trouble, so I cast all the blame on Glenna. By making her the guilty party, I could avoid any responsibility. In truth, I couldn't let anyone know who I was because I had this entrenched belief that they wouldn't like the real me, so I created a persona in my head of being Mr. Hip, Slick and Cool. Hell, I was so good at playing this role that I believed it myself! I know now that this was clearly an example of self-defeating behavior in the addictive personality. We make our problems out to be about others, and in doing so, we never have to take any of the responsibility or blame.

The tragedy in this particular situation was that Glenna bought the lie. She believed that she was responsible for our problems, so she tried to change herself in hopes of fixing me. But in reality I had put her in a no-win situation and no matter what she did or how hard she tried, it just wouldn't have worked.

I believe that my attitude that day in the hospital was the straw that broke the camel's back. That was when she finally decided that enough was enough. It was over. Our relationship changed and things were never the same between us. A year later we were divorced. I was to pay $200.00 a month in child support, an amount I was already paying before our divorce became final.

After our divorce, the only thing that Glenna and I had in common was our daughter, and I became a weekend father. Now, like all addicts in active use, I loved my daughter, but I had no clue how to build a healthy relationship with her. As a matter of fact, my concept of being a weekend father was to pick her up at her mother's house on Friday night and take her over to my parents. Then I'd spend thirty minutes with her, finding out about her week, and then I'd be off to spend the next two days drinking and getting high with my friends. On Sunday afternoon, I'd sober up enough to pick her up and take her back home.

I also had this false sense of entitlement when it came to our daughter. Now I knew I wasn't parent of the year, but my thinking was that with me paying child support, I should be able to give more input than Glenna was letting me have on the subject of raising Diane. What a joke that was! In truth I was so out of control with my drug use that I couldn't even hold down a job, and for the most part my parents paid my child support for me.

When I first heard that Glenna was dancing in a biker bar across the street from where she lived, I lost it. Of course, I judged her. I wondered, "How could she? What kind of mother would do that?" She also had a new boyfriend named Mike, who was a member of a well-known motorcycle club here in town. His club name was "Caveman," and he wore the name proudly. Glenna moved in with Mike. They lived in a small duplex behind a fire station. Glenna was now drinking more, and after moving in with Mike, she started using heroin. Soon after that, she started selling it to maintain her habit.

Well, being the self-centered, grandiose asshole that I was, I got angry. I didn't feel this was the type of environment my daughter should grow up in. (Like I could have done better at the time.) So I started to cause Glenna and Mike problems. I went out of my way to give them a hard time when I would pick up Diane. I was arrogant and acted like I was better than they were. The sad thing was, at the time I believed it. Again, in truth, I'm sure Glenna had her own problems with her addiction that created problems with our daughter, but all in all, she was a good mother and she took very good care of her. Diane was in good hands—even Glenna's friends loved her, and they were all very protective of her.

In November of 1970 I was introduced to a girl named Jackie. Roger and my brother Rich picked her and her friend Karen up hitchhiking one afternoon. I was attracted to Jackie the first time I saw her, even though she was pregnant when we met. I asked her for a date. It wasn't long before we were living together. My family and several friends warned me not to move in with her, but of course I wouldn't listen.

In December of the same year several tire companies got together to talk about buying a rubber mill. They contacted a company out of Akron, Ohio, and by June of 1971, they were setting up the first working rubber mill in Arizona. I was hired on as their first employee and was involved in every phase of its conception, from the assembly of the mill itself to its operation. I learned a lot about the tire industry and I took my position there seriously. There were concerns about it being too hot in Arizona and how the heat could affect the product outcome, but with a few adjustments, we made it work. The name of the company was "Arizona Strip Stock Incorporated." We called it A.S.S. Inc. for short.

Jackie and I moved into a trailer that she found for us. She was now eight months pregnant and having a hard time getting around. A month later she delivered a beautiful baby girl, Jane. When Jane was two months old we moved again. Our next move was to a duplex behind the Circle K on East Van Buren. I worked my job at Arizona Strip Stock while Jackie stayed home and took care of her daughter. Jackie was a good mother, but I wasn't Jane's father, so unless I was asked, I didn't offer much help.

Because of my position at work, I tried hard to keep my alcohol and drug use under some degree of control. I would get high on weekends and occasionally on weeknights, but that was rare. I was told that if the company continued to do well, there would be opportunity for growth and I might be one of those who would benefit from that growth.

My job was demanding and potentially dangerous. The mill itself had two cylinders, each five feet in diameter, that moved at two different speeds; one very fast and one slow to create a mashing movement. The cylinders were strong enough to break down a ninety-pound bale of raw rubber. With the rollers both turning at different speeds against the bale of rubber, friction was created, which would heat up the rubber so that chemicals could be added and mixed in to complete the product. When I was running the mill I had to stay completely focused. That's why I never used drugs before work, or let my mind become sidetracked by other problems that could distract me. I had to keep my mind on what I was doing.

Not using drugs during work wasn't hard, but I did have one problem that kept rearing its ugly head often and was getting worse. Jackie was very jealous, and she was always accusing me of sleeping around with other women. Of course I wasn't, but if I was ever a few minutes late getting home, or if I ever made the mistake of looking at another woman, she would go off; yelling, hitting and throwing anything in her path. It wouldn't take much to set her off either. Sometimes she would go off two or three times a day. I always had some type of injury from a flying ashtray, plate, or whatever else she had in her hand at the time and, worse yet, I never saw it coming.

Then there were times when she would go weeks without so much as an unkind word. She had her loving side that I really enjoyed. During those times, she'd already have food on the table when I got home from work. She loved to cook, and she was very good at it! She was also a very sensual woman; she gave great body rubs and could make love for hours. As a matter of fact, sex was how we made up when we'd fight. The harder we fought, the more intense our lovemaking became.

My ambivalence was mounting in this relationship. I loved her for how she made me feel when she was kind, and hated her for how she made me feel when she acted out on her jealousy. I was in a constant state of confusion. "How can a person both love and hate at the same time?" was a question I would often ask myself.

Six months after Jane was born, Jackie became pregnant with my second daughter Jenny.

I was working Monday through Friday, ten hours a day. My job was secure and the rubber mill was working well in spite of initial concerns. We were even selling product to other tire companies in the Phoenix area. My relationship was starting to improve and I had another child on the way, so why did I feel so incredibly lonely? I didn't understand it. What was missing? I couldn't tell you. These questions had haunted me most of my life, but at this time it seemed as if the feelings were growing more intense. I tried to ignore them, and for the most part I did well, but there were times when I needed the help of a chemical to put things into their 'proper' perspective.

The duplex we were living in was too small, so we moved again. This time we moved into a larger apartment. It was a small complex with eight units in all. The neighborhood was full of drugs and drug dealers; not the best environment for staying clean in. But the rent was cheap, only $49.50 a month plus utilities. The money we could save would help us get ready for the new baby. Soon after we made the move, a friend named Billy asked if he could stay with us until he could get back on his feet. We had a small room off the kitchen that would be perfect for him. He offered to pay us $20.00 a month, so Jackie and I agreed. Billy was a heroin addict and he was just out of detox. Living with us would help him stay away from the people he got in trouble with. Billy seemed sincere when he said he was through with drugs. I knew he'd been through hell with his addiction. His family was tired of his bullshit and he'd burned all of his bridges with them. I was pretty sure he had hit bottom. Billy moved in that day. He really liked his room—it even had its own entrance, so he wouldn't disturb us with his comings and goings.

We lived in apartment two. Living next door in number three was a Hispanic family: Bobby and Matilda, and their six children, ranging from age three to fifteen. They had moved out here from Echo Park, a suburb of L.A., five months previously. Bobby supported his family and his own heroin addiction by selling drugs, and judging from the traffic going in and out of his apartment, he was doing well.

Of course it didn't take long, with an addict living next door, for Billy to relapse. It was Billy's third week living with us when Jackie came to my work. It was a Thursday afternoon. I was sitting in the office when Jackie walked in with Jane. She said "John, I think there is something wrong with Billy."

"Why do you think that?" I asked.

"Because he just sits in his room, his back against the wall, nodding out, and when I asked him if he was alright, he wouldn't answer. He doesn't look alright to me. He's talking real slow and he keeps scratching his neck and rubbing his face, like Bobby does. John, I think he's using drugs again." I told her that I would talk with him when I got home. She asked me to come home right after work. I told her I'd be there. She thanked me and then she left.

I walked through the door at 5:20 that evening. Jackie was cooking tacos, rice, and beans for dinner. Jane was asleep on the couch. The news was on television, playing low so it wouldn't wake the baby. Jackie pointed to Billy's room. "He's in there in the same position he's been in all day."

"I'll talk to him after dinner." I told her. She put dinner on the table. Before I sat down to eat, I stuck my head into Billy's room and told him dinner was ready. He told me he'd be right there, but he never came.

After dinner, I had my talk with him. I confronted him on his relapse. He denied it. After going back and forth with him for five minutes or so, I got fed up and told him to get out. When I told him to leave, he knew I was serious and he got scared.

"This is the first time since I went through detox," he blurted out. "Bobby from next door turned me on."

I was still angry. I took several deep breaths to calm myself down. "Okay," I thought, "Where do we go from here?" Then it hit me, "Maybe this isn't so bad." I was looking at opportunity dead in the eye. I was thinking, "I could use some walking around money or, even better, some extra money to help with the new baby. I know a lot of people that use drugs and are always looking for a deal. As long as I don't use them myself, I'll be fine. Jackie never has to know, and the drugs will pay for themselves." I was trying to rationalize it all in my head, but my gut was telling me it wouldn't fly. Oh well, I had to try. I was an addict and I moved right into that drug addict logic I was so famous for. The problem with this kind of thinking was that in the long run the logic never worked out.

"Billy" I said, "If you're going to get loaded, you need to be more discrete about it. Don't let Jackie find out. Next time go over Bobby's house. Anywhere but here." I sold out, no doubt about it, but how could I turn down such an opportunity? I had convinced myself I was doing the right thing, so Billy and I went next door to wheel and deal.

I knocked, and Bobby's fifteen-year-old daughter answered the door. She waved us in without saying a word, then walked over to the couch and laid down.

"You need to watch him better and put clothes on him when he's outside!" Bobby was yelling at his wife about their three-year-old son. The neighbors were always bringing him home with no clothes on. I laughed at the thought. I guess this time he was out in the street chasing a cat with only his cowboy boots on, and when the lady from across the street brought him home, Bobby got mad.

Matilda was in the kitchen getting a glass of water for one of their kids when Bobby started yelling at her. She spun around, and she looked angry! Bobby wouldn't stop yelling. She was glaring at him and when she'd had enough, she threw the glass of water at him. It sailed passed his head and broke on the wall behind him. Then she started to yell back, "Fuck you, you piece of shit! I hate you!! Maybe if you helped me with the kids I'd get more done!"

There was glass and water everywhere. He looked back at the wall and then felt his head and face to see if he was cut anywhere. "Matilda," he whined, "You almost hit me."

"Too bad I missed!" She was still angry.

"Matilda, you know I love you," he smiled and held out his arms, offering her a hug. She stuck her nose in the air and walked past him on her way to their bedroom.

"Want me to come back later?" I asked him.

"No man, she'll be fine. What can I do for you?" He told the kids to go watch TV with their sister. Bobby and I talked, while Billy and Bobby's nine-year-old son went into one of the bedrooms to play a game or two of Pong.

"I'd like to do some business with you if you're interested. I know a lot of people who use, and I think I can sell a lot of drugs for you. I can use the extra money, so what do you say?"

He smiled and slapped me on the back. He stuck out his hand and we shook. "Partners," he said.

"Partners," I repeated. We sat at the table and worked out the details. I told him what I thought I could sell for him and he made a list: White crosses, PCP, LSD, and marijuana. He walked into his bedroom and came back out with a jar of crosses. "Here's a thousand. Start out with these and I'll get you more," he told me.

I thanked him and told him that I didn't want Jackie to know what I was doing. He said he'd tell Matilda not to say anything to her. I said goodbye, walked out and put them into the trunk of my car, then went into my apartment.

When I walked in, Jackie was watching the 10:00 news while Jane was asleep on the rug in front of the TV. "How did it go with Billy?" she asked.

I told her, "He admitted it. I let him know how upset it made you. He said he was sorry and that it wouldn't happen again."

"Good, at least that's over with." She gingerly patted me on my butt and asked me if I was tired. I picked up the baby and put her into her crib. Then I took a quick shower and went to bed. Jackie was already asleep when I crawled in. I was tired but couldn't sleep because I couldn't get my mind off the crosses I had in the trunk of my car. I looked at the clock several times before I finally decided to get up around four o'clock. I got dressed, then went into the bathroom and grabbed a bottle of aspirin from the medicine cabinet. I went out to my car and emptied the aspirins out into the street. I then counted out 100 crosses and poured them into the aspirin bottle. I put the rest back in my trunk, all the time rationalizing my behavior.

I went back to my apartment with full intentions of going back to bed, but without thinking, I popped three crosses into my month before I hit the door. Inside my apartment, I took them with a swig of milk, then put the rest of the bottle in my pants pocket. I went to bed and made love to Jackie until 6:30. She cooked me breakfast; I ate, and then I left for work.

When I walked through the door at work, it was almost eight. I turned on the mill to warm it up. Running the mill was a two-man operation. I waited for my co-worker, Gary, to come in; he was scheduled to be there at 9:00. When he arrived, I was in my office already making drug deals. While I was on the phone, Gary checked the oil levels on the mill.

On a good day, we could produce as much as 800 to 1000 pounds of rubber stock in an eight-hour shift, but today wasn't one of those days. I was pre-occupied with my new business and spent too much time on the phone setting up deals. I sold all 900 crosses that day and by the second week, I was making an extra $200. Of course, it didn't take long before all my inactivity at work started to show, and after several warnings to pick up my production, I was let go. Jackie was upset that I lost my job, but she knew that I was having trouble at work with Jim, one of my bosses, so she had already been pre-warned. She expressed concern about no money coming in, but I told her that I had it covered and not to worry.

Now that I had more time, I could build my client base. I already had money stashed, and I was sure I could keep it coming in. I began selling drugs to some of the people at my father's halfway house. Joe O. and Bobby T. were always good for about three ounces of marijuana a week. Joe was a hairdresser and Bobby, his roommate, was a plumber. They were also good for four or five hits of acid a month. Then there was Bonnie, who worked in the office. She would go through three or four racks of speed a week. John P. would buy dime bags of heroin from me if he couldn't score from his regular guy, and there were others who came and went. I was so self-absorbed I didn't have a clue that I was undermining all my father's hard work. I was self-centered and grandiose and it blinded me from seeing beyond my own selfish wants. With all the drugs I was selling there, I was making a pretty good profit. At first, Jackie wondered where all the money was coming from, but she wasn't stupid and I was sure she figured it out. By this time however, I think the money was so good we both avoided talking about it.

My own use increased; I was now using daily. I even tried heroin once with Bobby, but it made me sick, so I never tried it again. Shortly after I tried the heroin, Bobby turned me on to Terpinhydrate, which was cough syrup with codeine in it. It could be bought in any store, over the counter. One day I gave Bobby a ride out to Tempe to drop off a pound of weed. On the way home Bobby pointed to a small pharmacy to his right and asked me to pull in. We went over to the flu section and Bobby handed me two bottles of Terpinhydrate and then he took two more and we went up and pay for them. The cashier looked at us with suspicion but sold them to us anyway. He put our bottles in separate bags then handed them to us. We turned into a liquor store closer to home and bought four pints of Thunderbird wine, and then we headed home. Bobby took one of the bottles of cough syrup from the bag, opened it, and put it up to his mouth. He tipped it back and drank the whole bottle down in three large gulps. His face turned bright red. He then opened a pint of wine and in the same way, being careful not to spill any, put it up to his mouth and drank half of the bottle. He made a face showing his teeth as he pulled back his lips as far as he could. He then shook his head and said, "Damn that's good!" Then he killed the rest of the pint. I pulled up in front of our apartments.

Bobby handed me one of the bottles of cough syrup from my bag. I opened it and then put it up to my mouth, tilted it back and drank the contents of the bottle. It had a sweet-tart, medicine-like taste. I liked it. He handed me a pint of Thunderbird and I drank most of its contents. I felt flushed, and a feeling of well-being came over my body. It took my breath away. When I finally caught my breath, I killed the rest of the pint. I sat there enjoying the feeling. We sat there for maybe ten more minutes, and then Bobby handed me another bottle of each and told me that they were for later. He said he needed to go and thanked me for taking him. I walked into my apartment, put the bottles on the table, and then sat on the couch with the TV on. Jackie and the baby were asleep in the bedroom so

I played it low. After settling in, I started to feel the buzz. I couldn't move; it was almost as if I was moving against the current of fast moving water. I felt a warm tingly feeling, from the top of my head to the bottom of my feet, most intently in my face, neck, and crotch. It was like being on the edge of an orgasm and not being able to get off. I didn't want the feelings to stop. I continued to fight sleep, but with very little success. I finally nodded off. Jackie woke me up at 11:30 and told me to come to bed.

It wasn't long before I was going through several bottles of Terpinhydrate and wine a week. I really enjoyed it. The use of Terpinhydrate became so widely used that they passed new laws saying that stores could only sell two bottles to the same person every other day. We were forced to alternate stores; a pain in the ass, but oh well. I was getting more out of control with my drug use, maybe even more so than ever before.

Jackie had our new daughter, Jenny, at the new County Hospital, on January 8, 1972. I still wasn't working and I had this, "I don't give a shit," attitude. Jackie and I fought daily.

Chapter Twenty-Seven

Busted

"Yeah, the ones you're calling wild
are going to be
the leaders in a little while.
The whole world's waking
to a new-born day and
I solemnly swear that it'll be their way.
You'd better help the voice of youth
find what truth is."
-- *Johnny Cash*

It was April of 1972 when my father called me. He told me there was a matter that needed to be cleared up and he needed my help to do it. He asked me to come over. I had a bad feeling. I tried to pump him for more information, but he wouldn't tell me over the phone. "Just come over now," he said, "and let's get to the bottom of this." I was paranoid and didn't want to go, but he insisted. I just knew I was busted. I don't know how I knew, but I did. Drug addict intuition, I guess. I wondered who told on me. Was it Joe, Bobby or someone new? I couldn't figure it out.

When I pulled up to the Maverick House, sitting in the front yard was Jim, my father's counselor, and Bonnie, who bought speed from me. My father was coming out of the office with a cup of coffee when I walked up. When I looked at Bonnie she couldn't look me in the eyes. "She's the one," I thought. It's funny, I had never thought she'd be the one. She and I went back a few years; I wouldn't have believed that she would betray me.

When I walked over to my father, he held out his right fist and opened it to reveal what looked like a rack of speed I had sold to Bonnie just two days before. "What are these?" he asked me in a rather loud, angry voice.

"Don't know, what are they?" I said, more scared than angry. I looked at Bonnie again.

She kept her eyes trained on the ground. She kicked at the grass. Jim sat there with his legs crossed and his left hand on his chin, watching as my dad and I talked.

"Where did they come from?" He was trying to contain his anger.

Again, I played dumb. "I don't know, where did they come from?" My fear turned into anger at being caught. Jim looked like he didn't know what to do and my father looked like he didn't know where to take it next. I don't think they expected me to respond this way and it threw them off. I had them, so I continued being hostile. I started to yell, "Why are you asking me?, I don't even know what they are. Hell, I've never seen them before and don't know anything about them." I got right up in my father's face. "Why, did someone say I gave it to them?" I looked at him; he didn't know what to do. He had been caught completely off guard.

"That's bullshit!" I screamed.

My father tried to calm me down. Bonnie walked away. She was pissed. Jim sat there not saying a word.

Then my father said, "Look son, I had to ask." He looked ashamed.

Pretending to be hurt, with my head down, I said, "I don't understand. I thought Bonnie and I were friends." I left it at that. I walked back to my car, got in, and drove off. I wasn't sure they believed me, but nothing more was ever said. I never saw Bonnie again. I don't know what happened to her. I never asked, mainly because I didn't care.

I thought, after that, I needed to be more cautious when it came to selling drugs to the people at the Maverick House. I became more selective, and they had to come to my apartment to pick them up. I didn't want any more trouble. Shortly after Joe and Bobby relapsed I stopped selling drugs to Maverick House people all together.

The last time I sold drugs to anyone at Maverick House was to Jimmy, a pothead and alcoholic. I sold him a couple of hits of Orange Sunshine, and then we went tripping together. I told my father I was going to a 12-step meeting for addicts and asked if Jimmy could come along. He was just happy that I was going and rewarded me with Jimmy's company. I now owned a light blue VW Bug convertible that I had bought from Bobby. That was the second car I'd bought from him because he always gave me a good deal, probably because I was Skip's son and he loved my dad. Jimmy and I drove around the corner from the Maverick House and stopped. I handed him the two hits of acid he had bought from me earlier and he put them in his mouth. I took two hits myself. I let him drive. I was flying by the time we hit the outskirts of Phoenix, heading into the college town of Tempe. Tempe is the home of Arizona State University (A.S.U. was known for its beautiful co-eds). As we crossed over the bridge, I was tripping hard. It felt like we were driving so slow that I accused him of stopping. I was starting to freak when the bridge appeared to be moving up and down, like the belly of a fat man sleeping. I was afraid that something bad was about to happen. I was beginning to hyperventilate while Jimmy tried to talk me down.

"John, you need to cool it!" he yelled. He was trying to reassure me that he was in control and that everything was alright. It began to rain as we crossed over the bridge, heading into downtown Tempe. Jimmy found a parking place and we pulled into it. We climbed out of the car and walked around for a while.

Jimmy and I were talking with two co-eds in front of the Valley Art's Movie Theater. That was the last thing I remember before waking up in three feet of water, in my car by myself, in the Indian Bend Wash in Scottsdale. My car was moving sideways following the current. A tow truck was hooking a winch to my front bumper so he could pull me out. After he had done so, he asked me for the $15.00 he said I had promised him. I didn't remember that, but I was glad to do it!

I waited thirty minutes, started my car, and drove to my parents' house. I went to sleep on their couch. I woke up the following afternoon around 1:00. My parents were at the kitchen table; my father was drinking his coffee and my mother her Mountain Dew. "Good morning," I said. They both nodded. Then my father asked me how the meeting was.

I was still clouded from the night before, but then I remembered he was talking about the 12-Step Meeting I told him Jimmy and I were going to last night. "The meeting was good, I learned a lot." I told him.

"Jimmy didn't come home last night." He was fishing for information. "Do you know what happened?" he asked.

"I kinda wondered what happened to him myself when he left the meeting to smoke a cigarette and never came back in. Someone said they saw him talking with Della outside. I looked for him for about thirty minutes or so. I guess he went home with Della."

My father said okay, and then put his coat on to leave. Before he walked out the door he said, "If he comes back, I'll let you know," and I thanked him.

I never saw Jimmy again, nor did he contact the Maverick House to pick up his things. I hope that nothing happened to him, but I guess I'll never know. I felt things were beginning to get out of hand with the people at the Maverick House. I had never felt right about it anyway, so I stopped selling to them all together.

It was mid-September of 1972. One day I woke up sick to my stomach. I had never been so sick in my life. I couldn't stop throwing up and I was weak; it took all the strength I had to even hold my head up. I thought I had the flu, but when I looked at myself in the bathroom mirror and my eyes were bright yellow, I knew I was in trouble. I had a high fever and was having a difficult time urinating. When I did go, it smelled bad and it was a caramel color. I had been around enough addicts to know what was going on. I couldn't take being as sick as I was, so I went to Jackie's doctor in Tempe. After several tubes of blood had been drawn and tested, my suspicions were confirmed when I was told that I had hepatitis.

"Have you drank or used any drugs in the past three months?" the doctor asked me. Of course I lied. I told him I drank one time a few weeks ago, and that I only tried drugs once in my life and that was marijuana when I was sixteen years old. I didn't think he believed me. It could have been that sideways look he gave me or maybe my own paranoid thinking. In any event, he gave me a special diet and told me I was going to be sick and that it needed to run its course. The doctor was true to his word. I was sick for well over two months. I was told to drink a lot of fluids because of my dehydration; he didn't want me to end up in the hospital.

Being so sick I couldn't really do much business, and the money I had stashed away was soon gone. With no money coming in, it put a lot of pressure on my relationship with Jackie because we were starting to get behind on our bills. It wasn't long before we were fighting more.

A month into my illness Jackie told me she had a job. She would start working at Bagdad's Plastics the following day. "Since you're so sick, my mother will watch the kids," she told me. She appeared cold and distant. When I asked her to tell me more about her job, she didn't want to talk. I felt helpless. I was sick and couldn't help my family. I was no longer in charge, and I hated feeling that way.

For the next month, I either laid in bed and slept or I was in the bathroom being sick. I still couldn't hold any food down, and in a little over two months, I had lost forty pounds.

With more testing and several doctor visits later, the doctor told me, "John, with all the drugs you claim you never did and probably some of the drinking you say didn't do either, along with your hepatitis, you now have major liver damage." I thought he was being an asshole. He continued, "So if you are ever thinking about using, don't! It could kill you." Well, I have to tell you, that scared me. Liver damage at my age? That was something only alcoholics developed when they got old, I thought. But I was just twenty-one. The doctor had to be wrong.

It was a good two months before I could eat again. Soups and small meals at first helped me gain the strength I needed to get better. After thinking about what the doctor told me about my liver, I made a decision to cut down on my drug use and just drink. "I'll stay away from the hard stuff and only drink beer. That won't hurt me. Problem solved," I thought. So, beer was all I drank. This lasted about thirty days before I got high again. One weekend I was feeling like my old self. I took several crosses to help me stay awake as I partied from Friday to Sunday afternoon.

Jackie and I were still fighting; this time it was because she was working and she wanted me to watch the kids, since I was better now. I couldn't understand why; I felt like she was trying to control me, and I wasn't having any of that, so we fought.

I decided that fighting was the perfect excuse I needed to justify walking out and getting high that weekend. I started out by taking five crosses as I drove over to Mary's house. On the way, I stopped and picked up a six-pack. I walked into her living room and saw Leonard, Tooter and Denny sitting there watching TV. Mary was coming out of her bedroom, and when she saw me she smiled. I took a beer and handed the pack to the rest of the guys. Mary was drinking a Coke so she declined. Denny walked into the kitchen to get an opener. He opened his beer in the kitchen, then walked back into the living room and handed the opener to me.

Mary was in rare form that night. She was really showing off; telling dirty jokes and flirting with me. We all pooled some money together and the guys walked over to Mac and Marge's to buy more beer. They were back in less than ten minutes with a case of Coors. We each took a six-pack and sat in the living room talking and drinking until 11:30. That's when Leonard announced he had to go because he needed to work in the morning. "Do you guys want a ride?" he asked Tooter and Denny. They both said yes. That left Mary and me alone.

We sat there talking in the living room for a while. She then went into her bedroom and called me in. When I walked in, she was lying on her bed. I asked her what she wanted, she told me that her mother wouldn't be home that night, and her father was still out of town. Before she finished talking I had my clothes off and she was starting on hers. We were up until 5:30 in the morning, having sex and playing. I didn't climb out of bed until two that afternoon.

I jumped out of the shower and was toweling off when she walked in with a cup of coffee. She told me she'd made breakfast and that it was on the kitchen table, then she disrobed and jumped into the shower herself. About the time I took my last bite, Mary stepped into the kitchen fully dressed with a towel wrapped around her shoulder-length blonde hair.

"What are your plans today?" Mary asked me.

"None," I told her. "Why?"

"Don't know, just wondering," she said. We talked for a while longer, then she starting clowning around. "We sleep together and now you're done. I feel cheap." We both laughed. I was really okay with this arrangement and I truly believe that she was, too.

"I thought I'd go over to the bar and hang out, wanna come?" I asked her.

"Go ahead. I'll see you over there later. I need to clean up around here first." She took my plate and cup and walked over to the sink.

I took five more crosses, told her I'd see her there, and left. It was 3:20 p.m. when I walked through the back door of Mac and Marge's. I sat at the bar and Marge put a draft in front of me. I took a five dollar bill out and handed it to her. They were cleaning the stage area, because every Saturday night at 7:00 one of the local bands came in and played. I stayed for the show and then went back to Mary's house and slept on the couch until the next morning.

I knew Jackie would be mad when I got home, but I didn't much care. I had that "screw it" attitude and told myself I was tired of her shit anyway. We argued daily, and quite frankly I was tired of it. If she didn't like it she could leave. I'm sure that subconsciously I knew I was wrong, but that was just too bad.

When I pulled into our driveway, I had a bad feeling. When I walked into the front door, the house was quiet. It didn't look like anyone was home. I walked into the kitchen to see what I could find.

As I entered the doorway—whack! "What the hell?" I saw a flash of light, and the next thing I knew I was on the floor. I looked up to see Jackie standing over me with a cast iron skillet in her right hand.

"Where the hell have you been?" she screamed. She had this wild, venomous look in her eyes that sent chills through my body. "You piece of shit, you could have called! I hate you!"

I was dazed and somewhat confused, but as I started gathering some of my senses I could see that she was angrier than I'd ever seen her before. She was still holding the skillet over me, so I had to be careful about what I said. I knew I was still in danger of her flipping out on me again, and that could prove to be fatal. "I'm sorry," I blurted out. I held my arm out to protect me in case she came at me again.

"You'd better be!" She raised the skillet higher. "You bastard!" She threw the skillet at me, and it hit the floor next to my head. Blam!! It scared the shit out of me!

"Baby, I'm sorry. I didn't mean to hurt you. Leonard, Tooter, Denny and I all drove up to Vegas." When I stood up, there was blood flowing from the gash on the left side of my head. I was covered in it. "I just got caught up in the thrill. I'd never been there before. You know I'm sorry." I had blood all down the left side of my shirt. She was really upset, but when I walked over to her she held out her arms, and the next thing I knew we were entangled in some of the most bizarre sex I had ever experienced.

Now that she was no longer angry, she bandaged my head, and I took four aspirins for the massive headache I had going. She left to go pick up the kids over at her mother's house and I fell asleep on the couch.

Chapter Twenty-Eight

My First Treatment Program

Jonathan Livingston Seagull
"Don't be harsh with them, Fletcher Seagull.
In casting you out, the other gulls have only
hurt themselves, and one day they will know
this, and one day they will see what you see.
Forgive them, and help them understand.
-- *Richard Bach*

My father asked me to take a ride with him one Thursday afternoon. He never spent time with me, so I went along hoping to help our relationship. We stopped in front of a very large white house with a sign over the front door that read "Maverick House."

"Let me show you around," he said. We were greeted by a balding young man. He was wearing a leather hat with sandals to match, Levi bell bottom pants, a flowered shirt, and he was carrying a man's leather bag that looked more like a woman's purse. My first impression was that he was gay and that I needed to watch out for him. My father introduced us. "This is John, my son, the one I've been telling you about." He shook my hand. Then my father turned to me and said, "John, this is Mike." I nodded as I continued shaking his hand.

I was becoming suspicious. Something was definitely not right here. I didn't know the Maverick House had a drug treatment program. Mike asked me to take a walk with him. As we walked, he started asking me personal questions about my drug use. I was very careful not to incriminate myself. As we talked, things started to make more sense. It didn't take a brain surgeon to see what was going on. We walked completely around the block and ended up in front of the Maverick House again. He had grilled me pretty good, but I was on guard—I had an answer to every question he asked. I told him I didn't have a drug problem and that I had never even seen a drug other than marijuana. I admitted I tried it once or twice but didn't like how it made me feel. Mike just listened as I continued talking. "Look, I have a few brews now and then and I'll admit there has been a time or two when I drank too much, but that's it—nothing major."

I was convinced he was buying it, but then he asked, "Why do you think your father is so concerned about you?"

I was taken aback by the question. "I really couldn't tell you. Maybe it was because I went over to the Maverick House a few times when I'd had too much to drink and got a little stupid." God was I good. I should have been a salesman. "That's really the only thing I can think of, but that happened over two years ago. I thought he had forgotten about it." I continued to talk and Mike continued to listen. I was sure he was buying it hook, line and sinker. I had him where I wanted him, or so I thought. It was about this time that I noticed my father's car wasn't where he had parked it. As a matter of fact, it was gone. It was then that I realized I'd been set up. It was all planned out ahead of time.

I was angry but I didn't say anything. When we got to the door, Mike opened it and invited me in. He started showing me around, when we reached the sleeping area he said, "This is your bedroom, pick out a bed." He pointed to a set of bunk beds on one side and a single bed on the other wall. "Are you hungry? If you are, the kitchen is at the end of the hall. Help yourself." I was angry, but tried not to show it. He told me to settle in and that my things would be brought to me tomorrow. I wondered who all was involved in this scheme.

"This is bull!" I said out loud.

Mike closed the door behind him. I was sitting on my bed with my head in my hands, thinking about my situation, when I heard a knock at the door. I called out, "Come in." It was Mike again. He told me there was a group meeting at seven and that I needed to be there.

At about five o'clock, people started arriving home from work. A few of them introduced themselves. One of them was a Hispanic man named Tony, who identified himself as a heroin addict, and asked me why I was here.

"I'm here because I was set up by my father and God knows who else." I was angry just talking about it.

"That's not right," he said. Of course I agreed. He excused himself and was back in less than a minute. "It's getting to be group time," he told me, and then he held out his closed hand and said, "Here." He handed me two hits of Orange Sunshine. "Group's a lot more interesting when you're tripping," he said.

I couldn't agree with that more, so I took them. "Thanks," I said, and I walked out with him to the living room. There were seven of us including Mike, who was the group leader. There were three women from across the street and the three of us living here.

Mike had us identify ourselves as we went around in a circle. I remember him asking who wanted to talk. A girl named Jeanie spoke first, and she told the group how her drug use had come between her and her family. As she talked her voice changed. It sounded further away, then I realized it was the acid kicking in. I noted a large picture over the mantel above the fireplace. It looked like an Indian chief in full headdress. The left side of the chief's head was starting to melt. All the colors on that side were running together into a stream, and then into a puddle that gathered along the edge toward the bottom of the picture. I was completely engrossed in the melting Indian head. I tried redirecting my thoughts by changing my focus. I remember thinking I was going to be caught if I didn't cool it. The next thing I remember is waking up next to Jackie the following morning. I was a bit confused about what had happened, but glad I was home. I was angry with my family for their interference.

I didn't have any contact with them for almost three weeks. When I did speak to them, my experience at Maverick House was only mentioned, but never talked about.

The fighting between Jackie and I continued to escalate and become more violent. I was drinking a lot, and my chemical use was more out of control than ever. I had slowed down on the Terpinhydrate, but I was using more speed.

I was also becoming paranoid, probably because of all the speed I was doing. When I wasn't loaded on drugs, I was drinking. I began having major anxiety attacks. These attacks would haunt me several times a day, both day and night. I never knew when they would hit. I only knew that they would render me helpless and I hated feeling that way. Yes, life sucked, and if the truth be known, it had been that way for what seemed like a very long time now.

I hated my life. When I wasn't using something, I would have a panic attack, and when I was high, I no longer enjoyed it. I needed to be high to feel even half-way normal. I was afraid much of the time and I didn't know why. I would tell myself to stop, but no matter what I did, the feelings only got worse. I became angry with myself for being so weak and out of control. I was losing it fast. I went to bed with these feelings and woke up with them, if I could sleep at all. I couldn't turn it off, and speaking of getting high, I couldn't even do that. When I used I didn't feel high, I just didn't feel. I was numb.

I felt lost at this point in my life; I couldn't even make decisions. I was rapidly losing all hope of ever pulling out of it. Jackie was beginning to ask what was wrong. Of course I would deny that I was having any problems. I didn't want anyone to know. What I was experiencing was in and of itself a severe form of depression. I was pretty sure Jackie could see that there was something seriously wrong with me, no matter how hard I'd try and hide it.

I was having difficulty putting a sentence together. I knew what I wanted to say, but my mind was racing so fast I couldn't get it into words before the thought would just fly by. I was aware of all that was happening to me, but knowing it only made it worse. My awareness only made me more self-conscious. I began to hide from people so they couldn't see what was happening to me. I felt like I was on a fast train going in the wrong direction and I couldn't get off. My panic attacks were getting worse, and the thought of killing myself entered my mind several times a day. I couldn't turn it off. I felt totally and completely hopeless, scared, and alone. What's more, I didn't trust anyone, not even my family.

I had this feeling of detachment—nothing appeared real anymore. The problem was that I'd been feeling this way for a very long time. I was stuck in a hell I couldn't get out of. I wanted out so badly, but I couldn't find the door. I was looking for a tiny bit of hope, something to hang onto to help me get through this.

Several months before this, my mother had given me a small green piece of felt that was enclosed in plastic. On one side of the felt was a picture of the Virgin Mary, and on the other side was a picture of Jesus hanging on a cross. I found it in a junk drawer one day when I was looking for something. It was a message from God, an answer, some hope; it was something I could hold on to. It helped me get my mind off the emotional hell I was in. I carried it with me everywhere. I didn't care what I was doing, it was always with me. It was the only tangible proof that there might be the slightest bit of hope for me. I was on the edge. I would tell myself, "Five minutes. Please God, just five more minutes." This was how I lived, day in and day out.

I bought a gun one day from a neighbor. He knocked on my door asking me if I wanted to buy it. He was $20.00 short and he needed to sell it to make his rent. It was a cheap .38 caliber five shot and it was already loaded. I gave him the twenty and asked him not to tell anyone I had it. Jackie already thought I was crazy and would tell me so several times a day, so I didn't want her to know I'd bought a gun.

I hid it in the bathroom underneath the sink. It was wrapped in a small hand towel and then in a large coffee can, way in the back of the sink cabinet. I couldn't tell you how many times through the course of any given day that I would go into the bathroom, take that gun out its hiding place, and put in my mouth. I was convinced that I just couldn't take another minute of living this way. There were times I would keep it in my mouth for up to an hour, trying to gather enough courage to pull the trigger. I can still taste the gun metal that I tasted so many times before, contemplating those many hours, trying to put myself out of this miserable existence. In the end, I just couldn't do it. Somehow, I would convince myself that, just maybe, things would be better tomorrow. Of course, they never would be, but I kept hoping.

I was emotionally bankrupt. If there was a way out of this suicidal hell, I couldn't see it. So I stayed stuck. Looking back now, I've often wondered if those who have never kissed the edge of suicide like I have can truly understand the limited choices I felt that I had. Since I felt I couldn't trust anyone, that distrust kept me from the people who really cared.

I thought it would be wonderful to escape this nightmare, but then I thought that escape would just put me squarely back into the hell that had driven me there to begin with. I was trapped in a cycle I didn't know how to break, and I was its slave.

One Sunday evening around 9:00, I sat drinking a beer in front of the television. I couldn't tell you what I was watching because my mind was racing, and I couldn't turn it off. I drank so much that I finally passed out. I was awakened by sounds of my daughter Jenny crying. I watched Jackie walk out of our bedroom and into the girls' room. Jackie changed her, then went into the kitchen to warm her bottle. I followed them into the kitchen, and took a beer out of the refrigerator. Then I sat at the kitchen table. While Jackie fed Jenny, I drank a beer.

Knowing our relationship was in trouble and had been for a while now, it was not uncommon for us to be in the same room for hours and not talk. This night was no different. I continued to drink long after they went to bed. Jackie woke up at seven and got the kids ready to take over to her mother's house so she could go to work. When she came into the kitchen, she asked me, "Have you been there all night?" The tone in her voice expressed the disgust she had for me. I didn't want to fight with her, so I ignored her. She left for her mother's house at 7:45.

I continued drinking until late in the afternoon, my thoughts running away. I tried to stay focused; the beer helped. Then this thought came to me. "I must be crazy. That's it. I'm not firing on all cylinders and I need help." That's when I decided to walk up to the State Hospital and commit myself, and so with nothing more than the clothes on my back, I headed in the direction of the State Hospital. With every step I took, I became more convinced that this was what I needed to do. I used to listen to my mother talk about her patients and their bizarre behaviors. The more I remembered what she said about them, the more I just knew this was my answer.

I walked to the entrance, then up the long driveway to the guard station and announced that I was here. Standing inside was a gentleman who looked to be about fifty-five years of age, or so. He was dressed in guard uniform, wearing a brown jacket with yellow lettering over the left pocket that read, "Arizona State Hospital." A nametag on the right side said that his name was "Ted."

"Can I help you?" Ted asked.

"I need help," I told him.

"What's the problem?" he was all business, not appearing to be the least bit concerned. He never even looked up at me.

I got angry at his apparent disinterest. "Hey look man, my mind is really screwed up and I need help, okay?" I was losing control.

"You're drunk and you need to leave." Then he pointed to the street.

I was not happy. He was not hearing me, so I repeated myself. "Listen man, I need help and I need to be admitted." Again, he told me to leave. "Screw you, man!" I yelled.

He then picked up the phone receiver and dialed 7-1-1. I stood there as he helped the person behind me, ignoring me. It wasn't long before a State Hospital van pulled up with more guards. I watched the side door open up and two guards jumped out. Then both front doors opened and two more guards climbed out. The guard driving the van walked up to me. He stood towering over me by about a foot, and then he pointed to the street and yelled at me to leave.

I was confused and didn't know what to do. I got even angrier. "Screw you, too!" I yelled out. They then escorted me off the property. I was devastated. I couldn't believe what had just happened. I walked home with my head down and my feelings hurt. I was thinking, "I know I'm crazy, Jackie thinks I'm crazy, my neighbors suspect that I'm crazy, but I couldn't convince the people at the State Hospital that I'm crazy." What a loser I was. I now felt completely hopeless.

Soon after my experience at the State Hospital, I think I gave up hope of ever recovering from the emotional hell I was in. The thoughts of killing myself continued to haunt me. I didn't feel I had any reason to hang on, but I didn't have the courage to end it. I think it was at this time that I just stopped trying and gave in to my despair. I wouldn't leave my apartment, not even to take out the garbage. I was always afraid, and when I would try to leave, it would trigger a panic attack. If I used any drugs at all, other than alcohol, it was when my friends would bring them over. And using them, at this point in my life, seemed to only make me feel worse, so I started to tell them no. They could see there was something wrong with me, no matter how hard I'd try to hide it, so they would come over less and less.

I wouldn't take a bath or shower and I'd wear the same clothes for weeks at a time. I was living in an apartment with three other people and I was oblivious to their presence. I was obviously depressed and existing on borrowed time, and I knew it.

Chapter Twenty-Nine

God, Where Are You Now?

"There are two types of people in this world;
smart people and intelligent people.
Smart people learn by their own mistakes,
and that's good, but intelligent people learn
by other's mistakes and that's better."
-- *Wallace L. "Skip" Carter*

Two months after the State Hospital fiasco I was sitting on the couch one afternoon, wallowing in my despair, when I began thinking about all the times in my life that I had resorted to prayer when my life got out of control. I realized that I hadn't prayed in a very long time. Well, my life was more out of control than ever before, so I prayed. I prayed like I'd never prayed before. "God, I know I've asked you for help so many times, and when things got better I wouldn't follow through. I am sorry for that, but this time I need you more than ever. Please help me."

I realized I was pleading, but I didn't care. I truly believed this was my last hope. I prayed harder than I had ever prayed before. I prayed with my heart, and it felt good. I was beginning to feel a ray of hope as I sat there, and then I heard a knock at the door. I started to freak. I quickly moved back into my denial, and I panicked. I rushed over to the window and peeked through a crack between the curtains, trying not to move them. It was Black Wally and Jim B., friends of my father.

"What do they want?" I wondered. I tried to be real quiet. I didn't want them to know I was home.

There was more banging followed by Jim yelling, "John, we know you're in there, and we're not leaving until you talk to us." They continued knocking and yelling out my name. They wouldn't leave so I finally opened the door, but I kept the screen door locked.

"Hi guys," I said, trying to keep my composure.

"John, your father's worried about you. He hasn't heard from you in a couple of months." Jim put his face up to the screen, cupping his eyes with his hands trying to get a better look inside.

"Tell my father I'm fine. I've just been busy is all, and I'll call him when I get the chance." My voice cracked.

Then Wally put his head up to the screen door and yelled, "Bullshit, I ain't buying it. Your father thinks you're in trouble, and we were sent to find out and that's what we're going to do."

I was feeling anxious, and that anxiety quickly turned into a panic attack. I tried to close the door, but Jim must have anticipated my next move.

He pushed his hand through the screen door, putting a hole in the screen and pushing on the other door, preventing it from closing all the way. Then he forced himself through with Wally at his heels. Jim could see I was in trouble. He had me sit on the couch. Then he spoke in a calming voice, letting me know he was aware of what was happening to me. "Now slow down your breathing, okay?"

I started to breathe more evenly. Knowing he was one of my father's counselors at the Maverick House helped. He told me to close my eyes and to just concentrate on his voice. I did what I was told.

Then he said to picture a body of water, like a river, or ocean. "Now, concentrate on the water. What color is it?"

"A light blue-green," I told him.

"Can you see and hear the waves, the up and down motion? Can you feel the spray of the water as the waves break along the shoreline?" I was so engrossed in listening to his voice as he took me through this meditation that it completely brought me through my attack.

I then poured out to Jim and Wally the truth about what had been going on with me.

They both sat there and listened to me talk. Jim sat next to me and Wally was in the recliner across from me. I told them everything; all the drugs I'd used, the problems I was having with Jackie and my thoughts of suicide. When I finished I looked over at Jim. I half expected him to tell me I was nuts. Well, I already knew that. Instead, Jim asked me if I wanted help. I told him that I was ready. He said okay, but that I had to trust him. Wally agreed to help in any way he could.

Trust was still an issue but I was desperate. I knew I couldn't do this on my own—I had already tried, quite obviously with very little success. So I took a risk. I needed the help and they seemed sincere, so I told them that I'd do whatever they asked me to do. Besides I needed to trust someone, because if I didn't I knew I'd be dead soon. Jim asked me more about my symptoms. He told me he'd worked with people before with similar problems. He asked for some paper. All I had were some white paper napkins I took from the napkin holder sitting on the kitchen table. I handed him a couple, then he took a pen from his shirt pocket and started to write.

"This is what I think is happening to you," he explained, as he wrote on the napkins. What he told me made perfect sense. He called it the depression cycle. I believe that what Jim showed me that day saved my life, and although I had several relapses after that, I still believe that was the beginning of my recovery. He also explained that along with my depression, the inability to cope and all the chemicals I'd used in my lifetime, I was now suffering from an anxiety disorder more commonly known as "panic disorder." I felt relief knowing that I was not alone, and that what was happening to me could be explained. As he talked, I just knew that I was going to be okay. I didn't know how or when, but for the first time in a very long time, I felt some hope. We talked for a while longer, and then they announced that they had to leave. Jim assured me he'd be back the following day, and then they both left. That night I found myself actually looking forward to the next day, and seeing them again.

Jim came to my house the following day. We talked more about my fears and other symptoms that I'd had over the past few months. The more we talked, the more relief I felt. He expressed genuine concern, and with his help, I felt safe, something I hadn't felt for a while. Just before he left, he asked me if I felt better about my situation. I told him that I did. That's when he asked me for my gun. He reminded me that I had agreed to trust him, so I told him where it was. He took it with him when he left. Each day either Jim or Wally would come over and spend at least an hour with me, long enough for me to know that they were there for me. They made no demands, just let me talk and gave me reassurance. My panic attacks came less often, and the thought of killing myself was replaced with hope and the dream of getting my life on track. Each day I waited with anticipation for their visits. Then the day came when Jim felt I was ready to leave my apartment. I was scared. I wasn't convinced that I was ready, but knew I needed to try.

When I stepped outside my apartment I immediately began hyperventilating, my throat felt like it was closing and I was sweating profusely. I wanted to run back inside, but I didn't. I was not going to give in to my fear—not this time! Somehow, I knew that if I didn't take a stand, it would be over for me.

Jim could see I was in trouble, so he started to talk me down. He reminded me that I was in control and that I needed to go at my own pace. He went on to say, "John, all I ask is for you to go as far as you think you can go, and then, one step further. You can do it."

"I'll try," I told him, but I was terrified. I knew that trusting him was more crucial then ever before.

"That a boy, John," he said, "I just knew you could do it." I knew that I was at least willing. I stood outside my apartment for about ten minutes before I was ready to go back in. Not bad for my first day. Jim agreed. He then said, "Now see if you can make it just one minute more. I'll time you." He looked down at his watch. That minute felt like an hour, but I made it. "You did real well out there today. I'm really proud of you," he told me when we went back inside, which gave me even more hope.

The next day I not only stayed outside for thirty minutes, but I also walked out to the street. I didn't step out in the street, but getting there was a major accomplishment for me. I proceeded the next day with more confidence. I sat outside, in my yard, talking with Jim and Wally.

Jim expressed how he felt about working for my father as a counselor at the Maverick House. "Your father's a wonderful man to work for," he told us. "I love my job, and I'd like to think I help a lot of people." As he spoke I could see the joy in his eyes. Wally and I sat there, listening intently, as Jim talked.

Wally looked tired. He worked a full time job for either the city or the county, I really didn't know. He also spent a lot of time helping others with their recovery. Wally once told me, "You can't keep it unless you give it away." I didn't understand what he meant by that until years later. We sat there and talked for over an hour.

When Jim announced that he had to leave, I realized that I had spent all that time enjoying myself and not being afraid. I was on the road to recovery.

A few days later, I was able to cross the street. When I reached the other side, I felt confident that I was going to be okay. I was able to develop the knowledge I needed to help me divert a panic attack before I lost control. I also learned that stress triggered them, so I worked on limiting the stress in my life by talking about things before they had a chance to become stressful, and by using the stress reduction exercises that I had learned from Jim.

Within the month, I was meeting Jim and Wally at the Maverick House several times a week. Some days were better than others, but, for the most part, I was coping. I was also attending a few 12-Step meetings there—this time with a new attitude.

One day Jackie came into the living room as I was putting on my coat, getting ready to go to the Maverick House for a meeting. She told me she didn't like me much anymore. That I was more like one of her children and that she had lost respect for me. I couldn't say I blamed her. Let's face it, I was not the man she signed up to be with, and now that I was in recovery I was growing, but not in the direction she was hoping for.

A few days later, we had a huge fight about why I was going to "those dumb meetings." That was it for me. I walked out with nothing more than the clothes on my back. My father told me that I could move into a motel he had rented from the county called the Stone Motel. His plan was to move the old Maverick House there because they were expanding and needed more room. The place needed major repairs that could take over a year to complete, so he said he'd let me stay there to help watch the place.

"You can stay in number nine," he told me. I thanked him as he handed me the key.

Then he walked me out of the office and said, "You know my secretary Ilene lives next door in number eight." I said I did know her but not very well. "Good! Keep it that way. She's a very sick woman." I told him I'd keep my distance.

Now Ilene was a very attractive woman—she was 5'-6" tall, 110 pounds, and she had shoulder length blonde hair. She was thirty-two years old—eleven years older than I was. She also happened to be one of the most attractive—and by far the sexiest—women I had ever been around. She was hot! She lived next door with her three sons. When I got to know her better she told me she had two other sons who lived with their father. Now, honest to God, I had full intentions of honoring my father's request for me not to get involved with her, so I avoided her as much as I could. I really didn't want the stress of another relationship anyway.

I got a job as a helper hanging sheet rock with Pete, a resident of Maverick House. He said he'd teach me the trade if I wanted to learn. It was tough work, and I worked really hard. Two weeks later, I had a second job unloading trucks and stocking the job sites with the sheet rock to be hung. I was working sixty hours a week. When I'd get off of work I would be tired, so when I'd get home, I would take a shower, which would help to refresh me, and then I'd go to a meeting. After the meeting I'd come home and go to bed. I was finally back in control of my life (or so it seemed) and I really felt I was doing well.

After one very demanding day at work I was more tired than usual. When I got home I climbed into the shower, hoping it would refresh me enough so that I would be able to continue with my daily routine of going to a meeting. I owed my life to that program and the people in it and I didn't want to slack off now. As I got out of the shower and began to dry myself off I heard a loud knock at my door. I put the towel around my waist and looked out the window to see who was there.

It was Ilene, holding a plate of food. I opened the door just a crack and she asked, "Have you eaten yet?" I told her that that I hadn't. "Good," she said. "I have some left-over chicken, corn and mashed potatoes. I hope you're hungry." I told her that I was, but that I had just gotten out of the shower and only had a towel on. I asked her to give me a minute to get dressed.

What happened next blew my mind! She pushed the door open and walked right by me on her way to the kitchen. As she walked by she announced, "You don't have anything that I haven't seen before." I didn't say anything; I just watched her go by. She walked into the kitchen and set the plate on the kitchen table. Then she turned toward me and we made eye contact. Her eyes went up and down my body as she studied every inch of me. I felt very uncomfortable, yet aroused at the same time. She must have sensed that because she started to undress. She was beautiful; my heart was beating so fast I thought it would explode. I was in complete shock. She then walked up to me and we kissed. We had two hours of the most incredible sex I had ever experienced. She confessed two weeks later that she had planned the whole evening.

We were in love. There was no other way to describe it. She was good to me. She cooked, she washed my clothes, and once a week she cleaned my apartment. We were with each other whenever we weren't working. This time it was different; I'd found my soul mate, my life long partner. She loved and respected me, unlike Jackie, who had treated me badly. I was at her apartment every night at 6:30 for dinner with her and her boys. I'd play with them after dinner while she'd clean up the kitchen, then she would get them ready for bed. After they went to bed we'd watch TV until they fell asleep, then we'd make love in her living room or at my place until late in the evening.

On weekends, she would send her boys over to their father's house and we would enjoy two days of uninterrupted lovemaking. She was an incredible woman. I don't think I had ever had it so good. I was truly happy. Of course, we were lying to my father about our relationship, but I always suspected that he knew.

Ilene and I went on this way for almost five months. Then one night, after a very nice dinner and some great lovemaking, she told me she was pregnant. I lost it! I was *furious*! Yelling at her, I asked, "How could you let this happen?" Then I told her I didn't need another kid. This made *her* angry, and she told me to get out. So I left. My thought was that I already had two kids, what the hell was I going to do with another one? I didn't want to play anymore.

Things changed that night. This was the beginning of some of the most bizarre behaviors I had ever seen in a person. This was when I discovered just how sick she really was.

Now remember, I was in recovery, and had been going to 12-Step meetings almost every night, and then I had met Ilene. Just like any good addict still in their disease, I replaced my program of recovery with my new found love.

Wally told me that I wasn't ready for a relationship. He'd say, "You're not healthy enough," or "When the sex starts, the learning stops." I didn't want to hear it, so I started to avoid him.

My father used to say, "John, there are two types of people in this world; smart people and intelligent people. Smart people learn by their mistakes and that's good, but intelligent people learn by others' mistakes and that's better." I didn't seem to fit into either category.

I should have listened to the wisdom of my father when he told me not to get involved with Ilene. My father loved me, and he didn't want me to get hurt. But he was smart enough to know that there comes a time in a person's life when we just have to watch a bad situation unfold around the people we love, praying that they survive their situation and learn from it. He knew the lessons would be hard, and he also knew that if he intervened I would continue to repeat the same behavior over and over again.

And, just as my father had warned me, Ilene turned out to be a very sick woman.

The next day she launched her campaign to get even with me. She must have considered my reaction to her being pregnant a declaration of war because she prepared for battle. That morning at 6:00 I heard banging at my front door. I was still in my underwear when I opened the door to find two Phoenix police officers standing there. "Can I help you?" I asked. I was still half asleep.

One of the officers grabbed my left arm with his right hand and pulled me in to him. He looked angry as we stood there facing each other. He began to yell, "You are such a piece of shit!"

I didn't have any idea what he was talking about. My heart was fluttering; I was scared. I just kept my mouth shut. What else could I do? I was standing outside in my underwear with a very angry police officer calling me names. "Just play it out a little longer and I'll figure it out," I thought.

Whether or not I had done anything, at this point did not matter. Ilene had called the police and told them about our disagreement. She had (apparently very convincingly) explained to them that when she told me she was pregnant, I got violent. Ilene came out of her house about this time with a black eye, her head swollen, and it was apparent that her nose and head had been bleeding. It looked like I was going to jail. I asked them if I could put on some clothes before they handcuffed me.

On the way to the police car Ilene started to cry. "Please don't take him, I love him. I know he's sorry. I forgive him." She was sobbing. I was in awe—she was good! She was a true master. What a performance.

The officer who uncuffed me said, "You're a very lucky man." He was trying to intimidate me. He continued, "You have a good woman who really cares about you. If it were up to me I'd take you in, but it's not." I kept quiet. He leaned up to me, put his mouth up to my ear and said in a low voice, "By the way, if she calls us again I won't hesitate to arrest you." I just looked at him. He continued, "Pieces of shit like you, who beat up defenseless, helpless women, need to know what it's like to get their asses kicked." I was in complete shock. He walked over to Ilene and said something to her I couldn't hear. She nodded. I stood there, bewildered, as I watched the two officers drive away.

She looked at me with her big brown eye, the one that wasn't swollen shut. She had this self-satisfied grin on her face. I felt sick to my stomach. I couldn't believe it. I didn't say a word; I turned to go inside. Just as I started to close the door behind me, I heard her say, "You really don't know who you're messing with, do you? You may want to rethink your position. I love you and I know you love me. You'll come to realize that in time." When she spoke, it sounded hollow.

"What really happened to your face?" I had to know.

She smiled and said, "A pot, I beat myself in the face with a kitchen pot."

I couldn't believe what I was hearing. I stepped inside and closed the door. It was late so I got ready for work.

At work I thought about what she had done to me all day. "How could she do something like that?" I thought. To be honest, I was scared. I thought, "If she could do something like that, what else is she capable of?"

It didn't take long for me to find out. I didn't see her for the next three days. I was beginning to think it was over. Then at two a.m. on the fourth night, I was awakened by a loud banging. It sounded like all hell had broken loose. Someone was throwing pots and pans against my bedroom wall from the other side. This lasted almost an hour. I didn't say a word. I just lay there with my pillow over my head and tried to muffle the sound. She was really freaking me out.

At 1:30 the following morning, I was awakened by sirens. Police and fire trucks were pulling into the parking lot. They ran over to Ilene's door and her oldest son let them in. She had taken an overdose of sleeping pills. She left a suicide note explaining all about how I got her pregnant then walked out on her. In the note, it also said that she couldn't live without me. After they loaded her into the ambulance, the same two officers that came to arrest me just five days before were at my door and they were not nice. I tried to tell them how wrong they were about me, and what she was doing, but my words fell on deaf ears. They wouldn't listen. Instead, the same officer who had been so threatening before pushed her note in my face and screamed, "If she dies, I will find a way to charge you with her death!"

I didn't know what to do. I was losing a war I wasn't even fighting. As I lay in bed trying to get some rest before work, I prayed she wouldn't die.

I arrived home from work that evening at six o'clock. Ilene was sitting in the courtyard in front of her unit. She said hello and I nodded to her as I unlocked my door. "Did you have a good day at work?" she asked, as if nothing had happened.

I was still angry with her from the night before, but I didn't want to set her off again, so I responded with, "Work was rough today with all that went on last night. I didn't get much sleep." Then I closed the door behind me.

After I calmed down, I went in to take a shower. I put on a clean pair of Levis, walked back into the living room and turned on the TV. I had to be at a meeting in an hour, and I needed to finish getting ready. I was trying to avoid thinking about Ilene. I was putting on my socks and shoes when I heard a knock at my door. I looked out the window and saw her. I tried to ignore her but she only knocked louder, then she started talking through the door. "Come on John, open the door. I'm sorry about how I've been acting. Please John, let me talk to you." I was afraid she'd go off on me again. She walked back to her lawn chair, lit a cigarette, and then sat back down.

Ten minutes later she was back, knocking even more aggressively then before. She pounded on my door screaming, "Come on, we don't have to do this. We can just be friends." She was almost pleading. I felt so bad I opened the door. When I did I got one of the biggest shocks of my life. She was standing there without any clothes on. That's right, she was naked. I have to tell you, she was fighting a great war. Then I thought, "If I were ever in a battle I would want her in charge, because she knows all the right moves to win."

She threw her arms around me and started rubbing up against me. At the moment, I would have agreed to anything. I hated her for doing this to me, but I was too weak to stop. Oh, how I wanted to, though! I knew I couldn't give her what she wanted, but this was neither the time nor the place to tell her. We made love until early morning. We didn't really talk. When I would try, she would start kissing me. I passed out at 4:00.

I woke up the next morning at 9:00. Ilene was nowhere to be found and I was late for work. By the time I got there I was three hours late and my boss was pissed.

I was angry about what had happened and I was panicked that I had given her false hope. I needed to tell her we couldn't go on, but I was so tired. I hadn't gotten much sleep the night before. I thought, "I'll avoid her tonight, and then I'll tell her tomorrow."

On the drive home I was really tired, I nodded off several times. When I got there Ilene was nowhere in sight. I felt a momentary relief. My plan was to take a shower and go to bed early. I undressed and stepped into the shower. I felt relaxed, looking forward to a good night's sleep.

I was washing my hair when I heard the shower door open. It was Ilene. She had taken the extra key to my unit from the Maverick House office and let herself in. I was terrified but I had no options for the night. I was an emotional zombie being led around by this woman. I was afraid, but I was also intrigued, wondering just how far she would take it. She left to go home around two a.m.

Chapter Thirty

WITH HELP FROM AN ANGEL

"Not everything that is faced can be changed;
But nothing can be changed until it is faced."
-- *James Baldwin*

"When the wind stops blowing...Row!"
-- *Anonymous*

The next day was Saturday and Ilene let me sleep in. It was 11:00 when I woke up. I lay there for a while thinking that I needed to talk with her, and then I took a shower. I dressed, then went looking for her so that we could finally get all the cards out on the table. She wasn't home, so I walked over to the Maverick House to see if she was there. Harry, who was sitting behind the desk in the front office, told me that she had been there around 9:30 and said she was going to the swap meet. I thanked him and walked back home.

I was hungry so I drove over to Carrow's Restaurant for a bite to eat. I figured that I would talk to her when she got home. I thought, "I'll offer her help with the baby. Hopefully she'll understand." I walked into the restaurant and sat at the counter, then ordered breakfast and a cup of coffee. When the waitress was finished with the other customers, she came back and started joking around with me. It had been awhile since I had laughed and it really felt good. I forgot all about wanting to talk with Ilene.

And wouldn't you know, it was right about that time that Ilene came walking through the door. She was enraged, and she had no problem expressing it. She started screaming at me in the crowded restaurant. "Are you sleeping with her, too?" Before I could answer, she turned and yelled, "Well, bitch, are you sleeping with my boyfriend?"

I couldn't believe what I was hearing. The restaurant became ghostly quiet, as all of the customers were completely stunned. I could feel everyone's eyes on me. At first I was embarrassed, and then I got angry. "Ilene, knock it off!" I yelled.

This caused her to catch another gear. She turned back toward me and screamed wildly, "Is this why you don't love me anymore, over this bitch?" She had a crazy look in her eyes that scared the hell out of me.

I tried to calm her down, but she was out of control. She reached over, slapped my face, then turned and ran out of the restaurant. She jumped into her car and drove away, almost hitting several cars as she fishtailed going west, toward home. As I looked around at the others in the restaurant, the silence seemed to scream at me. It was several moments before everyone went back to what they had been doing before the scene had begun.

The waitress and I just looked at each other. "What the hell was that about?" she asked me. I explained to her what was going on. She reached over and put her hand on my shoulder and squeezed it gently. She asked me if I was all right. I told her that I was sorry for what had happened. She poured me another cup of coffee and just smiled. I told her I was a little nervous about going home now, but I had to tell her once and for all that it was over. She smiled again and then went out to serve her customers one more time. She was back in less than a minute.

When she came back and topped off my coffee she said, "I'm worried about you going back home to that situation tonight." She looked very concerned as she spoke. "Look, I get off of work in an hour. If you like, you can come over to my place. There are just my two children and me. We'd love to have you. I'll cook a nice dinner, we can watch some TV, and then you can sleep on my couch."

Now, I couldn't say that I didn't like the offer—I did. I was anxious about facing Ilene, but in my old style, I didn't want to deal with the problem. So I found myself telling her yes when she asked me again.

Her name was Sandy, and I spent the afternoon playing with her two children while she cooked dinner. When we sat down to eat at the dinner table, I noticed how wonderful her family treated me.

And then, of course, one thing led to another and I was sleeping with Sandy that night. It didn't take me long before I forgot about Ilene altogether. That's the way it is when you are in trouble and not using your head. You do the same thing all over again as if you did not learn a thing the first time. Here I was, having a baby with a lunatic, and I was jumping into bed with someone else.

We ended up going on a picnic the next day. As we sat on the lawn, I asked her children if they wanted to hear a true story about an Angel and Wood's Canyon Lake. They all moved in close. "When I was a kid around eight years old, I came to Wood's Canyon Lake with my father, his friend Andy, my brother, and Andy's son, Drew. After we set up camp, Drew, my brother and I decided to swim to the other side of the lake. When we reached the other shore, Drew and my brother got out to rest. I wasn't tired, so I just turned around, like I was swimming a lap in an Olympic-sized swimming pool. Well, that was one of the biggest mistakes I had ever made in my whole eight years of living on earth."

Sandy's daughter scooted closer to me, her eyes were wide and she blurted out, "Why? What happened?" She was sitting cross-legged, Indian style with her elbows resting on her legs and her chin in her hands leaning forward.

I continued, "I got tired about a quarter of the way back, but instead of turning around, I kept on swimming. Halfway across I was so tired I felt I couldn't go on. I was afraid I couldn't make it back to shore. I was confused and couldn't think of what to do next. I tried dog paddling for a while, hoping that would help me rest, but my arms felt like they were rocks, so it didn't help much. Then I saw a speedboat coming toward me. I started waving my arms hoping they would see me. It took every ounce of strength I had, so you can imagine how scared I was when they passed right by me, three feet to my right. They didn't even see me. I started to pray; there was nothing left to do. I was so tired I stopped fighting and let my body go limp. I felt so much better as I let my body go. I went under. My arms were above my head as I went toward the bottom, feet first. I could see the water change colors. It went from a lighter to a darker blue. I felt the temperature change; it got cooler as I headed toward the floor of the lake. I was at peace. I felt calm. I thought that I would die and I was really okay with it.

"I prayed "God, if you are real, I hope you'll be waiting for me when I get to the other side." I kept on praying as I went down even further. I couldn't tell you how far I went, but just before I passed out, I remember seeing a bright light below me. The next thing I remember I felt the bottom. I opened my eyes and saw that I was on my hands and knees in about two feet of water. I stood up. I felt water logged, my body was so heavy. Then I wondered how I got there and why I wasn't dead. I looked out on the beach in front of me and saw my father and Andy. They were talking and drinking beer. I looked behind me and Drew and my brother were still on the other shore.

Who saved me? I was full of questions. I couldn't see anyone around me and the lake was almost empty except for a few boats. Whoever it was, I wondered why they didn't stick around. I would have liked to thank them. Then I remembered my prayer. I knew then that God must have had a plan for me, because I ended up on the shore somehow and there was no other way that I could see—I have always believed that an Angel brought me to shore that day."

Sandy and her children sat there in complete silence with their eyes fixed on me as I spoke. When I finished with my story, her daughter asked me, "Do you think the Angels are still there?"

I told her, "Angels are everywhere, they are all around us. Angels are here to help us if we just ask. They are God's protection for us all."

Sandy looked at me and smiled.

It was completely dark by this time. There was only the light from a kerosene lantern that Sandy had lit just a couple of minutes before. We all helped load the car for our trip back home. I was anxious. I knew I had to face Ilene soon and I was not looking forward to it. Sandy sat next to me as I drove. She rubbed the back of my neck gently. She knew my concern. There was very little conversation. We were all tired and the children had fallen asleep in the backseat.

"Can you stay another night?" she asked me when we had finished unloading the car. I wanted to, but I knew I had to get this over with, so I told her no. She looked disappointed, but said she understood. "Will you call me later? Or tomorrow?" She knew I didn't have a phone. I told her I would, kissed her, and then I left.

I walked out to my car and opened the door. When I did, the inside light came on. There was a note, folded in half, under the windshield wiper. As I reached for it, my heart was pounding in my chest so hard that it was difficult to breathe. She knew where Sandy lived. How could I be so selfish, putting Sandy and her kids in such danger? My mind was going a mile a minute. I felt panic, and then I was just pissed.

I sat down in the car and read the note. "You and that bitch are in so much trouble. I know where you both live." She hadn't signed it, but I knew it was Ilene's handwriting. I started my car and headed home. I did this without any thought of the consequences or understanding of how advanced my adversary was in the art of war. I was about to find out.

When I walked up to Ilene's unit, the lights were out. I banged loudly on her door, but there was no answer. I was still pissed. She had proven to be unpredictable at best. I could feel my heart beating in my throat as I walked over to my unit, half relieved she wasn't there. When I walked in I turned on the lights. I waited for her, knowing I had to get it over with. I turned on the television, mostly for company. At 2:45 in the morning, I was so tired that I decided to go to bed and deal with it tomorrow. I fell right to sleep.

I was awakened by a loud bang that sounded like a cannon going off. I looked at my alarm clock—4:45, it read. I don't know why, but I rolled out of bed. I heard two more bangs and realized that someone was shooting through my bedroom wall. I just laid on the floor next to my bed, too afraid to move. I watched as the two slugs from the gun went through the wall and lodged themselves into the wall on the opposite side with very little damage. I was frozen with fear! Mass confusion set in and I couldn't move. I waited to see if the shooting would continue. When it appeared the shooting had stopped, my next thought was to get out, so I jumped out of my bedroom window. I was only in my underwear but I didn't care, I just wanted to get as far away as I could. Of course, I didn't take into consideration that her bedroom window was right next to mine, and being the warrior she was, she had anticipated my every move. She was waiting for me as I climbed down from the window. She reached over and put the gun to my head, then she said, "Run." And run I did. I ran through a field of bullhead stickers, weaved my way through traffic, and finally across a second field. As I crossed Monroe Street entering the driveway of the Maverick House, I heard her laughing uncontrollably. It sounded evil.

I was convinced now more than ever before that I was out of my league with this woman. She had several years of experience on me, and why I continued to hope for different results out of the same behaviors was beyond me. I needed to change my thinking, because what I was doing wasn't working. I finally figured out that I was going about it the wrong way. I was trying to be rational and do the right thing. She was angry and felt slighted, so she didn't care. You know what they say, "Hell hath no fury like a woman scorned." She wanted me to suffer. This was payback, and that was evident. I had to change my tactics or die trying. I couldn't call the police. I was afraid they would send the same two who had responded before, and that I would end up in jail instead of her.

Harry, who was sitting in a lawn chair smoking a cigarette, watched me run across the street weaving in and out of traffic in my underwear. He was laughing his ass off as I ran up to him. Harry always woke up at four a.m. so that he could drink a cup of coffee and have a cigarette before he opened the office at six. He would tell people that was the time he would get right with God. He was laughing so hard I thought he'd fall on the ground any second. His eyes were even watering.

I looked back to see if Ilene was behind me. She wasn't. "Shit Harry, what the hell are you laughing at? She tried to kill me!"

"I knew when I heard the first shot it was you and Ilene. What did you do to piss her off?" Harry asked me. I didn't answer him.

When I sat down in the lawn chair next to him he wasn't laughing anymore. My legs felt wobbly and I was sick to my stomach. Harry got up and went into his unit to get me some clothes. He unlocked the front door, we walked into the office and he sat down behind the desk. As we talked, he began arranging his papers. I was nervous as hell, afraid that Ilene would come through the door any minute laughing and shooting. But as I sat there it became evident that was not going to happen.

Harry walked over to the coffee area, then handed me a cup. I put my coffee on the desk in front of me, then began telling Harry some of the things that were going on between Ilene and me.

"Did you really think you were hiding it?" He wanted to know. "Most of the people around here knew you and Ilene were together, including your father," he said.

"I was afraid of that," I told him.

He continued, "We really didn't know how bad it was, but I became concerned when a police officer came in and asked for her a week or so back. She was back in the kitchen, so I went to tell her. She went out to his car and they talked. When she came in, she had a gun stuffed in her purse. She tried to keep it hidden, but I could see the butt sticking out and I knew what it was. I knew then that there was going to be trouble. I didn't know to what extent, but I just knew." He looked at me as he took a sip of his coffee.

I told him I didn't think I could call the police because of my fear of me going to jail and not her.

I was tired, afraid and confused. I sat there mulling over the events of the past hour, and as I did my feelings started to change from fear, to anger and then to rage. Who the hell was the woman to treat me this way? I was furious! "I'm not taking this shit." I stood up and headed for the door.

"Where are you going?" Harry asked.

"I'm not going to take this shit. I'm going home."

Harry looked at me with concern and then yelled to me, "Don't do anything stupid!"

Without saying another word, I walked out.

On my short journey home, I was telling myself to be careful. I needed to deal with her once and for all. I just couldn't live this way for even one more day. Besides, I hadn't been to a 12-Step meeting or talked with my sponsor in several months and my ability to cope appeared to be diminishing at this point. I guess what they say in the program is true: The program only works when you're actively working it. The key phrase here is "actively working it," and I sure wasn't doing that. I continued thinking on my stroll into the unknown that since it was daylight, she would be smart enough not to try anything while people were awake and could be watching. I guess I didn't understand women.

I walked up to my unit; the door was locked. Of course it would be, I'd left via the bedroom window. I heard the door open from Ilene's unit. When she stepped out, she was still laughing. She said, half joking, "You looked so cute running across Van Buren in your jockey shorts. It kinda turned me on." I looked at her with raised eyebrows. I noticed she had no gun, which was a good sign. She continued laughing, and it was really starting to piss me off. The more she laughed, the angrier I became. All that I could think about was that she was crazy. She told me to wait. She was back in less than a minute. She had the spare key to my unit. She unlocked my door and let me in.

I thought as I walked past her, "For someone who tried to kill me an hour ago, she's being awfully nice now."

She stood outside my door and asked if we could talk. I was reluctant, but I agreed. I invited her in and we sat on the couch. I sat on one end and she sat on the other end. She spoke first. "Look John," she said, "I don't want to hurt you."

I butted in with, "You could have fooled me." Then I asked her about the gun.

She started laughing again and said, "If I had wanted to kill you, you'd be dead. All I wanted was to get your attention and maybe scare you a little bit." It was clear to me she was enjoying this. She went on, "It looks like I accomplished that."

"Where is the gun now?" I asked. She told me it was in her unit and that she was out of bullets.

There was something about Ilene that I really enjoyed. Maybe it was that fine line she walked. The one that kept me guessing or wondering if what she did next was going to be good or bad. That intrigued me in a scary sort of way, and this was one of those times. Looking back at what happened next, I can see just how sick I was.

As Ilene and I sat there talking, she moved closer to me on the couch and before long she had her hand on my leg. I couldn't understand it, but with all the excitement that I had just gone through, the smell of her perfume, together with the physical contact I was experiencing, I was incredibly turned on. I had to fight it. She must have sensed my struggle because she started to come on to me. We were moving into dangerous ground and I could see it coming. She moved even closer to me on the couch. My head said fight, but my body said go with it and deal with it tomorrow. I got pulled in again. What was the power this evil woman had over me?

"I know I'll be sorry tomorrow," I thought, but right now I refused to look at the consequences. We were together until well into the afternoon. I felt ashamed as I lay there. This woman was using me; she was playing me like violin. When you want to have sex with the woman who shot at you just a few hours ago, something is terribly wrong. You can't lose your self respect on any level without losing it on all levels at the same time.

I wondered how I could face Sandy again. Hell, I couldn't even look at myself in the mirror. I was in worse shape now than I had been when I was using drugs. I seemed to be out of control all over again. I wanted to give up. No, that's not true. I gave up. Before the week was out, I was drinking and using speed again. I also ignored the several attempts that Sandy made to contact me. I just couldn't face her again.

Ilene didn't like my drug use. She learned just what an asshole I could be when I used, but for the most part, she tolerated it. I didn't care anymore. I did what I wanted and enjoyed it even more if she didn't like it. I felt a rage inside of me that kept me on the edge.

One night I came home drunk. I was angry because I had been confronted by the general manger at the construction site I was working at about my drinking. He yelled at me, so I knocked him on his ass and he fired me.

When I arrived home, Ilene was coming out of her unit on her way to the store. "How are you this evening?" she asked.

"It's none of your damn business!" I screamed at her. I was still mad about being fired. Of course, that pissed her off. That's when she told me I was a loser and to stay away from her. Well, I had finally done it. I had freed myself from her by placing myself back into the prison of drug and alcohol addiction. I guess it takes what it takes.

After losing my job and Ilene telling me to stay away, I had nothing to keep me in line, and it wasn't long before I started using worse than ever. I stayed loaded for weeks at a time and I was back hanging out with old friends. I saw David, Tommy's uncle, one day at the Exxon on Van Buren. When he saw me, he asked if I had heard what happened to Tommy. I told him I hadn't. He then told me that Tommy was dead—that his wife had stabbed him when he came home loaded on glue one night. I told him that I was sorry to hear that. It was hard to believe, and I felt sad.

A few weeks later, I was sitting at Pete's Fish and Chips on Van Buren when Tooter and his cousin Jerry came in. We talked for awhile, and then I left. A week later I heard that Jerry had been killed trying to break up a bar fight. My friends were dying like flies.

It wasn't long after Jerry was killed that I ran into Jackie, my ex, in a laundromat. She said she was glad to see me and told me that she just lived two blocks away.

I asked her about the kids. She told me that they were fine. "They're spending the night with my mother tonight," she told me. "Why don't you come over? I'll cook you dinner, and we can make a night of it. It will be fun." She was excited. Then she threw in, almost as an after thought, "As friends of course."

I said, "Of course." She helped me fold my clothes, and then I followed her home.

On my way to her house, I asked myself, "What are you doing John? You know better." But in the end, I justified to myself that it was okay and we were "just friends." My mind was full of justification; that's how I lived my life and I was good at it. I helped her carry the laundry in, then sat on the couch and waited while she put it away. My gut was telling me I would be sorry tomorrow. As she walked by me, heading for the bathroom, she said, "There's beer in the fridge. Help yourself."

It was 7:30 in the morning when I opened my eyes. We were facing each other about six inches apart. She was looking at me. "Hello," she said.

We talked as we ate breakfast; catching up on all the events of the six months that we had been apart. There's no doubt in my mind that we both probably lied to each other that day. I didn't care much. My mind was already on how I was going to get away gracefully. After a quick shower, I walked back into the living room wearing a pair of blue jeans. I noticed she had my laundry basket sitting on her couch and she was going through it, putting my pants and shirts on hangers getting ready to hang them up in the hall closet.

"What are you doing?" I asked her. I was angry.

"I just figured that after last night and this morning, we were back together again and I thought I'd help you with your stuff."

I was furious! How could she be so presumptuous and calculating? I had no intention of moving back in. Oh, I knew there would be a price to pay, but nothing like this. Again, I think back to the wisdom of my father, "Lessons are hard." I was so sick of fighting.

She could see where I was going with this. That's when she became angry and when she looked at me sideways, I knew I was in trouble. In her anger, she threw my clothes down on the ground. When I bent over to pick them up, she came at me kicking and screaming. I threw her off when she jumped on my back, punching me from behind. She came at me again. I had forgotten how violent she could get. I tried to reason with her but she wouldn't listen. She was out of control. I fought her off long enough to get my shoes on, grabbed what I could of my clothes and ran out of the house. She screamed at me all the way to the car. I was losing clothes with each step I took. She was so mad that I couldn't understand a word she was saying; she was cussing at me in Spanish. I threw my clothes in the back seat of my car, jumped in and drove away. I could still see her in my rear view mirror when I turned the corner, heading back toward familiar ground.

I drove in the direction of Mac and Marge's. I came out of my trance as I pulled into the parking lot, and then went in and sat at the bar. "How are you John?" Marge asked me. While she spoke, she was already drawing me up a draft. I took a dollar out of my pocket and handed it to her. When she came back with my change, I ordered another one. "Are you thirsty?" she asked. I told her that I didn't feel like talking about it. She brought me another beer, then took another dime from the bar in front of me.

Around three that afternoon, some of the regulars started coming into the bar. There were Roy and Jimmy. Roy still had grease on him from the cars he worked on at his brother's gas station. Trailing them were Charlie and his little brother Larry. They were both sheet rock tapers just getting off work. They all sat at the same table. When Roy saw me at the bar, he invited me over. Soon after I sat down, Mary walked in and announced that there was a party going on at Ted and Ida's house, one block over, and asked if anyone wanted to go.

"I'll go," I told her.

The others declined. Mary and I arrived at the party around six. It was dark outside. I was already drunk when I got there. Leonard was there with Freddie and Ernie from the Dupa Villa Projects. Ernie turned me on to some crosses, which enabled me to drink more. I continued drinking until around 8:30. I was feeling hungry because I hadn't eaten since ten that morning, so I decided to drive myself to Denny's. Everyone at the party told me that maybe I needed to sober up a little, but I thought I could make it.

I turned into the Denny's parking lot. I sat there with my foot on the brake looking for a parking space, hoping to get one close to the entrance. I looked to my left and through the west window were eleven, maybe twelve police officers gathered around several tables pushed together. I looked to my right and there were seven police motorcycles side by side, and a parking space right next to the end bike. Well, as drunk as I was, I had no business trying to fit my car into that parking space, but try I did! The only problem was that I made too wide of a turn, and when I did, I hit the first motorcycle in line. As it fell, it knocked over the next motorcycle in line and suddenly I had created, without intent, the domino effect. I freaked! As I looked back to my left, I watched all the officers stand up at the same time. One was pointing his finger at me. I turned back and as I watched the last motorcycle fall, I realized that those police officers were all now running toward me. It was time to go!

I punched the gas pedal in an attempt to get away. Without stopping, I turned left, fishtailing onto the main road. The light was red, but I didn't care. I ran it. I was so scared that my right foot was shaking up and down uncontrollably. I just knew there was a platoon of police behind me and they were coming up fast. I ran another red light. There was no doubt in my mind that there was at least one officer back there keeping score. I blew the light again. I could see them all around me. I cut in between them. They didn't expect me to turn and it gave me the edge. I made it back to the party, but they were hot on my tail.

George was outside wondering what all the sirens were about when I drove up. He could see that I was in trouble by all the police starting to pull up behind me. He yelled out some directions. I took off again, hoping what he told me would work. Knowing the neighborhood better than they did must have helped. I was able to get far enough ahead of them for me to pull back up to the party, open my door and run inside. I hid behind the couch. When I opened my door to run inside, I left it open. Standing next to my door, wondering what had just happened, was Robert. Now Robert and I looked so much alike we could have passed for brothers. As I hid behind the couch, I was looking out the front door, and my eyes were fixed on Robert. I have to say that he probably never knew what hit him as seven or eight police officers converged on him from all directions. I didn't know that one person could withstand such a beating. The more he protested, trying to tell them he didn't know who owned the car, the more they beat him. He appeared to be unconscious when they threw him into the paddy wagon and drove away. I was so upset that I had to drink another beer to calm myself down. I never saw Robert again, and I guess I have always felt guilty about what happened to him. I can only hope that someday, if he survived, I will be able to make amends.

I couldn't tell you what happened next. I don't even remember leaving the party. I woke up around 3:00 p.m. the following day on Mary's couch.

Two weeks later, I was late picking up my daughter from her mother's house. When I arrived, her boyfriend Mike threw me some attitude. That made me angry, so I gave him attitude back. He and I argued back and forth out in their front yard. Glenna got upset and told me to leave. She wasn't going to let me take Renee' but with a lot of talking on my part, she gave in.

We were driving to my parent's house. I was driving down McDowell Road when Jimmy Hendrix came on the radio. I was singing along, really rockin', when I noticed Renee' standing over by the passenger door, not saying a word. "Are you okay?" I asked her, and then I turned down the radio so I could hear her answer.

Renee' was a very smart little girl. She could speak very well for an almost-four-year-old. What she told me next broke my heart. Now I loved my daughter and would never hurt her in any way if I could help it, but unknowingly I had hurt her very deeply when I yelled at her mother and her boyfriend. She said to me, "Daddy, I don't want you to come and get me anymore."

I was devastated; I could feel my heart breaking in two. "Why baby?" I asked.

"When you pick me up you fight with mommy and Mike and it scares me."

I couldn't believe what I was hearing. Was I so self-centered that I couldn't see what I was doing to my little girl? I didn't realize how I was affecting her. I didn't have a clue. In my devastation, I drove to my parent's house and dropped her off. I was so disgusted with myself that I left without telling her goodbye. How could I ever face her again? What she had said to me stayed on my mind all weekend. I couldn't turn it off. I felt ashamed. She was right; I needed to change my attitude toward Glenna and her boyfriend. But how could I do that without losing face? I didn't know, so for the next year my family picked her up. I would only see her when I'd go and visit my parents and she was there. I loved my daughter, but I didn't know how to have a relationship with her, so my visits, when she was there, were short and superficial.

Chapter Thirty-One

I Did It My Way, But It Didn't Work

"Dear Landlord, Please don't dismiss my case.
I'm not about to argue, I'm not about to move
to another place. Now each of us has his own
special gift and you know this was meant to be
true and if you don't underestimate me I won't
underestimate you."

-- *Bob Dylan*

My father knew that Ilene and I were no longer together. He could feel the tension between us when I went to the Maverick House to see him, so he asked me to stop coming over as much, at least until things settled down between us. It was around this time that my father took over another complex from the county, which he planned to use to expand the Maverick House. It was a ten unit apartment complex. It had been vacant for some time and was in need of repairs. He had a target date of six months set before he would open its doors. He asked me to move over to the new place, hoping to cut down on all the tension between Ilene and me. Besides, Maverick House would be moving across the street soon and Ilene and I would have to move out anyway. I was glad he made the offer. I needed to get away from her before we killed each other.

I started hanging sheetrock again, this time on my own. Pete had long since relapsed and disappeared. I was working at a job site in Scottsdale building apartments. The job would last two months, and when you're only making two-and-a-half cents a square foot, you have to hang a lot of rock to make any money.

My boss knew it was my first time out on my own. He liked my work, but would tell me often that I needed to work faster. "Don't worry about making mistakes. If you do, let the tapers fix them." I took his suggestion and it worked. The tapers did fix them and I was able to increase production.

My first month, I didn't drink on the job. I drank at the bars after work. However, very soon after that, I started drinking when my work was done for the day, just before I left the site. Then I began having a few beers at lunch and before long I was drinking all day. It wasn't as if I was the only one. We all drank on the job back then. Toward the end of the job, I was also using crosses again. At first I used them to help me get through the day, but within a week I was taking them by the handful.

When the job was finished in Scottsdale, Lenny, my foreman, had no more work. He told me about a company that had a big project going in Del Webb's Sun City, which was a retirement community that they were building in phases. He gave me the foreman's name. They hired me to hang sheet rock and whatever else they saw fit to have me do. I'd leave for work at 4:30 in the morning, start work at 5:30 and work until 2:00. The job was very demanding, and drinking was not tolerated because of the age of the residents who were already living there.

One morning, in my third week working there, my car broke down. It was a Wednesday, and when I told my foreman, he was upset because he was already short staffed. "If you don't make it tomorrow I'll have to let you go," he told me.

I told him I'd be there. Then I called my father and asked if I could use his '64 Olds.

"Sure," he said. "It's just sitting here at the house, not being used."

I thanked him, and he sent Vance to pick me up. Vance was driving my mother's new VW bug when he arrived an hour later. I was waiting outside for him when he pulled up. We headed back to my parents house in Tempe. I stayed there for a while and visited with my mother, then left to go back to Phoenix.

My father had just taken the Olds out of the garage. He'd recently had it tuned-up, the oil changed and the a-frame replaced on the driver's side, and it ran great. As I drove down Van Buren I recognized my brother's friend hitchhiking going in the same direction. I pulled over to pick him up and when I stopped, he ran over to the car. When he opened the door to get in, he looked at me. His eyes got real big and he looked frightened. He asked me if I was Richard Carter's brother and I told him I was. Then he backed out of the car and turned around to run, yelling, "I'm not getting in the car with you man, you're crazy!" He was so scared that he dropped his backpack and didn't come back to pick it up.

My feelings were hurt. I couldn't stop thinking about it. It not only hurt my feelings but it reminded me of what had happened with my daughter and what she had told me. It looked like my wall of denial was starting to show signs of weakness and I didn't like it. It forced me to question how I must appear to others. Then sadness started to take over. I didn't want those around me to have to walk on eggshells or be afraid of me. My mind continued to attack me as I drove down Van Buren filled with pity for myself. By the time I pulled into Mac and Marge's parking lot, I was ready to do some serious drinking. I needed to forget for a while and what better way to forget? So I walked in through the back door and up to the bar.

When I sat down, I ordered a beer from Mary who was helping Marge out. She set it down in front of me and said, "The first one's on me." I thanked her, than set my money down on the bar. I couldn't stop thinking about what had just happened with my brother's friend. I was sorry that he felt that way. Then my mind went back to my daughter and moved right into all the shame I had felt the day that she told me not to pick her up anymore. I hated the way I was feeling, but I wasn't drunk enough yet to turn it off. I continued to drink throughout the evening. At eight o'clock, the band started to play. They were an all girl band, and they were good. They stopped playing around 11:00.

I knew I was drunk when I decided to leave the bar at 11:30. When I told Mary that I was going, she expressed concern about me leaving as drunk as I was. "Are you okay to drive?" she asked me.

"Me? Of course I am! You know I'm a better driver when I've been drinking. I'm more relaxed," I told her.

She looked at me sideways and said, "Yeah right! Why don't you sleep on my couch tonight?" she asked.

"No really, I'm fine. See you later."

She looked angry when she said, "I hope so."

I said goodbye to Marge and walked out the same door I had walked in.

On my way home, I stopped at Circle-K and bought a loaf of bread and some lunchmeat to make sandwiches. I also bought a six pack of Coors. I looked at the clock on the wall as I paid for everything. It was almost midnight. I jumped back into the Olds and headed for home.

Ilene was outside on her lawn chair smoking a cigarette when I drove up. When she saw me she asked me how I was doing. She looked very pregnant and I felt guilty about that. I told her I was fine. As I passed by, her mood changed. "You smell like you've been drinking," she said to me with contempt.

I didn't want to fight, so I said, "Goodnight," unlocked my unit and stepped inside. I turned on the television, then walked into the kitchen to make something to eat. I opened a beer, then sat down in front of the TV. I ate two sandwiches, washing them down with my beer.

When I looked at my watch, it was 2:30. I had to be at work at 5:30, and I knew I had an hour's drive one way. "If I go to bed I might not wake up in time," I told myself. I went into my bedroom, where I kept my jar of white crosses. I took ten of them to help me stay awake. Through the course of the next couple of hours I continued to take the pills with my beer. I left for work at 4:30, and I brought my jar of white crosses with me in case I needed them throughout the day. I put them under the front seat of my car.

When I stepped outside it was windy and the sky was gray. It looked like it might rain. When I arrived at work, my foreman met me at the gate to let me in. When he did, he smelled the alcohol on me and asked, "John, how much have you had to drink?" He appeared to be more upset than angry when he said it.

"I was drinking last night, and when I woke up it was late, so I rushed out of the house without brushing my teeth. I'm sorry." He was already mad at me for missing yesterday and I didn't want to get fired. He told me he should send me home, but he was short-handed and couldn't do that. He asked me to stay away from people. I told him I would and promised him that I'd never do it again. He looked frustrated when he walked away.

At around nine o'clock, the wind was blowing hard, which made it very difficult to carry the sheetrock. I couldn't get much done. There was a rumor that a tornado was coming our way, and the foreman was listening to the radio to stay informed. It was 11:30 when we were told to pack it up. With the way I was feeling and the difficult time I was having hanging the rock, I was sure glad we were told to go!

I pulled out of the job site and to my right was a Circle-K. I pulled into a parking space in front of the store, got out and went inside. I walked over to the cooler and grabbed a six pack of Coors. At the counter, I asked for a pack of cigarettes and paid for them both with a five dollar bill. She handed me the change and I left. When I jumped back in my car, I opened a beer with the opener I had on my key ring, and headed home. There were very few cars on the road, probably because it was near a retirement community and there were tornado warnings all over the radio.

For whatever reason, my mind was a collage of the past: Jackie, Ilene, what happened with my daughter, my brother's friend, my relationship with my family and all the people I had hurt through the years with my chemical use. I was feeling sad and remorseful over what I had done to the people I loved. I wondered how my life would have been different had I not used drugs. I was angry with myself for letting things get so bad. The words my daughter spoke still haunted me. I asked myself, "How bad does it have to get before I say enough is enough?" In the next few minutes I was about to find out.

Driving back to Phoenix, I couldn't tell you how fast I was going, but it was estimated by police in their report that I was traveling between seventy and eighty miles an hour. This was confirmed by several eyewitnesses playing football in a nearby open field at the time of impact.

I shouldn't have been driving that day, and if I could go back and change the next few minutes of my life I would, but I can't. There are times in our lives that, because of our own selfish decisions and with no regard for others, we make choices that will forever change the course of our lives and the lives of those others. There is nothing we can do or say to change it back or to rectify it. Oh, if only we could, because some of these choices will haunt us for the rest of our lives. At best, all we can do is ask for forgiveness and hope we can make it up by helping others to not make the same mistakes.

As I continued driving, I was looking to my right and observed what looked like several teenagers playing football in an open field. They stopped playing and all eyes were on me as I passed by. The events that took place next seemed to happen in slow motion and will forever be branded on my mind.

I watched as a silver-gray 1971 Buick made a left hand turn, directly in front of me. When it did, I watched the face of a panic-stricken elderly woman with short pepper gray hair look toward me with both hands over her mouth as she screamed. Her eyes were wide as I came toward her. I could almost smell her fear. There was nothing I could do. The driver of the Buick had pulled out in front of me. There was no time for me to even step on my brakes, let alone slow down. I watched in complete horror as their car rolled several times, then come to a stop facing in the wrong direction about a hundred and fifty feet in front of me. I felt like I had hit a steel wall. My car just stopped.

I watched my drywall hammer go past my head with such force that it broke out the front windshield. Before it hit the ground, I watched my hood come up and slap the top of my car and when it did, the top caved in on me. The engine and transmission buckled up and created a wall of scrap metal to my right. At the same time, the left fender wrapped around the driver's side door to entomb me. I could feel both my knee's break through the metal panel dashboard and my chin break the steering wheel. I was trapped and bleeding from my face and knees. I was hurt, but I was more concerned about the couple I had just hit. I was terrified!

People began running toward my car, and several of them tried to get me out. I heard one person say, "He's trapped!"

I was beginning to freak out! My heart was pounding in my ears. I asked someone about the people in the other car. No one would tell me. I asked myself over and over again, "Why?" Of course I knew the answer, but I didn't want to admit it to myself. Now, because of my decisions, one, maybe two, people were dead. How could it get any worse?

I started to pray. In my terror, I was unable to think clearly. It was difficult to put words together. I could only come up with two. "Forgive me." I said it over and over again. I was overwhelmed. My mind was going in five different directions. I began to think, as if in slow motion, what if I had stopped drinking yesterday, last week or a month ago. I started to hyperventilate. I needed fresh air. I tried to open my door but it wouldn't open. I was gasping for air. I started to panic, and then I must have passed out.

When I woke up, there were firemen working on my driver's side door. They were asking me how badly I was hurt. I was trapped and needed to be cut out, but because my gas tank was ruptured, they had to call another station that had a new machine called "the jaws of life." I was told that they would be here soon. "I'm okay," I told them. "I can wait. You need to help the people in the other car." An officer stayed with me while the firemen ran over to help the couple in the other car. I was beginning to gather some sense about me as I did some of the deep breathing that Jim had taught me when he was teaching me how to get through a panic attack.

Then I remembered the beer and white crosses I had in the passenger side of my car. I searched for them through the twisted metal wall. I could see the crosses. I tried to reach through the metal to either push them back under the seat, or pull them through to my side so I could hide them. It didn't take long before the officer began to wonder what I was doing. He walked over to the passenger side of my car and watched me as I tried to hide them.

As our eyes met, he asked me, "What are you doing?" I was petrified with fear!

I didn't know how to answer him. He had just caught me red-handed trying to hide illegal drugs after hitting two people at a speed of up to eighty miles an hour. What could I do? Things were looking bleaker by the minute. I was in so much trouble that all I could think about was going to prison. I had taken my chemical use to a level that even I couldn't comprehend. Then I remembered what they used to say in the 12-Step program I used to attend. If we continue to use chemicals, there are only three directions they will take us; jail, an institution, or death. I had no defense and I knew it.

What happened next came as a complete surprise. The officer reached into the passenger side of my car and picked up my jar of white crosses and the five remaining beers. Then he said, "You won't be needing these anymore. There were several eyewitnesses that said there was no way you could have avoided the accident. He pulled right in front of you. There was no way you could've stopped. That's what my report will say. You know, from the looks of your car you're a lucky young man. You could have been killed." He turned and walked away. I watched him put the beer and crosses into the trunk of his car. They were never mentioned again.

Another fire truck rolled up with the equipment that was needed to get me out of my car. It was just a minute or two before they had me out and into an ambulance on my way to the hospital. In the emergency room I was examined by an intern. They took x-rays and did a complete physical exam. I had no major injuries. I needed ten stitches in my chin where I was cut by the steering wheel and five stitches in each of my knees. I was told by the E.R. nurse, "You're fortunate to be alive. You must have an angel with you."

"I know someone up there must care," I told her. Then I asked her about the couple in the other car.

She told me, "The lady died and he is hurt badly and in intensive care in critical condition."

I felt guilty. I didn't care what anyone said, I felt responsible. The nurse could see I was upset, so she tried to comfort me. "I know you feel bad about the accident, but it wasn't your fault. The lady in the car was already in a wheel chair from an accident her husband caused two years prior. He had bad eyesight even back then, and he definitely shouldn't have been driving today."

I thanked her for her kindness, but it wasn't much help. I know it wouldn't have happened if I hadn't been drinking, high on speed, and driving eighty miles an hour. Until my dying day, I will always feel some degree of responsibly for her death and the injuries to the old man about whose life I am still uncertain. Even in death, my grave will not shelter me or remove my lingering guilt.

I lost my job because I couldn't work with the injuries I sustained in the accident. The next few idle weeks, with too much time on my hands to think, really took a toll on my mental health. I was depressed and struggling with my thoughts. I became obsessed with all the events over the previous several months.

It appeared that my life plummeted to a new depth. I was drowning in self-pity. I thought about my accident. I thought about my daughter and I thought about my family. I couldn't turn those thoughts off. The emotional pain was too great and I was collapsing inside. I felt like I was losing my mind. The thought of suicide began again to frequently raise its ugly head. When you have a hollow feeling inside, death waits for you like a stranger at the door. It was as if I had a big hole in my stomach. I felt so lost, I even started to blame God, even though I knew, somewhere in the back of my mind, that He had something to do with saving me in the first place. Life was moving so fast that I gave up any hope of catching up with it.

Chapter Thirty-Two

The Devil Had Me By The Foot

My life?
Hell, what life?
Again I went to bed with my thoughts
and again I woke up with my thoughts,
if I could sleep at all.

One afternoon, about three weeks after the accident, Jackie knocked on my door. She had a laundry basket filled with the clothes I had left behind the day I had left in such a hurry. She wanted to tell me she was sorry about what happened the last time we were together. I thanked her and asked her if she wanted to come in. She sat next to me on the couch.

"How are the kids?" I asked her. I had been thinking about the children along with everything else.

"They're doing fine," she told me. We continued to talk and as we did, she started inching her way closer to me. Then without warning, she tried to kiss me. I turned my head to deflect the kiss.

"Jackie," I said, "I think it would be best if it was over between us." She started to cry. "It's not about you," I tried to explain. "It's me. My head isn't on straight, and I don't think I could handle the stress of a relationship right now."

She looked at me with concern and said, "Look, we don't have to be together forever, just for tonight." And again I told her that I just wasn't ready.

I could see she wasn't getting it. Having come from a dysfunctional family herself, she not only had no boundaries, but she had no respect for another person's boundaries either. She didn't understand a thing I told her. That's when she moved into the next phase of dysfunction, and that was to try to wear me down. I have to tell you, it worked like a charm! She told me in a joking voice, "Just shut up." She stood up and walked behind the couch. She started rubbing my neck and shoulders. The seduction was pulling me in. It felt so good—I allowed it to happen.

As I watched her put on her clothes, I lay there feeling angry with myself for not holding my ground. There was no doubt in my mind that this was going to come back and bite me in the ass. I didn't know how or when, but I just knew it would.

I drifted in and out of sleep for a time, and then finally got out of bed around ten. I needed to pick up some boxes from the store so I could get ready to move. I hated moving, but it needed to be done and today was a good day to pack. My father wanted me out on Monday and I didn't want to disappoint him again.

At 10:30 I left my unit, heading for the grocery store. When I stepped outside, Ilene was sitting in her lawn chair, smoking a cigarette and drinking a cup of coffee. I told her hello as I started to pass by.

"How did it go with your new girlfriend last night?" she said without sounding upset. So I told her it went fine, and thanked her for asking.

"I'm happy for you," she told me.

I knew Jackie and Ilene had never met, so it's no wonder she thought Jackie was someone new in my life, but I didn't feel the need to explain it. Besides, she was being too nice, and that made me nervous. I told her I had things to do. She smiled at me as I turned and walked out to my car.

At the store, I loaded my car with boxes, and then drove back home. Ilene was still outside when I arrived. I unloaded three boxes and carried them to my unit. I set them by my door and reached into my pocket for the keys. I set the boxes inside and headed back for more. When I did, I saw Ilene heading my way with another load of boxes. She put them down on the floor next to the couch.

"Could you use some help packing?" she asked. I didn't answer her because my thoughts were on her and how pregnant she looked, so I didn't hear her. She took my silence as a yes, then picked up one of the boxes, went into the kitchen and started packing.

I watched her as she stretched up into the cupboards to take things down. As I watched her I found myself wanting to be with her. I know it sounds crazy, but in spite of all I had gone through with her, I just wanted to be with her. After all, she was pregnant with my baby, wasn't she? Somewhere in all the madness, I still was thinking in the moment and not remembering the lessons of the past.

She caught me staring. "Earth to John. Do you want me to pack up your bathroom when I'm finished with the kitchen?" She was almost done and ready to move on. I was embarrassed that she had caught me staring. She slapped me on my shoulder in a playful manner and asked me again.

"If you don't have anything to do, I could sure use some help," I told her.

"What am I doing?" I thought two seconds after I said it. "I must really like getting bitten in the ass, because I sure am setting myself up for it."

She finished the kitchen and started in the bathroom. I stacked the kitchen boxes on the floor next to the couch. As I was setting the last one from the kitchen down, she was already bringing me a box she had filled with bathroom items.

"Don't hurt yourself," I said.

She smiled and in a half-joking way said, "I didn't think you cared." She looked sideways at me and chuckled, then went back into the bathroom to finish packing.

"I want her, but I don't." I thought. "What the hell does that mean?" I was confused—there was no doubt about that. Was I hoping

Jackie would catch us? Was I just crazy, or—worse yet—completely insane? I was a mess.

It didn't take long before what I was hoping for happened. I felt so close to her at that moment. She was so gentle that I felt drunk with desire. I lost all control. "What am I doing?" I asked myself several times throughout the day and well into the night. The bottom line was, even with all the rationalizing I was doing; I still knew I was wrong. We finished packing around eleven that evening.

Does the term "sick codependent" mean anything to you? I didn't understand it at the time, but that's what I was. I was trying to fix myself by using these women. The other side of that was that I was involved with two women doing the very same thing to me. I guess it's true what they say about sick people attracting sick people. I see this so clearly today. It's no wonder I always became involved with sick women. A healthy woman wouldn't have tolerated my sick behaviors even for five minutes.

I moved the following Monday. Ilene helped me load my car and Jackie helped me unload it and set up my new apartment. Now that was a balancing act. To this day I still don't know how I pulled it off, because neither of them knew the other was involved.

When Ilene and I loaded the last box in my car, she kissed me and said, "I'm moving myself this weekend. Here's my new address." She slid it into my shirt pocket. "Come over and visit me now and again." We kissed again and I left. I never did go see Ilene at her new address. I always suspected she had an undiagnosed mental illness.

The next time I saw her was when she came to my house about a year later. She said, "I sold our son, and you'll never find him. This is your half." She threw $150 at me. Then she turned and walked away. I was told several years later, by my father, that he read in the paper that Ilene had committed suicide.

Jackie was waiting for the next load to arrive so she could put away the rest of my things. We had plans to go out to dinner, then to a movie, if we weren't too tired. We had everything put away by 2:30 that afternoon. We took a shower and laid down to take a small nap. As she slept, I lay there asking myself, "Why?" For a person who didn't want any more pressure in his life, I sure was creating it. I was one sick son of a bitch. I felt like an inexpensive whore who walked Van Buren Street. I was weak and getting weaker by the day. The more involved I became with this woman, the less control I seemed to have. This just added to my feelings of hopelessness. I felt like I was in a bottomless pit and the devil had me by the foot, pulling me down. I was going under fast.

Chapter Thirty-Three

A SOLEMN FAREWELL

"I would rather live the rest of my life sober
believing that I am an alcoholic,
than live the rest of my life drunk,
or even just a little drunk,
trying to convince myself that I'm not."
-- *Black Wally*
Phoenix, Arizona

There I was, with my life out of control once again. The problem was that it seemed worse than before. The months I had worked my recovery program and the benefits I had received were some of the best days of my life. I wanted those days back, but how? I realized that if I was ever going to develop any degree of sanity I needed to stop using, but where did I start? I had no answers. I knew how I had done it before, but how could I go back and face those who had gone out of their way to help me? I was the one who had stopped going to meetings, so I should be the one to fix it. The problem was, I couldn't do it on my own. I had let my pride get in my way and it was killing me.

It was September of 1973 and I was twenty-two years old when my little brother Vance entered Saint Luke's Hospital for bypass surgery. Vance was probably on his way to becoming an addict if he wasn't already one. He was sixteen years old and weighed close to 400 pounds. He hated his size and wanted the surgery to help him lose the weight.

Vance had a wonderful personality, and he had many friends. Both of our parents worked nights, so his friends would go over to our parents house and get high in the backyard. For as long as that went on, I was surprised that the neighbors never complained. They must have known.

One day, Aunt Betty came over to visit our family. She knew how unhappy my brother was because of his size. She showed him a section of the newspaper. The article talked about a local doctor who was doing this new surgery called an "Intestinal Bypass" that enabled people who were morbidly obese to lose weight. He grew more and more excited as he read through the article. They both talked it over with our parents and it wasn't long before he was in the hospital being prepped for surgery. His first day in the hospital was filled with blood work and all the tests needed to prepare him for surgery the following day. Our family and many of his friends dropped by to wish him good health. He was in good spirits and talked about how great life would be for him when he lost all the weight. He had wonderful hopes and dreams. I couldn't remember ever seeing him so happy and we were all excited for him.

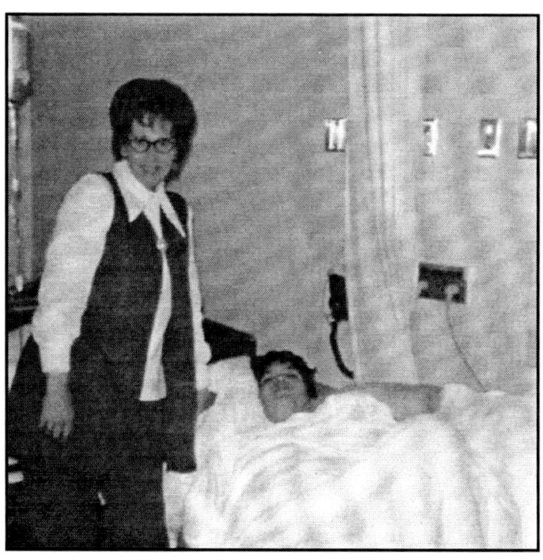

My aunt Betty and my brother Vance

The surgery started off as planned. When they wheeled him into surgery at 9:00 a.m. our family, as well as some of his friends, were there. It was 12:30 when his doctor came in and gave us a report on how well it went. My parents thanked him, then asked when they could see him. "He'll be in the recovery room for about an hour, and then he'll be taken back to his room. You can see him then." He asked if we needed anything else and then he left.

My brothers and I went to the cafeteria to get something to eat. It was hard for me to sit there with them. We didn't talk much. I realized that we really didn't have a whole lot in common. We never spent time together. As a matter of fact, we each had our own set of friends, and sometimes we crossed paths. The only time we spent any real time together as a family was at Sunday dinner, when my mother would cook for the whole family. The unspoken rule was that we were expected to be there or have a doctor's excuse if we weren't.

We finished our food and went up to Vance's room hoping he'd be there. He was lying in bed when we arrived. He was still groggy, just coming out of the anesthesia. My mother was sitting at his bedside holding his hand. He was rubbing the bandage over his incision and complaining about being in pain.

Steve stepped out and came back with a nurse. She was carrying a syringe. She rolled him on his side and plunged the needle into his right hip. He winced. She told us that should help his pain soon. It wasn't long before he fell back to sleep. He continued to go in and out of sleep for the next eight hours or so.

That evening a young man came into Vance's room and said, "Hi, I'm Hector and I'm your brother's aide for tonight. I'll be coming in to check on him when I can. If you guys need anything, just let me know." Through the next few weeks, I could see that Hector really enjoyed his job, and he went out of his way to do it well. He not only was there for the patients, but for their families as well. Hector had a lot of compassion for Vance. He worked hard to make his stay there as comfortable as he could, considering the circumstances that took place while he was there.

Vance did well for the first three days. He was surrounded by family and friends around the clock. He was in pain, but for the most part, he continued to be his witty, smart-ass self. Vance was fun to be around. He was always making people laugh, but by the end of the third day, he was starting to lose his edge. He was irritable and couldn't seem to stay awake.

At first, we thought Vance just needed rest so he could continue to heal, but by the following day, when he woke, he appeared to be hallucinating. I wondered if one of his friends turned him on to drugs, but no one would admit it.

Hector worked the day of Vance's surgery and then was off the next two days. When he came back, he couldn't believe the change in him. "Something's not right," he told us. "He should be doing better than he is. I expected to see him walking the hallways today." He read Vance's medical chart at the end of his bed. He noticed the fluid intake and output ordered for him was not being charted.

By the end of the following day, Vance started lapsing in and out of consciousness, and the times he was awake he appeared confused and unaware of his surroundings. He would pick at the air, or if you stood by him, he would pick at your clothing as if he were picking off lint that wasn't there. His lips were so dry that they were cracked and bleeding. He had this distant stare as if he were looking right through you, and he looked so bad we were beginning to wonder if he would even make it through the night.

When the doctor examined him, we were told that Vance was in renal failure and that his kidneys were almost completely shut down. Vance needed to be on dialysis and the doctor ordered it to start immediately.

I didn't understand all that was happening, but as with all crises that took place in our family, we all moved into crisis mode. Crisis mode is a trance-like state where we begin to function on automatic pilot. The problem is that in a dysfunctional family like mine, it's more the norm, rather than the exception.

Two days after we were told about Vance, my mother ended up in the hospital suffering from valley fever. Then my father was diagnosed with lung cancer and needed to be operated on for a partial lung removal. So, for a short period of time, they were all there in the same hospital together.

The beauty of crisis mode is that once you're in it, you can add to it and function even better than before. Help from extended family allowed Steve, Richard and me to take shifts at the hospital.

When my parents were released, friends from the neighborhood, along with our family, all came together and helped out as they each recuperated from their illnesses.

Believe it or not, I was actually staying clean and sober. All of my focus was on my family. I was needed and that was rare. I had always been the one who couldn't be counted on, so they had stopped asking a long time back. But now it was different. I was given another chance and this time I would be there. It also made me feel better about myself, knowing I could help. For the first time in a very long time, I felt like I belonged. I also noticed that the feelings of hopelessness were gone. It sounds selfish thinking of myself in this crisis, but that was the nature of the beast. When you're needed, that empty feeling sometimes goes away. It was that empty feeling that had caused some of my problems to begin with.

Vance's condition continued to decline. When he was conscious he was hallucinating, and because of his size, he was so strong the nurses couldn't handle him. He would push them away. However, for some unknown reason, Vance would listen to me and my brothers. When we told him to do something he would, so it was requested that one of us be with him at all times. On those rare occasions when one of us was not available, the nurses would tie him down. I didn't like it when that happened, so I tried to stay available at all times.

Around three one afternoon, I relieved my brother Richard. He had been with Vance since seven that morning and he complained about being tired. I turned on the television in his room and sat next to him in a chair to watch it. Two hours into my shift, the room filled with a truly awful smell. It gagged me. I thought Vance may have had a bowel movement, so I removed the sheet he had over him to check. When I did, what I saw turned my stomach.

There was a twelve inch gaping hole where his staples had been, and what looked and smelled like human waste was oozing out of the hole. I had to fight throwing up.

Vance was so incoherent he didn't have a clue about what was happening to him. He was covered in that ooze—he had it in his hair, all over his face, even in his mouth. I was horrified! I grabbed his arms, holding them down so he wouldn't continue to smear shit all over himself. I was screaming for help in between my gagging. The door flew open against the wall, and several nurses and an aide ran in to see why I was screaming. When they saw what was happening they looked shocked. One ran out to get the doctor, who was sitting behind the nurses' station charting. It was mass confusion. I wasn't sure anyone knew what to do. The doctor called for some order, he needed to start treating Vance. I was asked to leave the room.

When they cleaned him up, they were able to see more clearly what had happened. During Vance's surgery, the doctor had removed several feet of his small intestine. Where he had reconnected it had come apart, causing all the waste to leak into Vance's abdominal cavity.

I sat out in the lobby wondering what to do next. I was thinking I couldn't ever imagine ever seeing anything like that again. It was that hideous. My thought at the time was that my little brother was dying and I needed to let the rest of the family know.

When I called my parents, my father answered the phone. "Dad, I don't know what's happening, but I don't think Vance is doing well." Then I told him what I had seen.

I can still hear the fear in my father's voice that day. He didn't want Vance to die, in spite of all the problems between them. They were always arguing. You see, Vance was the oldest of the second set of children in our family. Steve, Richard and I had moved out several years earlier and we each had families of our own. I know now, looking back, that Vance was like me. His drug use and behavior created major problems between him and my parents, so they had a lot of unfinished issues that needed to be addressed. The reason they had so many issues, I thought, was because my father would use the same tactics during a problem as he had with me. He would attempt to confront the problem head on, but in the end he would let his guilt get in his way.

I believe my father loved my brother very much, but, as with me, he didn't know how to build a relationship with him. My father would attempt to set boundaries, but because of his feelings of guilt he was rarely—if ever—able to stick to them.

I knew that my father didn't want to live with unfinished business, but now he might have to. It was at that minute on the phone, telling him about my little brother, that I forgave my father for all the bad blood we had between us, and that's when our relationship changed. I will always believe that my father tried to do what was right with each of us, but in the end, I realized he just never knew how.

My parents were angry about what happened with Vance at Saint Luke's Hospital, so that night he was taken by ambulance to Good Samaritan Hospital. They immediately admitted him to the intensive care unit. His condition was critical but stable. He had his own room with lots of windows and a private nurse around the clock. He was hooked up to a heart monitor, and several IV's were started in his ankles because the veins in his arms had collapsed.

Vance continued to go in and out of consciousness. When he was awake, he had no awareness of his surroundings. He was more out of control than ever before, and he was hallucinating all the time. My brothers and I were there 24/7, and because I had no job I pulled the graveyard shift. During the day, I would either go home and sleep, or go over to Jackie's house and rest over there; it depended on how I felt after my shift.

After relieving Steve, during one of my shifts, I sat next to Vance's bed reading a book that my mother had given me a few months before, "The Power of Positive Thinking," by Norman Vincent Peale. My mother was always trying to get me to read his books, hoping it might change my life for the better. I never had the heart to tell her that I couldn't read very well and that I only understood about a quarter of what I read.

Around two o'clock, the nurse excused herself. She told me she'd be right outside and that if I needed her, I should just step outside and let her know. Vance was still out of it when she left the room. I went back to my book, reading the same paragraph over and over again, trying to understand what it was telling me. That's when I looked over at my brother. He was staring at me and he was smiling. He didn't have those empty eyes as if you weren't there. He was looking at me.

"Happy Birthday," he said. I was shocked. He'd been out of it a little over four months now. How could he possibly know that in two days it would be my birthday? But he did! He smiled at me when he said it. Then he told me something that will stay with me the rest of my life. "John, I'm worried about you. I'm afraid if you don't cool it on the drugs, you may die soon." That really blew me away! How could he possibly know the extent of my drug use? I never used around him, but he knew that, too. I didn't know what to think. I sat next to him, holding his hand, pondering his words in my mind. I was deep in thought when I looked back at him, then watched him close his eyes and fall back to sleep. He was asleep for several hours before he woke up again. When he did, it was if nothing had changed. He was back to hallucinating as badly as before.

I have never told a soul about what transpired in that hospital room on the evening of February 16, 1974 until now, and for the most part I have always honored his request. I couldn't stop thinking about what my brother told me, and because he went back into his previous state when he woke up again, I began to question whether he had said it at all. Following this line of thinking, I justified drinking five beers that morning. But in reality I knew that he had said it, so from that day on I never used another mood-altering chemical again.

I spent not only my 23rd birthday, but also my first day clean and sober, on February 18, 1974, in the hospital with my brother Vance. I have never regretted my decision to stay clean, and again it showed me, as I have seen so many times in my many years of sobriety, that God speaks through people. I will forever believe that God spoke though Vance that day.

Vance went through all of March and most of April with very little change. He had massive bedsores on his spine, butt, feet and legs. I believe that the hospital staff was truly doing all they could to make Vance as comfortable as possible. Even Hector, from Saint Luke's Hospital, would come by when he could, to see how we were all holding up.

By mid-April, my brothers and I were tired, having been with Vance almost daily since September of the previous year. We were all feeling the toll it was taking on us. On April 22, 1974, when I walked into the hospital to take over my shift, most of my family was there. Steve told me Vance was awake and alert enough to know who people were. He just woke up and started talking to the nurse as if he were waking up from a nap. The doctor who examined him said there was no reason Vance couldn't be moved to his own room in the main hospital. "We'll keep the private nurse for a few more days to be safe, and if he continues to improve the nurse can go too." Then he asked Steve to bring the family together in the waiting room because he had something to tell everyone.

The doctor came in when we were all settled and sat between Aunt Betty and my father. He explained that it looked like Vance was on the mend, then he explained what his plans were for his continued recovery. "You are all very tired, and from here on out I want you to start taking care of yourselves. Vance will be all right tonight. Just go home. I don't want to see anyone back here for at least twenty-four hours. Is that understood?" With some reluctance, we all agreed.

After they moved him into his room, we said goodbye and left. As I walked through the hospital lobby, I looked at a clock on the wall. It was 5:35 p.m., so I left for home.

When I arrived home I took a shower, got dressed, then left for a 12-Step meeting at the Maverick House. I got there just in time to hear Black Wally speak. "I would rather live the rest of my life sober, believing that I am an alcoholic, than live the rest of my life drunk, or even just a little drunk, trying to convince myself that I'm not." I cannot tell you the number of times I've heard him speak those words in past meetings. It felt good to be home again. After the meeting, Wally walked over and welcomed me back. I thanked him for caring.

Wally and I walked through the back office door and joined Harry and Wild Bill for some conversation and a cup of Harry's coffee. Old Wild Bill was on a roll, telling jokes using his W.C. Fields impression. He was funny and it felt good to laugh again. God knows I needed it.

I got up the next morning around nine o'clock, ate a bowl of cereal, and then took my ten-speed out for a ride. I had no destination in mind, I just rode. My apartment was less than a mile from the hospital where Vance was. I'd had no conscious intention of going there but I was heavy in thought, and when I came out of my trance-like state, I found myself straddling my bike, looking up at the back entrance of the hospital.

I knew Vance's doctor would be angry with me if he saw me, so I turned to leave, but something was wrong. I couldn't tell you what or why. I just knew, because I had this uncontrollable urge to go in. It was almost as if I was being led. I decided to go in through the back stairs, so I couldn't be seen. When I walked into my brother's room, he sat up to greet me.

I said, "Hello."

He said, "Hi, I've been waiting for you."

"Well, I'm here," I said.

Then he told me, "I've been calling you all morning."

I looked at him, wondering what he meant. It was then that I realized that something was wrong.

He asked the male nurse if he could give us a few minutes alone. The nurse left mumbling something about getting some ice. Vance asked me to come closer and held out his left hand for me to hold. I reached out with my right hand and held his in mine. He pulled me down to face him. "You need to do something for me."

"Sure, what is it?" I asked him.

"You need to tell Dad something for me. Tell him that I love him and that I forgive him." Now that I was face to face with him, I noticed he had no color. His voice was low and it was becoming more difficult to hear him speak. His mouth was very dry and he spoke just above a whisper. With the other hand, he pointed to a section of the newspaper folded in half on a chair behind me. I turned to see. "You need to finish that crossword puzzle for me," he said.

I was confused. What was he saying? I didn't understand. The doctor said he was getting better, didn't he? "Vance, what are you saying? I don't understand." My head was spinning. Things were moving too fast.

Then Vance looked into my eyes and said again, "Don't forget to tell Dad that I love him and I forgive him." I told him that I would. He smiled and said, "John, I'm checking out." Vance squeezed my hand. And then he died.

I was still holding his hand, wondering what had just happened, when the nurse walked in. When he realized what was happening, he ran over to Vance and felt for a pulse on the side of his neck. I could see the disbelief on his face. He reached up above the bed, and on the wall was a red button. When he hit it, all hell broke loose. I still had my brother's hand in mine when several doctors and nurses came through the door. I was told to leave while they converged on him from every direction. I stood over by the door watching them try to revive him. I heard one doctor yell out, "Get him out of here!" Then a nurse opened the door and pushed me out.

I stood outside his room in shock, wondering what to do next. I couldn't think at first, my mind was clouded. Then it came to me that I needed to let my family know what had just happened. I went to the waiting room down the hall to use the phone.

"Hello," I heard my father say.

"Dad," I said, "I'm not sure what's going on here, but I think you need to get up to the hospital. Now!" I could tell by the sound of his voice that he knew what to expect when he got here.

It didn't take long for my family to get to the hospital. We gathered in the waiting room. The mood was somber. We all knew. We were just waiting for the doctor to make it official. My mother was staring at the floor, not saying a word; my father sat next to her. My Aunt Betty was there. She had her arm around Richard. I sat in a chair across from them. Steve had gone to the cafeteria to get something to drink for my mother.

The doctor walked in and noticed that Steve wasn't there. I told him where he was and he asked me to go get him. I ran down the stairs to the basement, and yelled at Steve that the doctor needed to talk with the whole family. He left everything there and we took the elevator up to the fourth floor. When we walked in a nurse was waiting. She told us the rest of the family had been taken to a more private room. She escorted Steve and I through some double doors at the end of the hallway, and then into the room my family waited in. When we were all together the doctor came in and told us that Vance had passed away. Even though I now knew for sure, I still didn't want to believe it. I felt numb.

I felt so sorry for my parents as I saw them sitting there in disbelief. I told my father what Vance had told me about loving him and forgiving him. I could see tears gathering in his eyes. He didn't say a word; he just walked away. My mother just sat there not saying anything. I felt so helpless. She was so distraught she needed to be helped to the car. We buried Vance three days later. He was put to rest in St. Francis' Cemetery on 48th street.

I truly believe a large piece of my mother died that day. She was never the same after that and through the years, until the day she died, my mother withdrew to her bedroom, only coming out to cook or do what had to be done. She became a lonely, bitter woman who emotionally distanced herself from the rest of the family and pushed everyone away. I truly loved my mother and I hated to see her live this way. When she died in 1986 I was almost glad, because her tortured soul was at peace.

Through the years, I've often wondered what kind of person Vance would have turned out to be, had he lived. This seemed to me an ordinary thought with the passing of a young loved one or family member, yet it has lingered in my mind throughout my life—at times with great intensity and imagination!

Rachel Carter center of the picture having her shoulders rubbed by Grandma Carter. Taken at the reception after Vance was buried.

Chapter Thirty-Four

A Path of Willingness

Behold the turtle, who only makes progress
when he sticks out his neck.
-- *Unknown*

What we resist, persists.
-- *Unknown*

The day before my twenty-third birthday I stopped my chemical use. I began going to 12-Step meetings again, reconnected with my old sponsor, and recommitted myself to the program. The problem was that I continued to feel that something was missing in my life. Again, I couldn't tell you what it was, because I just didn't know. I wondered at first if I was grieving the loss of my little brother, but six months into my program the feelings were still there. It didn't seem to matter that I was doing everything I was told, I just kept sinking deeper into my despair.

I would ask myself over and over again why I continued to feel this way. Again I felt different! I often thought about Chapter Five in the "Big Book" of Alcoholics Anonymous titled, "How It Works," where it states: "Rarely have we seen a person fail who has thoroughly followed our path. Those who do not recover are people who cannot, or will not, completely give themselves to this simple program. Usually those men and women who are constitutionally incapable of being honest with themselves." I often wondered if maybe I wasn't being honest. I didn't know, because it seemed the longer I stayed clean of chemicals, the more confused I became. I can't say that being clean at first didn't feel good. It did, but the feelings didn't last.

I was living on the unemployment check I received weekly for $105.00. At this time in my life I had no job skills or education because I had dropped out of high school in the ninth grade. By this time it was becoming harder to find a job without a high school diploma or G.E.D., and I didn't have either. I felt like a dark cloud was hanging over me, following me everywhere I went. I couldn't even face the rejection I feared would come if I asked for a job, so I just wouldn't ask.

I understand this today. When a person holds on to a negative thought, they only look for the evidence to reinforce what they already believe, being unwilling or closed to the possibility of anything else. Then taking that limited information for truth, nothing changes. This is what we call a self-fulfilling prophecy. You know what they say, "We are what we think all day long."

I was emotionally fragile and I knew it. I didn't know what to do. It seemed as if my life was as out of control as it had been when I was using. The anxiety I was feeling continued to trigger my panic attacks, and I was depressed all the time.

Jim, my sponsor, was frustrated with me because I started to pull back on meetings. When he would ask me about it, I would tell him I had more important things to do. I was still involved with Jackie, and that seemed to take more of my time. I knew my relationship was toxic and I needed to look at it, but I wasn't sure I could handle that major of a change in my life at this time. Therefore I continued to lie to myself, saying that it was temporary or I was lonely and needed to be loved. I just couldn't see that we were feeding each other's sick obsessions.

I noticed something critical. There has to come a time when we stop running from our deviant behaviors and begin to gather our assets. Instead of using blame as a predominant reaction or reason for what we do, we need to find those good things inside of us and use them as the reason for what we do. It all begins inside. Sometimes the beginning is very small. Sometimes just successfully getting out of bed in the morning is reason enough for feeling good about ourselves. It gathers momentum as we begin to see how we helped ourselves and then extend that help to others. Dysfunctional is a term we should use to describe *ourselves*—not others. As we gain momentum in gathering that which is good around us, it creates a force, like gravity, that draws others into our world and fills up the hollow places.

After six months on unemployment I was asked to participate in the C.E.T.A. program. C.E.T.A. was the "Comprehensive Employment and Training Act." It offered training for those who had no trade or work skills to find a job. It helped move them off unemployment. Through this program I was offered a job at Terros, in their crisis department. My training would help me develop skills in the medical and counseling fields, if I chose to pursue them. I started the following Monday. I was scared and filled with anxiety throughout the weekend. I was plagued with feelings of insecurity, inadequacy and panic attacks, but—for the very first time—I took a major risk, and I will be forever grateful that I did.

I was well received within the Terros organization. I was able to help other suffering addicts like myself; and I was good at it. I went back to school and excelled. I continued to work my 12-Step program and develop more positive friendships. With all of my accomplishments I felt better about myself, but even with all I was doing, I still felt that something was missing. I still felt different and I still felt stuck. Life was still a struggle and I was beginning to see why. I was still involved in this sick relationship with Jackie. No matter how many times I would tell her it was over, I would weaken and invite her back in.

Our relationship became more bizarre; one minute we'd be fighting and the next entangled in sex. I even stopped calling it love because no two people who acted like we did toward each other could be in love. Hell, we weren't even playing house, we were just two very sick people together.

It was a year and a half into what I believed was my recovery, but now that was in question. I began to see a correlation between my codependent relationship with Jackie and my ongoing recovery. I was stuck! It appeared that when I stopped using chemicals, my codependency was then activated, and it came out with a vengeance!

I now believe that in growing up within a dysfunctional family system, I developed underlying codependent behaviors. They masqueraded themselves as coping skills, but they were nothing more than survival tactics. In other words, my chemical use was my primary disease and needed to be stopped. However, when it stopped, my codependency was then reactivated. Because I did not understand this, the codependency would then become my primary disease. Those survival behaviors I learned growing up had helped me function in a world where reality changed often, but they denied me any growth or stability. I continued to be stuck in behaviors that I had developed as a child growing up in dysfunction; combined with my past chemical use, I never developed the emotional maturity to cope with problems as an adult. Meanwhile, my codependency continued to block my recovery. Yes, I had stopped my drug use, but when my codependency was reactivated, I was still in my disease. I simply had no control over behaviors that were still controlling me.

I once heard Earnie Laren, the author of the book, "Stage II Recovery" say, "When Alcoholics and drug addicts stop using alcohol and drugs, they are nothing more than codependents with alcohol and drug problems." I understand what he meant by this today. I came to realize that until I addressed my codependency and saw it for what it was, I would stay sick!

I now understand what the 12-Step program means when they say, "We need to work this program in all our affairs, and half measures will avail us nothing." Well, addressing my chemical addiction and refusing to look at my codependent issues was a half measure, as far as I could see. It wasn't until I became willing to look at my codependency and see it for what it was that I was finally able to receive the full benefits of my recovery. Those benefits included true mental health, the ability to enjoy life on a level I've never experienced before, and the coping skills that I had searched so diligently for in my disease. When I used the resources I developed as part of my 12-Step program on my codependency issues, my life changed!

One day, after working a graveyard shift at Terros, I walked into Jackie's house with full intentions of telling her it was over, but instead I found her in bed with another man. Thank you, God!! I truly believe today that was God doing for me what I was ready for, but had been unable to do for myself. That day I chose recovery!

I made a decision and a commitment to spend the next year of my life without being in a relationship. I would focus all of my efforts on my recovery. It was hard at first, but as hard as it was, I learned that the only way I could ever have a healthy relationship with another person was for me to be healthy first and foremost. So, as hard as it was, I can honestly say that it was the best decision I ever made for myself. It was my turning point and I have never regretted it. In being responsible for myself, with no outside interference from the pressures that came with being in a relationship, I was able to see my assets more clearly. I now love my life, and I believe that today I am a well balanced person. I have a lot to look forward to, and I haven't felt that "something missing" feeling in over twenty-eight years. Even my symptoms of manic depression, which I now believe were drug induced, went away after a few months.

My decision to work at Terros helped me to develop a career in substance abuse counseling, and in all my years working in this field, I have seen countless others make the same mistakes I did. Another thing Earnie Larsen says is, "If we do not address other self defeating learned behaviors as they come up in our recovery, we will never get beyond Stage I recovery." Stage I recovery is nothing more than stopping the drinking or drug use, and although this is a major accomplishment, the good feelings generated by it are short-lived.

I believe that many of these self-defeating learned behaviors could be codependent in nature and may lead us back to our chemical use, or create other behaviors in us that become just as damaging. We continue to see life as a series of up-hill battles and life continues to be a struggle.

Through the years I have seen this kind of dysfunction in virtually every dependent person I have worked with. I believe that every addict has several self-defeating learned behaviors that will continue to surface in their recovery. If those behaviors are not dealt with, they steal the addict's joy and keep him or her continually on their own personal road to destruction.

I know now that I was stuck, and the only way I could get through it was to face all my demons, and I had a few. I have left many wounded, and I will forever be sorry for that. I can only throw myself on their mercy and hope that some day they will find it in their hearts to forgive me. I'm not asking them to forget, just to forgive.

My chemical use and my codependent base behaviors brought me to a depth of survival that most animals never get to. Why I stayed there and continued to feed this obsessive compulsive lifestyle was beyond me, but that was all I knew. I used to beat myself up over it. I no longer feel the need to do that. As a result of my changed lifestyle I now have the ability to take charge of my life and I am responsible. I have the clarity to make more positive choices in my life and my behaviors no longer control me. No more wreckage, no more crises and no more wounded. I've learned that saying you're sorry means nothing unless you're willing to change your behaviors.

I've never met a person who *couldn't* do it, but I've met many who *won't*. Some will only work hard enough to get out of their pain, and then—the second they're out of pain—they stop making the effort. They never work all the way through the problem so they can move to the other side of it. Consequently, pain and crisis will continue to plague them. We can only pray that some day they will find the strength needed to get through it.

Recovery is an ongoing process, and I believe the willingness to go to any length must be absolute! Remember, if *our* way worked in the first place, we would have never been sick. So become willing, and never quit! With this new attitude and God's help, you can't fail.

John Carter at four years
clean and sober with son Sean.

EPILOGUE

I chose my own recovery path and it worked well for me. I personally feel that 12-Step programs are great for many reasons: One, they're free. Two, I believe the 12 Steps, combined with sponsorship and the support from those who have been there before are invaluable. And three, 12-Step programs are everywhere.

However, I do **not** believe that 12-Step programs are for everyone. There are many paths we can choose from. All it takes is a commitment to your recovery, an open mind and the willingness to go to any length. We must have all three for it to work. As we develop these rich ingredients in our lives, it enables us to change our attitudes and give us a new outlook on life. In addition, our mind automatically moves into solution-oriented thinking and becomes open to the positive change happening around us; and if we hit a wall—and we probably will—our mind will automatically seek out a solution.

I believe that all paths lead us to the same place, as stated by Don Juan in Carlos Castaneda's book, *The Teachings of Don Juan*, when he was explaining about the Devil's Weed. He said, "One path will have a heart and another path will not. One will lead us through a bush and the other around a bush." You choose your path, but may I suggest that you always choose the path with the heart.

John A. Carter
January 18, 2006

About the Author

JOHN CARTER has been a substance abuse counselor for more than thirty years. He started working at Terros, Inc. through the CETA program in November of 1974. John worked in the Crisis Unit, working on drug overdoses and other drug related problems. He also worked on the suicide hotline.

John went to school and excelled. In February of 1976, he was asked to go to work for St. Luke's Hospital, where he worked as a counselor's Aide until he became certified through the Arizona Board of Certified Alcohol Counselors (ABCAC) in 1977. Since that time John has worked as an administrator in several programs in Phoenix, Arizona.

John has started several programs working with DUI offenders, Probation and Parole. He is an educator and lecturer teaching about dysfunctional family systems, substance abuse, DUI education and substance abuse treatment. John is a Licensed Independent Substance Abuse Counselor in the state of Arizona where he now resides.